BY RICHARD P. HORWITZ   PHOTOGRAPHS BY KARIN E. BECKER

The STRIP

UNIVERSITY OF NEBRASKA PRESS   LINCOLN AND LONDON

An American Place

Manufactured in the United States of America

Publication of this book was aided by a grant
from the Andrew W. Mellon Foundation.

The paper in this book meets the guidelines for permanence
and durability of the Committee on Production Guidelines
for Book Longevity of the Council on Library Resources.

Library of Congress Cataloging in Publication Data

Horwitz, Richard P., 1949-
The strip : an American place.

1. City and town life – United States – Case studies.
2. United States – Social conditions – 1980-
3. United States – Popular culture – History – 20th century.
I. Becker, Karin E., 1946- . II. Title.
HN59.2.H67 1985 307.7′62 84-11897
ISBN 0-8032-2332-3 (alk. paper)

Material from the "Mac's and Mil's" section of Chapter 5
has previously been exhibited and published by the
Mary and Leigh Block Gallery of Northwestern University
in *Exploring Society Photographically*, ed. Howard S.
Becker (Chicago, 1981), pp. 60-67.

Contents

Photographs

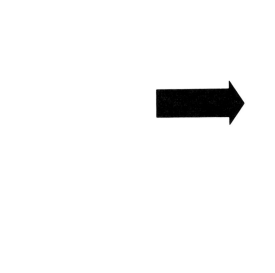

Preface

I t is hard to live or travel anywhere in the United States without encountering a strip. Americans may bemoan or celebrate that simple fact, but they tend to share a conventional view of the place and what it "represents." In the following pages, I intend to show that an alternative view is in order. We can and should make better sense of the strip.

Admittedly, my work here is difficult to categorize. It is more like a guidebook and a personal journal than a textbook. It may never find its way to a supermarket display; nor is it just for The Specialist. It touches most of the humanities and social sciences but never becomes attached. In that respect, what I have to say is unusual, and readers deserve some warning. Yet the subject is common enough. Place is a long-standing American, if not universal, concern. People around the globe have assumed that "folks around here" are the only "real folks" to be found. Of course we know exceptions, visitors with the "right attitude," but even then we cling to our own exceptionalism ("You'd understand if you grew up here") or crackpot environmentalism ("You must be from a weird part of New Jersey"). One of the first acknowledged works of American literature addresses this very issue. Two centuries ago in *Letters from an American Farmer*, Crèvecoeur's James asked, "What, then, is the American, this new man?" Like his immigrant creator, James never doubted that "new" places make for "new men."[1] And that faith persists. Despite modern mobility and mass communication we remain convinced that a place and a way of life are and ought to be intertwined.

I, too, am convinced that the connection exists, though not in the simple ways we often assume. Jokes about Cleveland, Orange County, and the state of New Jersey are as cruel as they are funny. Even confirmed Midwesterners are estranged from "amber waves of grain" and "American Gothic." If you see a restaurant on the coast of Maine with barnboard on the walls and fish nets on the ceiling, it is a safe bet that the designer hails from Boston. In such ways a place, its image, inhabitants, and their history form close but complicated connections.

This book is an attempt to untangle some of those connections but to preserve a sense of their integrity. It falls somewhere between phrenology and a postmortem. Yet between such extremes lies a variety of approaches. Each specialty and school within it has a rationale and protocol to recommend. There are modernists and postmodernists in the arts, quantifiers and interpreters in the social sciences, historians of society, symbols, and intellect. I might claim to tell you more than any one of them but never the whole story. The best I can do is to fashion my own story and warn you to remember the source.

The main source is supposed to be the strip itself, but I am also a key ingredient. My rendering of any place will be colored by a special regard for certain kinds of places, those that support particularly intimate, memorable, and diverse experience. This reverence might be attributed to personal quirks, such as my affection for small-town Maine and regrets since leaving. But I doubt such feelings are wholly unique. They constitute a bias to be watched but one that I hope you will come to share.

There are also undeniable influences of national history. For example, this book was prepared during an abrupt decline in the American economy. Presidents, pollsters, and talk-show hosts recognize less of the turbulent optimism of the 1960s and more popular resignation. Surely this change shapes my vision of the strip or at least the alternatives I can imagine. In my prose you might anticipate the strains of 1960s idealism and 1980s realism that are strains of the moment as well as the strip.

I wish that I could report some technique for dispelling such influences, but I do not have one. Instead, I try to work with them, to use my sensibilities to appreciate, attack, and improve conventional wisdom, to participate critically in popular and academic lore. My work does, then, have a method, at least in Durkheim's sense of the word, but it is hardly methodical.[2] It is a disposition more than a protocol, emerging as I read, worked in the field, and wrote between 1978 and 1982. Throughout the book I refer to the evolution of my method, but here I can illustrate it by describing the contribution of Professor Karin E. Becker.

I first turned to Karin for help in 1979, after realizing how closely my informants followed the academic line, including its failings. This was a source of frustration for them as well as me. Somehow, the mere thought of the strip belied their own true sense of the place and their hopes for its future. Even worse, those feelings, whether pride or disappointment, seemed so objective, immediate, and inevitable. They could barely articulate, much less change, them. The connection between this place and its inhabitants was more than a "belief," something to be captured with a pen or a tape recorder. You *saw* it. Since Karin is an expert in visual communication and documentary photography, I hoped she could help me envision the strip as my informants demanded.

She was, then, initially another informant. I invited her to accompany me to a strip and take a roll of "environmental shots" as she might for a *Life* magazine reporter, and she agreed. I jotted down some predictions, as is my custom, and asked her to think out loud with the camera. At first I was proud of myself for anticipating her moves. They were highly conventional. For example, she used a

telephoto lens to accentuate the clutter of signs above and a wide-angle to expand the pavement below. But I was surprised that Karin was so aware of these conventions and anxious to work with them. Since we shared this urge to learn through critical participation, we decided to work together.

Although we often, in fact, worked apart, with different goals and tastes, our methods evolved in parallel. Just as I had initially surveyed the literature and the setting of my informants, Karin began systematically to document the strip. With a 50-mm lens held at eye level parallel to the ground, she took frontal views of "whole" buildings and signs as they might appear to a pedestrian. She worked mainly in color to match common perceptions of this colorful environment. She made a special effort to select subjects that informants recommended: first buildings, "typical" signs, "beautiful" and "ugly" construction, traffic hazards, and the like. We both, then, started with an outsider's overview of the strip and its most remarkable features. Even as we focused our research, we regularly returned to such exercises in objectivity. For example, Karin chose some sites—empty lots, new construction, old buildings, entryways—to photograph monthly. Such procedures helped us recognize and control our sensibilities as they evolved and continually reminded us of the bigger picture, especially the importance of change. For example, they helped us check our affections for the place. Pretty pictures, sculptural renderings on sunny days with a bright blue sky, seemed less satisfying.

Karin eventually followed me to interior landscapes, to workplaces, workers, and their movements, and here we all worked more closely together. Informants suggested scenes to document and commented on the results. Since they helped us make and edit the tape recordings and photographs, this was truly a collective, evolving enterprise.

We hope the book reflects that spirit. For example,

Karin's choice of fast black-and-white film (Tri-X) represents a compromise between her ideals and the cost of reproduction, the dark settings I chose, and our informants' natural light. At the same time we tried to help readers trace the distinctive contributions we each made. The photographs roughly follow the text, but they are grouped to express Karin's own view of the strip and its meaning for inhabitants. Similarly, each of the character sketches was crafted with and ultimately released by its subject. My own voice recedes through the middle of the book, but, of course, I am ultimately responsible for the whole.[3]

There are, then, three key orientations in the book: (1) outside—an "objective," strongly visual rendering of the strip, (2) inside—the perspective of observers and participants in strip life, and (3) my own interpretation. Rather than blending them, I have tried to preserve a sense of their distinctiveness. The story unfolds in purposeful starts and stops that invite a reader to participate, as I did, in developing a criticism of the strip. As a result, the form may be a bit unconventional, but it is, I believe, true to the subject. It is more like a drive down the strip than a flight overhead.

Given, however, the perils of modern motoring, readers might at this point welcome a billboard or a map. We begin in Chapter 1 with an overview of the strip, its definition and treatment in everyday experience, geography, photography, advertising, history, law, economics, architecture, and planning. Common themes and their strengths and weaknesses appear in relief when related to the exchange between two noted architectural critics, Peter Blake and Robert Venturi. Although they teach the importance of the look of the strip, they also reveal the shortcomings of an avowedly visual, generic response. *The* view of *the* strip, despite its objective feel, is too mired in transitory projections. Arguments about what is right or wrong with it or what to do about it will be shallow unless they are framed closer to the ground.

We therefore turn in the second chapter to a specific strip and the Iowans who surround it. Here it is easier to see the people and events that shape visions of the strip as powerfully as the strip itself. In particular, we can see how stock responses to the strip express a consumer orientation with potentially awesome social, economic, and environmental effects. As "The View" suggests, the meaning of this strip is connected to wider cultural currents, but surrounding lore obscures their true connection, especially their connection to the changing culture of work. The search for meaning or remedies, even on the ground, will require more than a consumer's eye.

After Chapter 2, then, we turn to the particular stories of "insiders," the management and staff of a "typical" site, a Best Western motel. It is typical in that it occupies a middle ground among strip offerings, intermediate in scale, organization, and business maturity. Here, again, each worker's story touches main cultural currents, but I present those stories more or less in the raw, as people experience and tell them. It is my and their conviction that the meaning of the strip they know emerges most clearly amidst the minutiae of daily life.

In "The Carousel and the Strip" I offer my own assessment of the lessons in their lives by tying them to the history of the motel, Best Western International, and the other chains that have come to dominate the roadside. In particular, I argue that workers' frustrations on the strip are part of the evolving structure of the strip itself, a structure that it necessarily shares with American enterprise as a whole, including both the power of capital and mass markets. Consumer-oriented, "visual" critiques not only fail to enlighten the strip; they are part of the problem.

With this interpretation in mind, I invite readers to review the strip, to see how it looks with a greater sensitivity to the *exchange* between insiders and outsiders, workers and consumers. To promote contrast, we move from the generic or typical to the archetypal. Karin's photographs of McDonald's represent the most sophisticated and advanced of strip offerings while Diamond Mil offers her own reminder of primitive beginnings. Neither, of course, is a unitary ideal, but together they suggest both an impressive array of possibilities in the present and the narrowing of possibilities that the future portends.

I do not in the end, then, conclude that the strip is fundamentally good or bad. (It seems to me an impotent question, anyway.) But I do evaluate trends in the history of the strip that should inform our choices in the future. There is a tragic side to the strip, but it is neither peculiar to the place nor, I believe, thoroughly inevitable. Given my misgivings about popular perceptions of the strip, I cannot endorse popular solutions. For example, recent efforts to "historically preserve" the strip promoted by celebrants of pop kitsch seem just as miscast as those to "beautify" or eliminate it.

But I trust that my efforts to clarify our sense of the strip, to make it more historically and humanly informed, will help us remember the responsibilities we share, especially the responsibility to know our past and care about it. If we act on those memories, we might yet preserve the connections to place that are an enduring American ideal.

Acknowledgments

There are hundreds of people who contributed to this book in ways I cannot begin to detail. I was most impressed by the cooperation I received from residents of Coralville and the surrounding area. Most of them must accept my appreciation as a group because I failed to record their names or was encouraged to forget them. The following pseudonyms have been used to protect privacy: Kathy Yager, Frank Deleon, Jill (head of housekeeping at the Carousel), Barton Construction, Mitch Jensen, Bill Dixon, Rick Schmidt, Bader Manufacturing Company, Muriel and Stan Bidney, Tugger Tractor Company, Wilbur's, and Cecil. There are, however, many whom I can thank by name: John Allen, Mike Allen, Mark Alvey, Rina Azzam, Cary Beatty, Johanna Beers, Ruth Bonfiglio, Virgil Bowers, Charlie Bringle, Craig Christensen, Herb Cochran, Donna Epley, John Fisher, Tammy Freeman, Brad Gardner, Nadine Hain, Mark Hansen, Jim Harris, Henry Herwig, Barry Hokanson, Michael Kattchee, Doc Kennedy, Ermal Loghry, Susan Masters, Bob Mitchell, Alison Mochoskay, Dean Moore, Dick Myers, Bruce Nelson, Dorothy, Kevin, and William O'Brien, Millie Ollinger, Tim Peters, Craig Poock, Jim Reid, Farokh Roberson, Dave Schnoebelen, Jane Shaffer, Glenn Shoemaker, Steve Sprague, Dave Steckling, Jan Stephenson, Bill Stewart, Lee Strottman, Neil Trott, Jack Waite, Sara Weers, Bernie Westfal, and Mary Wilson.

My work has also benefited from the counsel of academic associates around the nation. In particular, Professors Howard Becker, John Caughey, Jay Mechling, Murray Murphey, and Connie Perin provided encouragement back in 1979, when field research threatened to overwhelm me.

I am especially indebted to the University of Iowa, which supplied my salary, two summer fellowships, and several grants for this effort. My debt to Professor Karin Becker should already be obvious. Steve Ohrn, the Iowa State Folklorist, also had much to add. My students and colleagues in the American Studies Program at the university supplied much-needed patience, support, and criticism. Special thanks go to Carrie Louvar and Susan Onderdonk, secretaries for the program; Professors Wayne Franklin, John Raeburn, and Al Stone; and my research assistants, Kay Aldrich, Dan Jones, Becky Leach, David Marc, and Robin Radespiel.

I reserve for last my public thanks to Noni, my wife, and our son, Carl, who have always indulged my curiosities while reminding me of the ground on which I stand. All of these people are due my deep appreciation, and it is to them I dedicate this book.

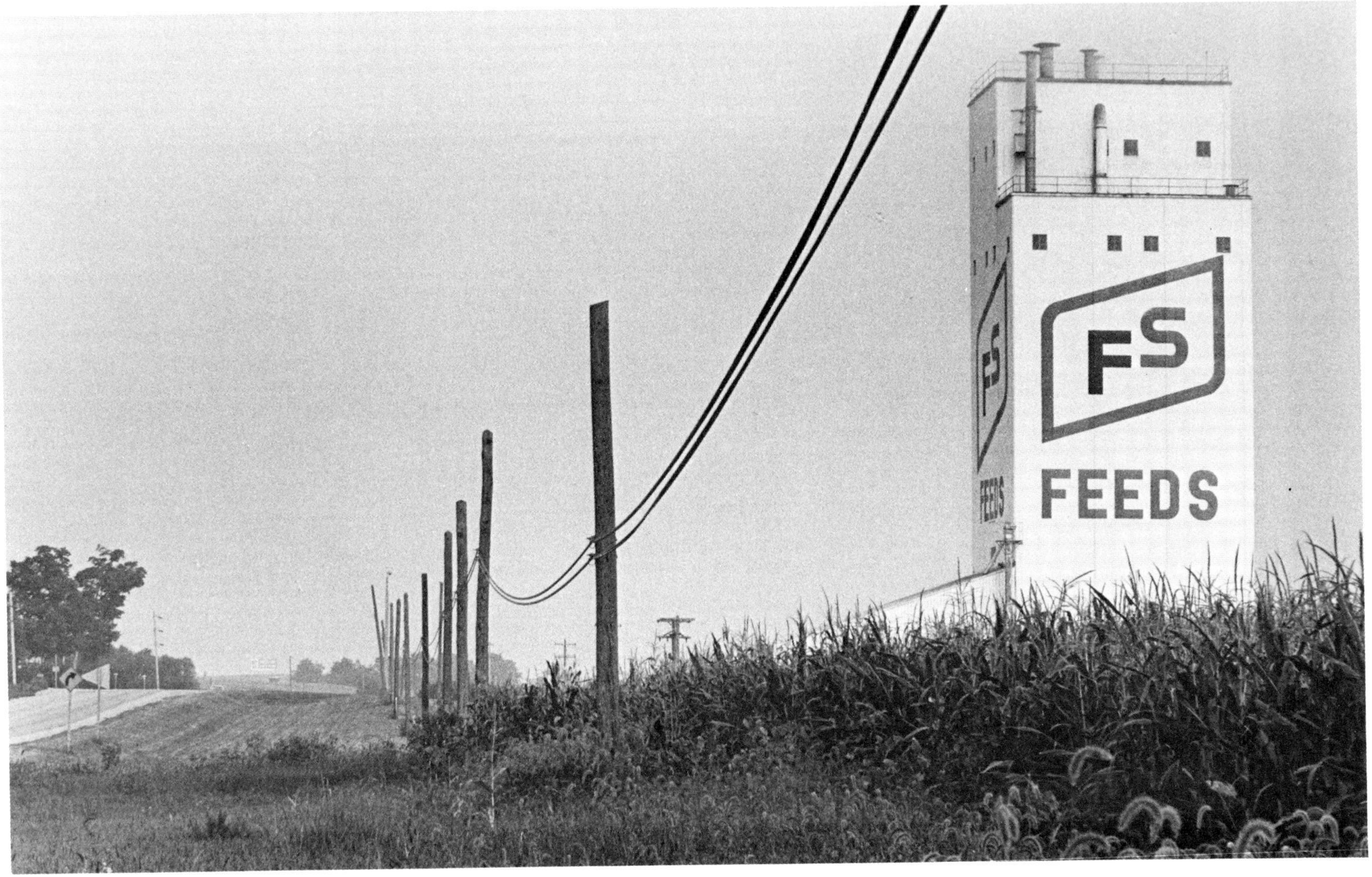
FS
FEEDS
FS
FEEDS

Chapter 1. The View

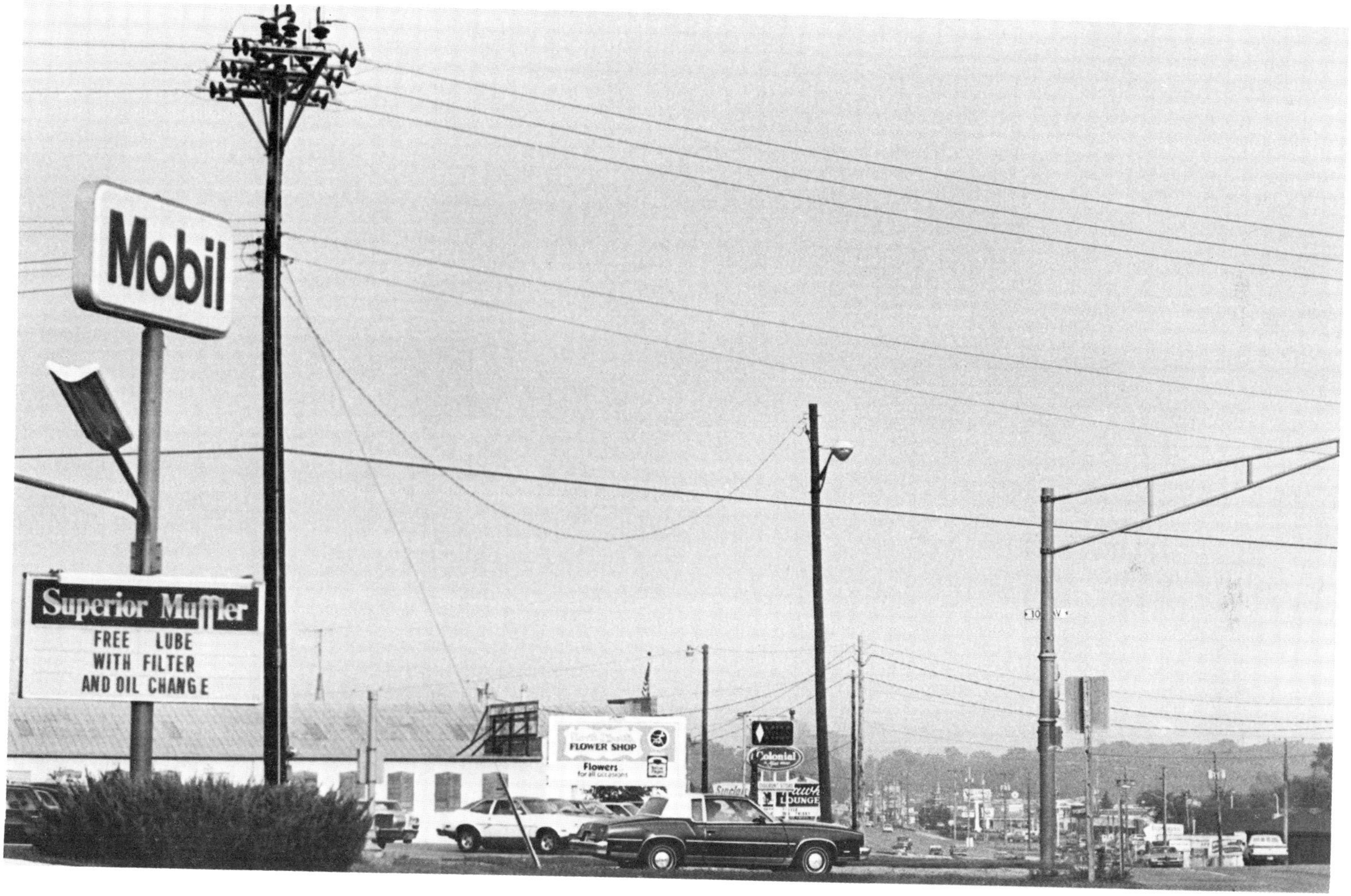
Mobil
Superior Muffler
FREE LUBE
WITH FILTER
AND OIL CHANGE
FLOWER SHOP
Flowers
Colonial
LOUNGE

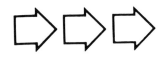

This book is about a place, an American place like ones you have surely seen. Even if you have only seen it through a dirty windshield, you will remember how it looks. Picture a highway lined with businesses—gas stations, motels, fast-food outlets, family restaurants, retail malls—all trimmed in asphalt and colored lights. Names like Mobil, Ramada, McDonald's, Steak 'n Brew, or such-and-such Plaza hover beside the road. The place is a strip, and ones like it line commuter routes in cities and suburbs and surround highway interchanges across the nation.

Drivers on long hauls measure their progress by standard strip stops, one tankful apart. Commuters have their favorite places to fill up, grab a gallon of milk, or buy a burger. They take turns stopping for the office doughnuts at a drive-up window on the way to work. Salespeople have favorite phones or mailboxes to use from their cars or motel rooms that are their homes on the road. Families frequent the mall for back-to-school clothes or one of the sales that have become part of our national calendar— January White Sales, Washington's Birthday, Summer Extravaganza, and so on. Kids hit the mall after school just to hang out or catch a movie, or they spend the evening cruising the strip with friends. At sixteen, thousands of them will get their first jobs scooping fries or working a register in some roadside establishment.

No strip is as striking as an unfamiliar one, one where you have not yet staked out routines and favorites. Who can forget that horrid night in what was to have been a pleasant family vacation? It is raining and the windshield keeps fogging up. You have been on the road ten hours since a misguided "early start," the kids screaming in the back seat while you try to find a place just to get things sane again. "I'm h-u-ngry." "When are we gonna stop?" "I have to go to the bathroom" . . . again. Whining. The pressure is on to find a safe place, anything reasonable. So, when a hazy line of incandescence can be seen off the ramp to the right, the driver (probably dad, who has been chewing Tums for the last forty-five miles) pulls off and leans against the wheel to spot the sign of a familiar restaurant, motel, or whatever (damn it!) midst the glare on some strip somewhere—the climax to a remarkable evening.

The strip is a site for such common American experiences or plain adventures. Instead of covered wagons limping to a trading post of Fort Laramie, we speak of Ford wagons and Holiday Inns. Even strip regulars tell tales that recall the frontier. Strips are the unfordable rapids and towering peaks of rush-hour travel. We rely on local scouts to recommend a bypass, a tangle of side streets like some obscure mountain pass between beds and jobs.

The point is not that these are heroic or, for that matter, pathetic tales. The point is that strips are places to which great meaning, from experience or lore, for good or ill, is attached. In fact, particular strips such as Ventura Boulevard in Los Angeles or Route 91 in Las Vegas have become legendary in their own right.

Mention the nearest strip and people easily speak of a near-accident, a bypass, a job, or a favorite stop. There are, too, a host of simpler sense impressions: the sound of traffic outside and Muzak inside, the sight of disorderly electric signs above or neat yellow stripes on the lot below, the smell of gasoline or a grill, the taste of fries or soft ice "cream," the feeling of midnight hungry or bloated full.

Against this wealth of impression, experience, and lore it seems odd that Americans also describe strips as "homogenized," uninteresting if not downright boring. For about three years I have talked to people about a strip near my home in Iowa, and their usual response is to rattle off all the others they know "just like it." It does not matter whether the conversation is in Maine or California or whether the person has ever been in Iowa. Strips are assumed to be standardized places.

This assumption was particularly evident on a day I spent chatting with motorists who waited to use a drive-up pay phone on an Iowa strip. Nearly all of them were businessmen from out of state who routinely use this phone in covering a local territory. Their attention was fixed on books of accounts and product lines, but I directed it to the landscape beyond their windshields. One young Chicago-based salesman, calling on service stations and rustproofing franchisees in the northern Mississippi Valley, gave a typical report. Looking up from the fat ring binder in his lap, he said: "Gee, you know, I don't really spend that much time here. Just do my job, and. . . . One day I hope I'll have my own stores and put someone else on the road. Ha! Yeah, I know a bunch of guys who've done it. Heck, my boss is only in his thirties. . . . But I do O.K. . . . [Nodding.] Pretty well—cover a lot of ground." He fiddles with the gold chain hanging to the third button in his open shirt and squints out the window. "Yeah, it's a strip, all right. Never really noticed. We've got a bunch of them in Chicago. I guess if you've seen one, you've seen 'em all."

This was not a criticism, just a statement of fact. For many people, like this salesman, the strip is just the undistinguished background for normal daily life. But for others it is a kind of safety zone. Part of the appeal of a national chain such as Holiday Inns is its very lack of distinction. A television commercial, for example, depicts a traveling family shocked by one unwelcome "Surprise!" after another till they meet the sponsor, who boasts, "No surprise!" If you are in a strange place, you can be comforted to know that there is fast and dependable (if undistinguished) service waiting at the nearest strip. In fact, dependability—basic quality, service, cleanliness, and value (McDonald's "QSC&V")—is the watchword of roadside commerce. Harried consumers demand it.

A manager of a prestigious steak house explains how uniformity is equally important for local trade: "If you're consistently good in all phases of your operation—food, service, atmosphere—you'll do repeat business time and time again, and if you're inconsistent you're dead. . . . One or two nights when the cook fouls up or a waitress is in a foul mood can kill you. . . . People come in the first time because they're curious. But if they come back, you better serve them the right cut of meat, done exactly the same 'medium-rare' or whatever, in the same atmosphere. . . . Our building is unique and the atmosphere is unique, but after you've been here three or four times for dinner it's pretty much standard and there's not a whole lot of stuff to look at any more; so then people are going to come back for consistency. . . . You've got to have it down to a science."[1]

In general, the more comprehensive and rational the procedures—finance, marketing, accounting, and management—the more likely a business is to succeed. Standardization pays. This is one reason that in their first year independently owned businesses in America fail at six to ten times the rate of their franchise counterparts.[2] It is no wonder, then, too, that strip developments, with their heavy capital demands and market competition, mean relative safety for consumers and providers of standardized commerce.

On the other hand, there are many people who resent this standardization even as they buy or sell it. A place deserving affection in America is supposed to be distinctive. It is "quaint," "charming," or "funky" in the way it is because of where it is. It should feel uniquely right, like a seaport in New England or a Spanish mission in the Southwest, not only because it is useful to be that way, but because it could be no other. To standardize across space or time is absurdly to deny nature, the lay of the land and ways of life that form a place in history.

Few people have spoken as passionately of this sense of place as Wright Morris, but his sentiment is familiar. In *The Home Place* he envisions what is right about "Lone Tree, Nebraska," like that monument to the plains, the grain elevator:

There's a simple reason for grain elevators, as there is for everything, but the force behind the reason, the reason for the reason, is the land and the sky. There's too much sky out here, for one thing, too much horizontal, too many lines without stops, so that the exclamation, the perpendicular, had to come. Anyone who was born and raised on the plains knows that the high false front on the Feed Store, and the white water tower, are not a question of vanity. It's a problem of being. Of knowing you are there. On a good day, with a slanting sun, a man can walk to the edge of his town and see the light on the next town, ten miles away. In the sea of corn, that flash of light is like a sail. It reminds a man the place is still inhabited. I know what it is Ishmael felt, or Ahab, for that matter— these are the whales of the great sea of grass.[3]

But if you are looking for sails or great whales, a strip seems more like a school of carp. It is not a safe place but a monotonous blight. It betrays the textured history that should distinguish any place. When franchises line the local highway, your town becomes everywhere and no-where: "My God, there's a Burger King in Missoula; we might as well be back in Reading!"

Here, then, is a full spectrum of reactions to the modern strip. It is an uninteresting background, a safety zone, or a threat. It is a place to ignore ("eh?"), welcome ("ah"), or despise ("bah!"). And it is easy to find representatives of every orientation on the strip, easiest perhaps to find critics. Yet, even those who have made a career of de-nouncing its growth admit to collusion. For example, Peter Blake, the author and photographer who made the strip a premier example of "God's own junkyard," admits: "Whenever I drive through Colorado, or Maine, or Louisi-ana, or any other state of the union with its homogenized highways, I look for the nearest Ramada Inn or the near-est Holiday Inn billboards with the color TV they promise in every 'suite.' I don't, in truth, look for the kind of idyllic lodge shown in [the photograph by Marion Post Wolcott,] plate 77."[4] Why, then, should people claim that a place is so alien, uninteresting or inhuman when they devote so much time, money, and talk to it?

I do not think it is because strips are dull. It was, in fact, a strip that inspired this book. That story, though, is a bit more complicated than usual. In 1977, I was teach-ing at the University of Minnesota, but, like most young Ph.D.'s, I was a migrant. I was spending that spring, as I had the past three, hunting for the next job, a miserable business. If you are "lucky," a band of professors fly you to their turf for a "visit," which is, in fact, a grilling. For one to three days, from dawn to midnight, someone will be trying to eliminate you from an impossibly long list of can-didates. The only compensations are a possible job, some free meals, and a chance to see a little of the country. Since someone else generally gets the job and the meals are spent feigning brilliance, I tended to con-centrate on the tourist dimension. Before each visit, I would study maps, trying to imagine what daily life might be like in a new place. When I flew to visit Iowa, I had guessed how far apart towns would feel and how big they would seem, given the size of their names on the map. I gathered that there was a city called Coralville on the highway between the airport in Cedar Rapids and the University in Iowa City. When I arrived I was anxious to check my predictions.

Imagine my confusion when the professor who picked

me up, John Raeburn, drove us to Iowa City by a strikingly long route with nary one sign of Coralville. I later learned that driving through Coralville entailed driving down a strip. Out of kindness and respect for my well-known urbanphobia, John had decided to bypass the infamous "Coralville Strip." He wanted to protect—and control—my first impressions. He later told me, "I didn't want you to get the wrong idea. Iowa City really is just a nice small town, and Coralville . . . well, it's just not like that."

In retelling the story of that experience, I have wrestled with its lessons. On the one hand, it makes sense only when we assume a strip has great evocative power. Running a gauntlet of commerce, John feared, might lead me to uncontrollable associations, tainting my image of an area he likes. On the other hand, John and I were brought together only because we were professors of "American Studies," a field that routinely harnesses such power in the name of cultural interpretation. We were literally circumventing a source that should be our stock-in-trade. So, the story ends and work on this book began with an ironic image: two experts in the study of American culture motoring around one of the most standard of American places, the commercial strip.

I cannot believe, then, that strips are uninspirational. A story they inspire may seem familiar, but it is familiar only in kind. In its individuality none is devoid of some genuine feelings. In this respect strip lore is like any other. Having heard shaggy-dog stories hardly interferes with enjoying a new one. In fact, a recognizable form invites participation. Think of all the hours folks fill as they improvise on strip themes—outrageous new franchises or near-accidents on Route 1.

A more promising explanation for the bad press strips attract might be their formulaic appearance. Strips do look alike. They are difficult to define apart from their appearance. Despite their prevalence and the volume of government polls, surveys, plans, and regulations, they

have no official, objective definition. For example, the common zoning category CH, or "highway commercial," is a better reflection of local politics than social and economic facts. Moreover, it includes large, planned retail centers like the suburban megamalls that have been a favored alternative to the strip since the early 1970s.

Certain economic conditions—the presence of strong auto-oriented markets and uncontrolled private development—may encourage but hardly determine a strip. Look at the kinds of criteria that national food and fuel franchisers use in choosing a location:

1. Traffic count (15,000—20,000 in 24 hrs),
2. Speed limit (35 mph),
3. Frontage (at least 125–150 ft),
4. Visibility (corner sites and liberal sign ordinances preferred),
5. Accessibility (two-curb opening on undivided thoroughfare preferred),
6. Favorable market conditions (high percentage of apartments, evidence of commercial neighborhoods, and families with both husband and wife employed),
7. Cost of land (especially frontage),
8. Competition.[5]

These conditions may promote roadside success. Indeed, they are the hard facts that led many strip dwellers to their present sites. But again, these can hardly be definitive. Many areas that meet these conditions simply are not what we would call strips—at least, not yet.

Even in physical geography there are important variations. Where development occurred in the 1950s or early 1960s (prior to the wave of limited-access legislation) businesses simply flank the highway. More recently they have been built on frontage or service roads that parallel a highway, or they line approach roads radiating from a freeway interchange. Roadside businesses leapfrog from choice, expensive sites off into the hinterland. A strip "ends," not with some change in land forms or the roadway, but where it simply no longer *looks* like a strip. There may be some way to represent all this legal, historical, economic, and geographic variation with numbers, but to my knowledge no one has.[6] Besides, when speaking of strips we have a sight in mind.

The landscape is dominated by signs and buildings that are franchise trademarks. Since much of their sales comes on impulse, from people moving at thirty to forty miles per hour, businesses make their service or product identifiable at a glance. Individually, then, they are designed to look familiar from the road. When haphazardly developed, one next to the other, the overall impression may be bewildering, but the look of each component is no surprise. We would be surprised if a row of shining pumps surrounded by pavement under a projecting canopy were anything other than a gas station. A smaller canopy attached to a large, windowed wing just as surely suggests a motel. These are the conventions of commercial architecture.

Their most sensitive critic is Robert Venturi. He calls his subject "pleasure zone architecture," "commercial vernacular," "roadside eclecticism," or simply the "ugly and ordinary." He and his collaborators have explored sprawl in articles, books, and a Bicentennial exhibition, "Signs of Life," for the National Collection of Fine Arts of the Smithsonian Institution. Their most detailed work began in 1968, including a studio course in the Yale School of Art and Architecture, and ended in a book, first appearing in 1972 and revised in 1977, entitled *Learning from Las Vegas*. Claims to legitimacy ranging from Michelangelo and the Italian mannerists to pop art have not shielded the authors—Venturi, Denise Scott Brown, and Steven Izenour—from charges of social and aesthetic irresponsibility, slumming it, or celebrating schlock. Yet the controversy surrounding the book cannot diminish its lessons. Venturi et alii can teach us to recognize more of what we see when we see a strip.

First, there is the long, flat roadway, an automobile promenade. The curbing is either broken or nonexistent, and there certainly are no sidewalks. Central, public places are reserved for vehicles. Nothing looks quite so out of place as a jogger on the strip.

Next to the road and inflecting radically toward it are towering electric signs, a mix of lighted words, pictures, and sculpture, glowing, blinking, or in motion. As marketing research confirms, the colors grab the eye; the yellow to red range of the spectrum predominates. A single pole can support signs at three orders of magnitude: freeway scale at the top for the most distant and speedy traveler, facade scale in the middle for approaching traffic, and close-up for people in the lot. In color, scale, and sheer candlepower, signs so dominate the landscape that they have come to symbolize the strip itself. For example, how did dad know where to go on that remarkable evening? By sighting the line of lights off the freeway.

Photographers routinely represent the strip by shooting a row of signs with a telephoto lens or multiple exposures that collapse the field of vision, piling sign upon sign. Each sign may look a bit wild, but crowded together they are only monotonous. These conventions have remarkable tenacity. In 1978, for example, I was interviewed by a local television reporter shooting a thirty-second story: the eccentric strip scholar. I was interested in how the reporter would handle my subject but warned him about photographic conventions. Standard strip shots are uninteresting and uninformative, clichés that reveal more about the culture of photographers, particularly their fascination with signs and depth of field, than their subject. Besides, I had struggled for more than a year in Coralville to develop my informants' trust. They demanded my suspending such preconceptions. No matter. My warnings certainly did not affect the five o'clock news. At twenty after, the station featured a rapid-fire, crooked collage of fast-food signs.

Although signs define the strip's stock image, they seem to defy classification. Witness the pop journalist

Tom Wolfe as he portrays the paramount strip landscape: "One can look at Las Vegas from a mile away on Route 91 and see no buildings, no trees, only signs. But such signs! They tower. They revolve, they oscillate, they soar in shapes before which the existing vocabulary of art history is helpless. I can only attempt to supply names— Boomerang Modern, Palette Curvilinear, Flash Gordon Ming-Alert Spiral, McDonald's Hamburger Parabola, Mint Casino Elliptical, Miami Beach Kidney."[7] Wolfe's description, like a conventional photograph, is good fun. The vocabulary in the sign industry itself is less fun but probably more powerful. In a salesman's terms, the strip is a market for "on-premise signs" to be distinguished by their "placement" (e.g., facia, roof, marquee, canopy, or pylon), "treatment" (e.g., revolving or with chasing lights on the perimeter), materials (e.g., letters of wood, aluminum, masonite, or plastic), and lumination (e.g., lighted with fluorescent or neon bulbs, indirectly lighted by spot lights, or unlighted). Standard installations include the "individual face-lighted," "individual back-lighted," "open-channel," and ever-popular "lighted cabinet."[8] Yet again, in whatever vocabulary, the image is one of individual variety and collective pattern or uniformity.

This is equally true when we consider on-premise asphalt, for behind the signs, off the pavement, is more pavement. Restaurants and motels blacktop a narrow band in front for customer drop-off or a few prestigious parking spaces. (Those spaces are generally full but signal more to the side or rear.) Gas stations are set a little farther from the road to accommodate pumpside bays, tanker deliveries, and room to turn around. The largest expanses are paved for car dealers, supermarkets, and shopping malls. Here, too, there are conventional photographic images. Switch to a wide-angle lens and crouch low to the ground. Now any pavement under foot becomes a broad foreground that stretches into the distance.

Strip buildings also have a conventional look. In addition to gas stations and motels, we have a standard image of supermarkets and malls. They enclose a massive, low space within rectangular walls and a flat roof. Smaller structures at least share a relationship to the road. They inflect toward it only slightly less than the signs that dwarf them. Together, building, lot, and signs give the roadside a diagonal orientation to invite right turns. In fact, their angles of inflection roughly tell the history of a strip. In its early days sites have an acute angle to catch speedy travelers. Angles become less acute as the strip is more fully developed and traffic more congested.

Still, in the midst of all this order there is some awfully fantastic or at least fanciful architecture: restaurants that look like castles or jacks-in-the-box, dining cars, cowboy hats, pirate ships, showboats, pagodas, pueblos, or Miss Kitty's saloon. How can such buildings be said to look alike? Venturi, Scott Brown, and Izenour say so by pointing to the simple, rectangular box upon which symbols, false fronts, roofs, windows, and all, are applied. They call it the "decorated shed," a radical departure from modern architecture with its "heroic and original," abstract, expressive, and monumental form. Instead of an organic design sculpted in concrete and glass, strip structures begin with a cheap, serviceable, single-story box under a flat roof punctuated with exhaust vents, transformers, and air-conditioning plants. The whole is then simply sheathed in modular, often patented decoration. Since the basic shed is so thoroughly decorated, it can be an architectural chameleon. For example, when beautification committees, zoning boards, and consumers of the 1970s objected to the garishness of roadside glitter, businesses could just slap on more earthy ornamentation. Gas stations were sheathed in barn board, antiqued brick, and simulated field stone. R. David Thomas, one of the founders of Wendy's Old-Fashioned Hamburgers, boasts how design flexibility is an asset: "With some minor changes we could sell almost any kind of food in these buildings. Also, we could change from a Gay-90s theme to space-age theme almost overnight."[9] (Wright Morris groans from afar.)

Nearly everyone seems to have followed McDonald's lead by applying new symbols of good taste. The founder of the hamburger chain, Ray Kroc, recalls those days in 1966 to 1967 when he finally succumbed to the complaints of Luigi Salvaneschi, a real estate manager in the corporation who held an Italian Ph.D. in canon law:

"Mr. Kroc, California is setting the trend for the rest of the country in community planning," he'd say. "How can we go into these towns and propose to put up these slant-roof buildings, which are absolute eyesores?"

I'd usually wind up getting mad and throwing him out of my office when he started carrying on about aesthetics and Michelangelo and blah, blah, blah. Yet, down deep, I knew he was right. The time was coming that we were going to have to make a major change in the appearance of our buildings.[10]

The "major change" did not much affect the building itself, only its decorations. Clay bricks were simply substituted for red and white tiles over the cinderblock core. The old slant roof remained, only hidden now behind a fake mansard. In fact, since McDonald's adopted it, the ornamental mansard roof has become a good-taste cliché on the roadside.

There is, then, good reason to conclude that strips look alike. To see one is to know one. The scale, color, size, style, and arrangement of its components are easily recognized, often intentionally so. Standard images are propagated by architects, sign salesmen, photographers, and the businesses themselves. Insofar as we see the "same thing" in Texas and New Jersey, they have succeeded.

But can this fact, alone, justify the reactions, the "eh?", "ah," or "bah!," that strips attract? I do not think so. At least I doubt that they can be directly traced to the architecture itself, though historians and critics have tried. They claim that some buildings or landscapes are unique and uplifting while others are imitative and debased. But these claims depend on slippery classifications. By highlighting a difference here or ignoring a difference there, they find variations among styles and styles amid chaos. Venturi, Scott Brown, and Izenour, for example, teach us to look at signs collectively but to assess buildings by their particular type. At the level of abstraction where Caesar's Palace, Burger King, and a supermarket look alike, almost everything does.

This is not to deny that there is a sameness about them, only that this sameness is purely physical, a matter of masonry, asphalt and plastic. Surely no two strips contain the same mix of structures in the same order, with an identical design history. Like strip lore, strip architecture consists of variations on some very general themes. Yet, critics protest, variations, shmariations—who cares if you see a gas station sandwiched between burger joints or a muffler shop between motels? It amounts to the same, standardized, commercial sprawl. Bah!

In general, I must agree, but not, again, on purely architectural grounds. If we were to reject every built environment that seemed standard, we would not have much left to admire. Surely the Greek Revival house, so beloved by modern preservationists, is as predictable as any fast-food outlet. It is rigidly simple and symmetrical in the center of its lot with cloned ornamentation—pilasters, porticos, friezes, and fake marble columns. Builders' guides, like those by Asher Benjamin, John Haviland, and Minard Lefaver, were the nineteenth-century equivalent of canned plans from the home office. In 1834, a New York correspondent for the *Architectural Magazine* in London complained of "Greek mania": "Everything is a Greek temple from the privies in the back court, through the various grades of prison, theatre, church, custom-house, and state house."[11] But did not this same "mania" give us beauties like the state capitol or Andrew Jackson's Hermitage in Nashville, Tennessee? I just do not see how we can dismiss any built environment, whether it is a roadside strip or a public monument, simply because it has the style of its day. Some buildings and landscapes are beautiful and others ugly, even if they are all somewhat the same.

Of course, Americans have never totally agreed on their aesthetic ideals. As Yi-Fu Tuan, among others, has observed, even dominant landscape ideals, those with powerful sponsors, have changed through history. In the seventeenth and early eighteenth centuries, America's destiny seemed pastoral. Easterners launched a drive westward to escape the city and turn a godforsaken wilderness into a pattern of neat farms reminiscent of the English countryside. In the mid-nineteenth century a middle landscape of garden villages such as early Lowell, Massachusetts, seemed to hold promise. But as cities in the Northeast-Midwest corridor grew with industrialization and immigration, the next best hope was an architected city. Between the 1880s and 1920s, social reformers, political bosses, commercial boosters, and architects for varying reasons entertained grand designs. Plans like those which Daniel Burnham showcased at the Columbian Exposition in 1893 and the even grander Chicago Plan that followed strove for a rational, interdependent, expansive mix of landscapes—pastoral, industrial, and residential.

Since then the distinction of central city and suburb has come to seem less complementary. Those enriched by urban opportunities took their families and wealth home at night, leaving the central city to decay. Now forced to choose among tenements and little boxes, Americans are increasingly attracted to the wilderness that early colonists shunned. More modern grand designs, like Columbia, Maryland, or "new towns" in the Southwest, are apt to stress fuller integration of social groups and economic functions in higher densities with both pastoral and "wild" preserves. But for many Americans the only beauty left is to be seen on their Sierra Club

calendar or a vacation in Yosemite. So, visions of an American Eden have been quite diverse—the pastoral, the garden city, the suburb, the wilderness—and each continues to have its advocates. Each can be said to possess a "natural" beauty, whether by divine or human design.[12]

But by all of these standards the strip is hopelessly, unnaturally ugly. It is incoherent, angular clutter. Compare the nearest strip with a farm in the Shenandoah Valley, the area encompassing Central Park in New York City, Marin County, California, or the Everglades, and there can be little doubt as to which is more beautiful. These are the sorts of comparisons that strip critics love to make. Whether they prefer the gentle balance of field and farmhouse, the tree-lined boulevards of a small town, the massive coherence of redeveloped cities, or the power and subtlety of wilderness, they see everything to abhor on the strip.

Books like *Man-Made America*, *God's Own Junkyard*, or *The Hand of Man on America* document ways that places like the strip betray whatever beauty God or His agents create.[13] In typical fashion Peter Blake complains: "Our suburbs are interminable wastelands dotted with millions of monotonous little houses on monotonous little lots and crisscrossed by highways lined with billboards, jazzed-up diners, used-car lots, drive-in movies, beflagged gas stations, and garish motels."[14]

Since the late 1950s, such charges have multiplied. Reformers have rallied to halt the visual pollution that strips are supposed to represent. They try to preserve the wilderness or historic sites, beautify highways, or revise comprehensive plans. And they can claim some victories. Environmental impact statements are now standard fare, even if aesthetics are still ordered à la carte. Highway beautification and historic preservation are nationally mandated, though subject to local resistance. Here and there citizens have united to stop the construction of a highway or a franchise, like doctors excising a tumor. Others treat the strip with sign ordinances or spring plantings.

But the results of this movement, like so many of the 1960s, have been discouraging. A strip developed in the 1970s may have a few more shrubs or mansard roofs than its predecessors, but it still pales before natural and architected wonders. Opposition to the strip has done more to enhance the opportunities for regulators and to soothe the conscience and loneliness of critics than to control commercial sprawl. Critics certainly still have reason to complain. For example, nearly ten years after the publication of Blake's attack on "God's own junkyard," a group of "Socially and Environmentally Responsible Geographers" (SERGE) offered identical assessments of the strip. They dubbed it "visual blight" and "excrescential geography." Pierce F. Lewis echoed Blake as he bemoaned "the belt of roadside ghastliness that envelops most American towns like the rind of some decaying fruit."[15]

Of course, one could hardly expect a few outraged academics and concerned citizens to triumph easily in a nation where economic and political power is at least formally decentralized. Local, state, and national governments, legislative, judicial, and executive branches, and innumerable committees and bureaus vie for authority, especially in land-use planning which affects private property itself. In few other areas do the rights of individuals or corporations so obviously conflict with the rights of the citizenry as a whole. Moreover, reformers, who are often volunteers with little expertise or resources, compete for government attention with businessmen, who must try to keep their own options open. Match some beautification committee against a multinational corporation with wealth and organization, a team of talented experts, attorneys, and lobbyists; and the openness of the competition hardly matters. Regulated procedures, studies, or statements eventually become just so much red tape, another game to be mastered.

But seldom are these fights won or lost on purely aesthetic grounds. Look, for example, at their treatment in law. Since the turn of the century, state and federal courts have broadened their interpretation of the government's role in controlling land use for the public good. But they have resisted interfering with property rights if only beauty is at stake. Early cases, such as the Supreme Court decision on billboards in *Varney and Green vs. Williams* (1909) or those in state courts on the limits to police power in zoning action, ruled that matters of taste cannot govern land use. Even after 1926, when in *Euclid vs. Ambler Realty Co.* the Supreme Court upheld the constitutionality of comprehensive zoning, "objective" considerations like property values or safety took precedence. Since then, *Berman vs. Parker* (1954), an unsuccessful challenge to the constitutionality of the District of Columbia Redevelopment Act of 1945, may be the only decision sustaining the exercise of eminent domain or police power on purely aesthetic grounds, and this case had the added strength of dealing with beauty in "our Nation's Capital."

The nine-year fight between Mr. and Mrs. Stover and the People of Rye, New York, provides a fine example of the legal and moral muddle that remains. In 1956, the Stovers began to protest high city taxes with an imaginative display. Each year amid great fanfare they erected a new clothesline on their front yard. By 1961, they were maintaining six lines that prominently displayed tattered underwear, old uniforms, rags, and scarecrows. Eventually the city prosecuted them for violating an ordinance that regulated the roadside in familiar terms: to guarantee clear visibility for motorists, pedestrians, and, of course, the fire department. These are the very terms in which most regulations for strip beautification are defended. But as the Stovers persisted, a more complex gnarl of issues had to be addressed. The Stovers claimed their rights to private property, freedom of speech, and due process, while the city stood for the hallowed public welfare.

After the usual course of appeals the case reached New York's highest court, which declared that the case was aesthetic at its core. Could Rye control the appearance of yards on its public streets? Did the people's eyes merit as much protection as the rest of their bodies? Referring to the precedent set by *Berman vs. Parker*, the court said yes. In 1963, the Stovers' appeal was dismissed.

The case has been cited as, among other things, an encroachment on the Bill of Rights and a triumph for aesthetic zoning. Certainly it dramatizes the questions of freedom and justice that visual reformers must face. It dramatizes, too, their legal vulnerability. Even with the benefit of a sympathetic court, a background of cries against visual pollution, and the precedent of *Berman vs. Parker*, the New York majority denied that aesthetics alone could justify the ordinance. In question was the ultimate reasonableness of the act. It could impose "no arbitrary or capricious standard of beauty or conformity on the community." The Rye regulation was upheld because, whatever its basis, it was reasonable.

Predictably, the dissent in this case and majorities in more recent ones found the criterion of reasonableness itself too broad and imprecise to uphold. Furthermore, the New York Court of Appeals referred to "property" and "real estate values" as well as "eyesores" in explaining its decision. In its judgment aesthetic considerations could be primary but not sufficient. The one clear lesson I see in this and ensuing judicial history is that critics who seek legal remedies for visual blight will need to broaden their arguments.[16]

When the roadside is discussed in other settings, it is even clearer that more than beauty is at issue. Listen, for example, to advertisers defend their work at a Rotary meeting or a public hearing. They are as dedicated as anyone to "appealing" displays, but surely they mean a special sort of appeal. When an executive says that her billboard is "impressive" or "attractive," she is referring

primarily to its influence on the market. The real beauty is in the ledger and only by happenstance on the road.

Occasionally a businessman will claim his towering logo or decorated shed is itself "beautiful," but critics will remain unconvinced. Their exchanges are unique in substance, but the ones I have seen, at least, follow a predictable course. The principals might be someone like Jake Alger and Doris Wright. Jake has been working as a prep man at his stepfather's car lot since the age of fourteen. At thirty-five, he and his wife finally save enough to start their own convenience store on the Wayco strip, but the custom sign, "Jake and Jan's" surrounded by chasing lights, violates the building code. Doris, who is president of the Wayco Citizens League and married to a prominent attorney, wants to see that the code is enforced.

When a hearing convenes to consider granting a variance, Jake explains his predicament, his misunderstanding of the code, and his desire to serve the community (club pins dot his lapel). His sign is not that bad, and replacing it could mean the end of his business as well as the service and taxes it provides.

Doris rises to extol the virtues of the code that she helped pass in 1969. She mentions the danger of distractions for motorists, pedestrians, and the fire department and closes with a snipe at "visual pollution."

All has been civil up to now, but Jake has already heard enough of this pollution business. Trying to control his temper, he suggests that the sign is "damned attractive," at least in the advertiser's sense, and "besides, *some* people have different taste." This is a classic counter, for nothing puts a liberal on the defensive so easily as a charge of intolerance.

Doris decides to let others speak.

The others rise to register their sentiments, mainly establishing the two groups who will form after the hearing. On adjournment, Jake's supporters grumble in one corner ("What does she know about running a business, anyway?"), and Doris's in another ("'Attractive' and 'tasteful,' my eye!"). Strip critics leave convinced that the real aesthetic issues have been addressed only as a guise for economic self-interest.

They have more trouble discounting such talk when it comes from people who should know better—art critics, historians, and practicing artists. The published arguments between Peter Blake and Robert Venturi illustrate the difference that credentials can make.

In the 1964 edition of *God's Own Junkyard*, Blake compiled a furious visual and verbal assault on "the planned deterioration of the American landscape." It was original, creative, and devastating, but his artillery was standard bore. He set photographs of commercial sprawl opposite hay stacks, seaports, and fine buildings. He shot suburbia from the air, strip signs with a telephoto lens, and pavement with a wide-angle, seasoning the whole with ironic quotations from the likes of Robert Frost and Herbert Hoover. The conclusion even begins with an excerpt from the decision in *Berman vs. Parker*. Any claims for roadside beauty are made laughable in Doris Wright style. For instance, he cites "beautylover Burr L. Robbins as saying that 'billboards are the art gallery of the public.'" Blake dismisses this by announcing (1) the greater wit of Ogden Nash's verse ("I think that I shall never see / a billboard lovely as a tree"); (2) the fact that Robbins' quotation appeared in the *Wall Street Journal*, which only a Philistine bureaucrat would take seriously; and most of all, (3) that Robbins was president of the General Outdoor Advertising Company.[17] In all these ways Blake provides a model attack on commercial sprawl and its self-interested defenders. Whether they have read his book or not, most strip critics borrow from Blake's arsenal.

But it could hardly prepare them for Robert Venturi, not a bureaucrat or billboard lobbyist but a practicing architect and published critic. Neither he nor his collaborators could be suspected of lacking wit or good intentions when they asked readers to see genuine artistic achievement amidst roadside sprawl, to "learn from Las Vegas." Their route to this position is complex and at times contradictory, but nonetheless a serious challenge to Blake and his followers.

The authors of *Learning from Las Vegas*, Venturi, Scott Brown, and Izenour, begin by asking for quiet. Let us look at strips dispassionately, "non-judgmentally," in the name of analyzing a new urban form. They coolly describe the commercial strip, its components and style as best exemplified in Las Vegas, and then compare it with grander architectural traditions. They find striking parallels between classical Roman architecture, particularly as it was recast in the Renaissance, and the modern strip. Both, for example, enclose intricate space within heavily ornamented walls. Their facades are vastly out of scale with their interior plans. One is oriented toward sculpted iconography for the pedestrian and the other toward electrographics for the motorist, but both blatantly advertise their purposes to the public. It is an "architecture of communication" in applied, conventional symbols. Like the Piazza, the strip is an "eclectic accumulation" of structures suited to fluctuating commercial demands.[18]

Once Italian architecture is viewed as it was used, the similarities are striking. In context, in use, bas-relief is the forerunner of the lighted cabinet, "the series of triumphal arches in Rome is a prototype of the billboard," and "the Italian palace is the decorated shed *par excellence*."[19] Their differences are more a matter of contemporary imagery, materials, and function than style.

If the historical, eclectic architecture of the Italian Renaissance lends respectability to the strip, modernism is its foil. The works of Le Corbusier, Mies van der Rohe, and Louis Kahn are presented as a neat opposition to both Rome and Las Vegas. They reject representation for abstract expression, ornament and contradiction for massive organicism, functionalism for pure art, and historical allusion for originality. The strip is "ugly and ordinary," explicit symbolism in space, while modern architecture is intended to be "heroic and original," pure flowing form.

Since modernism in architecture as in painting began with a rejection of slavish representationalism, this analysis seems only reasonable. We may be hesitant to locate the inspiration for strips in the Renaissance, but surely it is far distant from the concrete and glass giants that have been commissioned since the 1940s. Left to our own conclusions, we might find the strip architecturally irrelevant, nostalgic, or simply reactionary. But Venturi et alii are no longer willing to suspend judgment. From cool analysis the authors launch a polemical offense against modern architecture and its social and intellectual foundations. In so doing they advocate not just learning from but emulating the very junkyard that Blake condemns.

The real reactionaries, we are told, are the modernists. In aiming for subtle forms that are difficult to read, they interest only the leisure class. Theirs is an "establishment" architecture, no longer heroic and original, but boring and imitative. Photographed side by side, Le Corbusier's Monastery of La Tourette (built in Evreux, France, 1956–60) and Boston City Hall (by Kallman, McKinnell and Knowles, 1963) look as if they were drafted with carbon paper. As these designs reject classical scale and symbolism, they unknowingly enshrine "technological indulgence." In their historical precedents, materials, and expense, the megastructures of the 1950s and 1960s owe more to late-nineteenth-century industrialism than to current social or economic realities.[20]

At best, modernism represents a liberalism gone wrong, when the intelligentsia mistakes its utopian musings for practical beauty. "As Experts with Ideals, . . . they build for Man rather than for people—this means, to suit themselves, that is, to suit their own particular upper-middle-class values, which they assign to everyone." At worst, it represents their effort to impose an outdated or-

der on a diverse silent majority. "Only the very poor, via public housing, are dominated by architects' values. Developers build for markets rather than for Man and probably do less harm than authoritarian architects would do if they had the developers' power." The recent increase in architected public space—pedestrian malls, skyways, restoration districts, and the like—is just further cause for concern. In Venturi's world Robbins and Alger are right—*some* people, in fact *most* people, have different taste—and the Wrights and Blakes are the self-interested elite. "Manipulation is not the monopoly of crass commercialism. . . . Commercial interests and the billboard lobby manipulate, but so do cultural lobbies and design review boards, when they use their intimidating prestige to promote antisign legislation and beautification."[21]

With an aesthetic theory honed from pop art, the New Left, and the social sciences, Venturi, Scott Brown and Izenour finally, forthrightly, advocate the "ugly and ordinary" as an alternative. They admire the architectural complexity and contradictions that the strip affords. It is "a vital mess," reflecting the genuine needs of a diverse, auto-mobile citizenry. Towering signs, for example, may seem grotesquely out of scale to a modernist eye. But modernists are standing still. Passed at thirty to forty miles per hour, which is, after all, their normal pose, the signs are "just about right." Messages on the strip may seem vulgar, but they are honest in origin and realistic in cost. Technological allusions are closer to the TV in every American home than a modernist alternative, the robber baron's factory. The strip does not, indeed should not, disguise its commercial purposes with irrelevant, utopian pretensions. "Unlike urban sprawl architecture, [modernist] megastructures lend themselves to total design and to extremely beautiful models, significantly impressive in the boardrooms of cultural foundations or in the pages of *Time* magazine but unrelated to anything achievable or desirable in the present social or technical context. . . .

They are a bore as architectural theory and ultimately, as well as immediately, unresponsive to the real and interesting problems now."[22]

Yet the authors admit there is still room for improvement. High-design architects can work with the strip, improve upon its style, if they shed the snobbery and "technological voodooism" of their modernist training. After the bids are in, most of them have to, anyway. Even those who are still horrified by mainstream tastes can mine strip styles for their ironic potential. Venturi, Scott Brown, and Izenour ask their disenchanted colleagues to become jesters, to do for Las Vegas what Warhol did for Campbell's soup. "Irony may be the tool with which to confront and combine divergent values in architecture for a pluralist society and to accommodate the differences in values that arise between architects and clients. Social classes rarely come together, but if they can make temporary alliances in the designing and building of multivalued community architecture, a sense of paradox and some irony and wit will be needed on all sides."[23]

One could hardly expect the artistic establishment to feel either accommodated or entertained. The revised edition of Learning from Las Vegas lists 256 reactions to Venturi's work in English, French, German, Italian, and Spanish publications between 1960 and 1976, and more have followed.[24] Nearly all of them take his work seriously. In fact, it has quite an active following. For example, the Society for Commercial Archeology, formed in 1977, is dominated by Venturi disciples. The organization's News Journal and convention papers are filled with expressions straight out of Learning from Las Vegas. They advocate extending historic preservation to billboards and decorated sheds that defy modernist canons. Books such as Frank Rowsome's The Verse by the Side of the Road, a tribute to Burma Shave billboards, and John Baeder's Diners suggest that there is a market for the ideas of Venturi and his collaborators.[25] Complex-

ity and Contradiction in Architecture, in which Venturi details his aesthetic theory, has been translated into Japanese, French, and Spanish.[26] But most of his fans seem to be academics and journalists rather than established artists or critics.

The whole Venturi movement, if it can be so called, has a late-1960s flavor. The hybrid, pop-Yippie-radical jargon sounds again like children of the baby boom addressing their cold warrior or New Deal parents. This "establishment" is attacked on the one hand for technological indulgence and on the other for denying it full reign. Pleas for systemwide reform are mixed with naive moral relativism and capitalist ideology. "Live and let live" and "let the market reign" seem to me odd policies for anyone to the left of a libertarian. There is a good deal of unintended humor in a vision of fourteen Yale professors and students pursuing "social relevance" and "the Great Proletarian Cultural Locomotive" by getting into Las Vegas in 1968. I do not imagine that members of the proletariat would have felt much solidarity with the class if they had seen them at the "opening of the Circus Circus Casino . . .—attired to meet the situation in Day-Glo–decorated castoffs from the local Salvation Army Store."[27]

But the artistic establishment tends to gear its defense toward more purely aesthetic issues. They challenge the analogy of strip to Renaissance styles, the blanket condemnation of modernism, and generally the value of "architecture without architects." Ornament, complexity, and contradiction may have their appeal, but they do not seem to be used very effectively on existing strips or, for that matter, in Venturi's own designs. It does not take "intimidating prestige" or arcane aesthetic theory to conclude that strips are ugly.

If anyone should have felt challenged by Venturi's work, surely it was Peter Blake. The basis for his irony, juxtaposing sprawl and high design or nature, was deemed irrelevant if not sinister. The charges of manipulation and elitism seem to be written with Blake in mind. Moreover, the central opposition in *Learning from Las Vegas*—modernism versus the strip, what the authors call "the duck" versus "the decorated shed"—comes directly from *God's Own Junkyard*. The authors reproduce Blake's photographs and use them constantly to reach an opposing conclusion.[28] What could be more insulting than the sight of your own image of commercial trash touted as an architectural ideal? —an ideal, that is for all except the manipulative, reactionary, pretentious, boring, and self-interested elite.

Blake was amazingly gracious in his response, all things considered. As an editor-in-chief of the prestigious journals *Architectural Forum* and *Architecture Plus* as well as the recipient of the Architecture Critic's Medal in 1975, he could have simply ignored the insult that was at least implied. Moreover, he had anticipated many of Venturi's charges back in 1964.

Blake's original argument was geared more toward preserving landscapes than building utopias. He wanted to defend existing variety against the garish, consuming novelty that both commercial sprawl and pop art represent. He hardly relished the notion of legislated beauty: "Where any citizen is permitted a choice between degrading ugliness and beauty, the state has no right to step in and restrain the uglifier. No citizen is *forced* to look at 'pop art,' or listen to alleged musical compositions consisting of five simultaneously broadcast tape recordings of the mating calls of dromedaries, or watch supposedly prurient movies. He has a choice. But in America today, no citizen (except for an occasional hermit) has a chance to see anything but hideousness—all around him, day in and day out."[29] Given this reality, a policy of aesthetic laissez-faire, live and let live, is just naive. Commercial vulgarity already has sufficient sponsors without artists' help. In the hands of unregulated capitalists, the landscape will be robbed of whatever genuine variety remains, variety that Blake admires as much as anyone.

Furthermore, with works such as *Form Follows Fiasco: Why Modern Architecture Hasn't Worked*, Blake firmly established that he is no simple-minded modernist.[30]

But Blake chose the republication of *God's Own Junkyard* in 1979 as an occasion for a formal defense. The only difference between the updated edition and the original is a new introduction, more than half of which is a response to Venturi. It begins with an admission that the book betrays some of the emotionalism that was prevalent during the early 1960s. In hindsight it may seem too passionate, but Blake hopes that he made some modest contribution to the environmentalist movement that followed.

And then he turns to "the other side of the coin." He acknowledges that in fifteen years, he, too, has changed his mind on some of the issues surrounding commercial sprawl. He confesses: "Certain photographs I included as an example of God's Own Junk in my 1964 book now strike me as extraordinarily interesting—even beautiful. . . . Judging by the kinds of photographs I began to take on trips after the emergence of the pop-garde, it is clear that I had become less and less interested in established, certified, and acknowledged 'Grade A' Architecture, and more and more interested in the potentials of junk, both physical and visual."[31]

But Blake concedes little else to the pop-garde. He found it ironic, to say the least, that his photographs helped make Robert Venturi an overnight celebrity: "I must confess that I was absolutely stunned—and then vastly amused. Venturi, a man I admire with very little reserve, was not the first one to challenge do-gooders such as myself." Yet, judging from the rest of the introduction, his reservations are substantial. Blake notes Venturi "has said that 'Main Street is almost all right,' which is balderdash. Main Street, USA, is almost uniformly dismal, disgraceful, and frequently disgusting. He has glorified the Las Vegas strip, conveniently forgetting, I suspect, that the proliferation of highway extravaganzas like vast shopping centers, fast food chains, and similar razzle-dazzle merchandizing efforts have destroyed whatever stores and restaurants the traditional urban street still had to offer—and thus destroyed a significant part of the quality of urban life, including the quality of Main Street—which ended up (as a direct result) not even remotely 'all right.'" In a place like Grand's Restaurant in Philadelphia, a Venturi and Rauch design, Blake can see only "highfalutin' condescension."[32]

In other words, Blake accuses Venturi of learning the wrong lessons from Las Vegas. Rather than striving for excellence as an artist, a messenger of discontent and the ideal, Venturi abdicates to mediocrity. He is a "messenger of the Lowest Common Denominator" in a "capitalist, consumer-oriented nation." Blake closes his defense much like Venturi with an appeal to open-mindedness, even if "our best talents join the barbarians."[33]

I present the arguments between Blake and Venturi in some detail, not because either seems to have won in the end, but because together they take the most common reactions to the strip to their logical extremes. I began by suggesting that strips are powerfully evocative places. Americans usually, I would guess, react to roadside sprawl somewhat like the salesman I interviewed at that drive-up telephone in 1978. The strip is just a fact of American life to be shrugged off, "eh?," as ordinary. It exists, as most things do, for limited, practical purposes in our daily lives. But with a little prompting from an interviewer or simply in the course of normal conversation, people reveal strong impressions of a strip. They know how to use it or avoid it, how it compares with other places, how it provides memorable or uniquely forgettable experiences. And most of all they know how it looks.

The strip seems to defy definition on any but visual grounds. Whatever the legal, historical, economic, and geographic particulars, people know where a strip begins and ends at a glance. By following Venturi, at least in his

analytic mode, or mainstream photography, we can identify some concrete sources for this stock image. Like strip lore, strip landscapes are conventional. The shape of the roadway, the design of signs, parking lots, and buildings, their materials, colors, scale, and arrangement follow regular patterns. Even their evolution—for example, toward less acute orientations to the right and toward more "tasteful" ornamentation—is wholly predictable. Most consumers that I have talked with can guess the experience they should expect in a decorated shed by glancing at its facade. Businessmen, as well as the architects, advertisers, and contractors they employ, help their own chances for success by maintaining these strip conventions.

But when people abandon cool analysis or simple resignation, their reactions to the strip seem less purely visual. The sigh of relief, "ah," that can be heard from hassled highway travelers is more for their stomachs, bladders, and gas tanks than their eyes. A billboard lobbyist or franchisee who delights in a roadside display can hardly be expected to distinguish its aesthetic from its commercial merits. In denying that these two kinds of merits, visual and financial, should be distinguished, Robert Venturi and his collaborators take the "ah," pro-strip position as far as it can go.

Critics, on the other hand, tend to begin with a more purely aesthetic position. Natural beauty is in pastoral, wild, historic, or fine-architected landscapes, and the strip is simply ugly. Bah! Reform measures like sign ordinances may be justified in terms of public safety, but the real enemy is visual pollution. The common charge here is that strips look too homogenized to express the distinctive character that any beautiful place should possess. This is the sort of argument that Wright Morris championed in *The Home Place* and that Peter Blake presumed in *God's Own Junkyard*. It appears in one form or another in nearly every literary condemnation of modern civilization, alias "the waste land," but also figures in most of the grumbling that I hear in the doorways of fast-food joints.

Yet, I argue, it is difficult to sustain on strictly visual grounds. How could a place as crazy as a strip look boring, anyway? Even if it does, other architectural styles, such as those in the Greek Revival, seem to have matured amidst homogeneity. When this or some other allegedly universal aesthetic standard is challenged, critics tend to turn to credentials. If they can show that a strip defender like Burr Robbins or Jake Alger has an economic stake in sprawl, that is, has an impure social conscience, he can be quickly dismissed. Such people confuse aesthetic and commercial concerns, a distinction that critics will tend to preserve. After all, Doris Wright, the Supreme Court in *Berman vs. Parker*, and the People of Rye can hardly be considered revolutionaries. They do not take on free enterprise or the social order, just the visual pollution that anyone uncorrupted by self-interest should see.

Therein lies a problem. Midst excursions into aesthetic theory, the Italian Renaissance, Circus Circus, and grain elevators, nearly everyone stands accused of self-interest, if not for money or prestige then for personal Ideals. A response to the strip, "ah" or "bah," may begin with formal properties—the use of space, ambiguity, color, and the like—but seems always to end in character assassination. (I'm an artist; you're a barbarian. I'm for the silent majority; you're an elitist. I'm realistic; you're naive.) Those who claim their criticism is essentially visual must prove that their social conscience is pure or be dismissed along with their self-interested foes. Even "progressive" court decisions, such as *People vs. Stover* in New York, agree that aesthetics alone cannot justify reactions to the strip, at least in law.

Implicit, then, in all this talk of self-interest and credentials is the fact that these arguments are not strictly or even essentially visual. A strip is ugly or beautiful because of one's vision of society as much as anything else.

Blake's attack on the Junkyard bespeaks a view of the world where serious artists inspire a public thoroughly victimized by crude commercial villains. Venturi's defense of that junk suggests a world where designers humbly cooperate with businessmen who are only rational, in proper service of a pleasure-seeking public.

These arguments also tell of social history. Cries against "visual pollution" on the strip recall Kennedy-era liberalism and its descendants, movements for environmental and consumer protection. Similarly, defenses of the strip in Venturi style make the most sense in the context of all the other battles that set "the people" against the "establishment" during the late 1960s and early 1970s. The businessman's defense of the strip typically appeals to "the good life" that has been part of the Euro-American promise since colonization.

Moreover, Blake and Venturi ultimately justify their assessments of the strip in terms of what it represents. For Venturi it is the beauty of Everyman's fantasy. This is one reason he finds allusion so attractive. Las Vegas, he admits, looks like a mess, but the vitality in that mess is what it communicates or symbolizes. Here is a place for sheer, unpretentious, high-speed fun, where investors and consumers pursue their interests and critics are just a drag. For Blake or his followers it represents Everyman's nightmare. Vernacular neon or pop architecture may be acceptable if confined to museums, but in public view it is a frightening omen of the future Americans should expect if they entrust developers and their bureaucratic allies. The strip is a threat to Main Street and virgin lands, not just because it is ugly, but because it represents the worst tendencies of American culture.

In these ways a cruise down the strip is far more than a visual experience. It is a kind of projective test for American culture. Like an ink blot, it may first engage the eyes but inevitably stirs the other senses. It is as ugly or beautiful, as inviting or horrifying, as our memories and dreams. A critique of the strip, pro or con, in terms of its formal, physical features is only a beginning. Its true meaning is to be found in the ways it is used, both pragmatically and symbolically.

Most of the uses that I have emphasized so far are based on imaginative constructions. Blake and Venturi talk about the ways of life that a strip supports by imagining themselves in Everyman's shoes, and their conclusions might be guessed before they tie the laces. Blake steps into wing tips or desert boots and makes Everyman an urbane liberal. Venturi dons patent leather to become a conservative suburbanite. But Everyman, and surely Everywoman, do not conform to such a flat image. Furthermore, there is reason to doubt that either would know much about life along the road.

Most consumers have, literally, only a passing acquaintance with the strip. They are an important part of the scene, but surely there is more to it. The strip is a place for the production as well as the consumption of goods and services. It is a workplace, a place for labor, management, and government, and their side of the strip, the inside, has been too often neglected. In addition to imaginatively identifying with Everyman, a cruising consumer, let us look at and listen to those who staff the strip. They are its more permanent residents. They as much as anyone will be affected by efforts to reproduce, beautify, or abolish their environment.

The conventional view of the strip, then, seems too generic and self-absorbed. To improve we will have to engage other voices closer to the ground. By examining a particular place, its inhabitants and surroundings, we can gain a fuller and more accurate picture of the ways of life the strip affords.

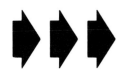

Chapter 2. The Hub of Hospitality

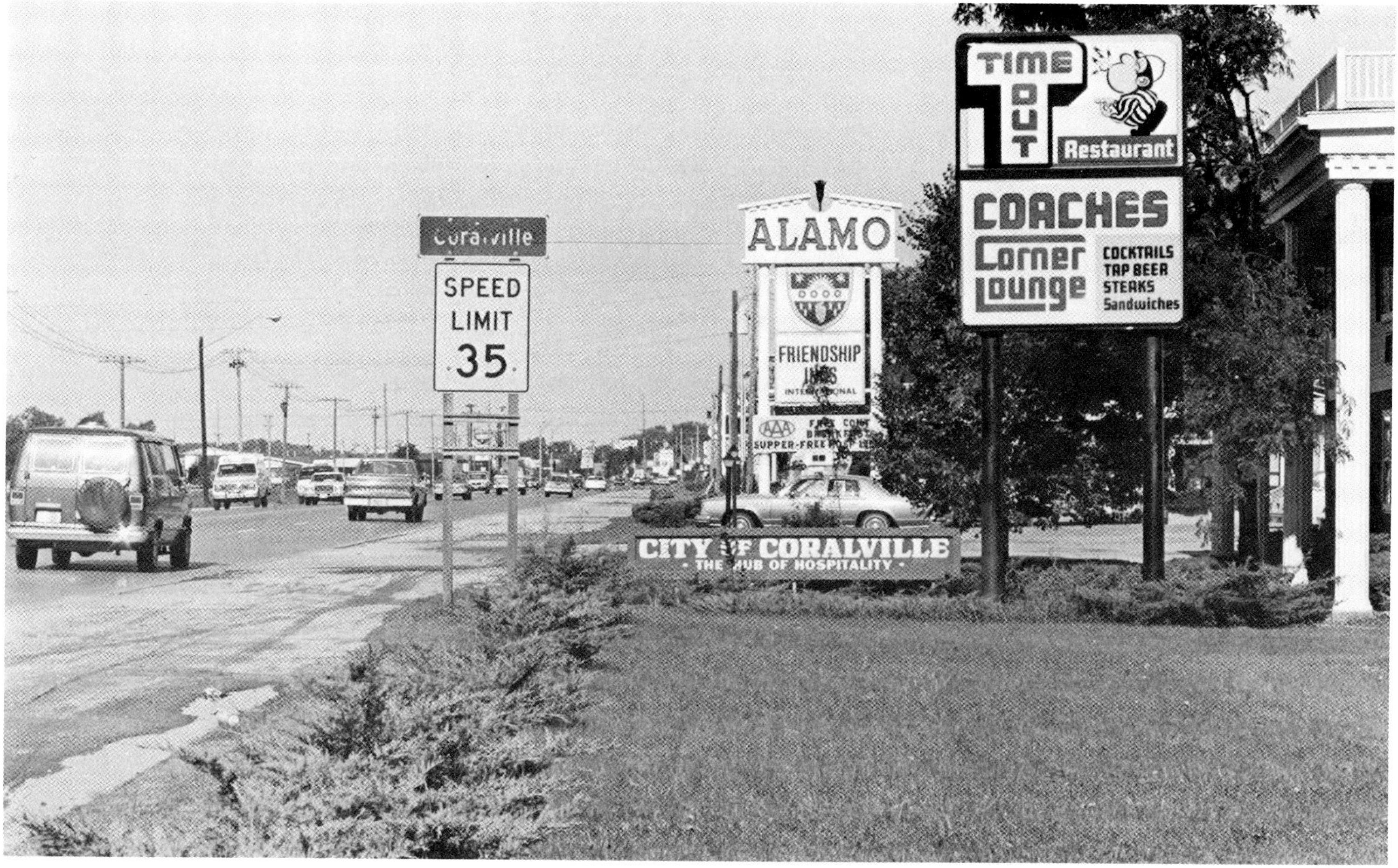

Coralville
SPEED LIMIT 35
ALAMO
FRIENDSHIP
TIME OUT
Restaurant
COACHES
Corner Lounge
COCKTAILS
TAP BEER
STEAKS
Sandwiches
CITY
CORALVILLE

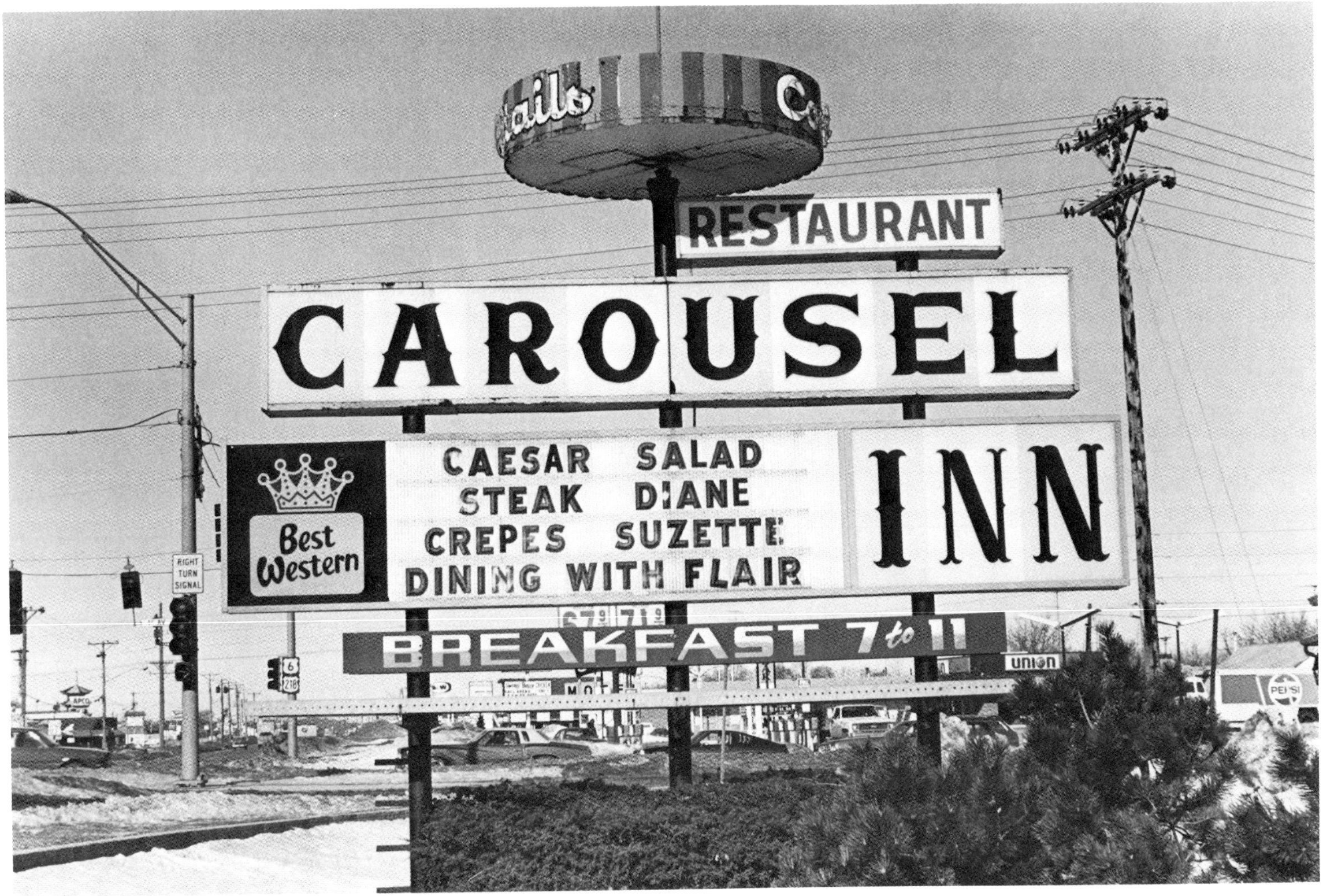
RESTAURANT
CAROUSEL
Best Western
CAESAR SALAD
STEAK DIANE
CREPES SUZETTE
DINING WITH FLAIR
INN
BREAKFAST 7 to 11
RIGHT TURN SIGNAL
union
PEPSI

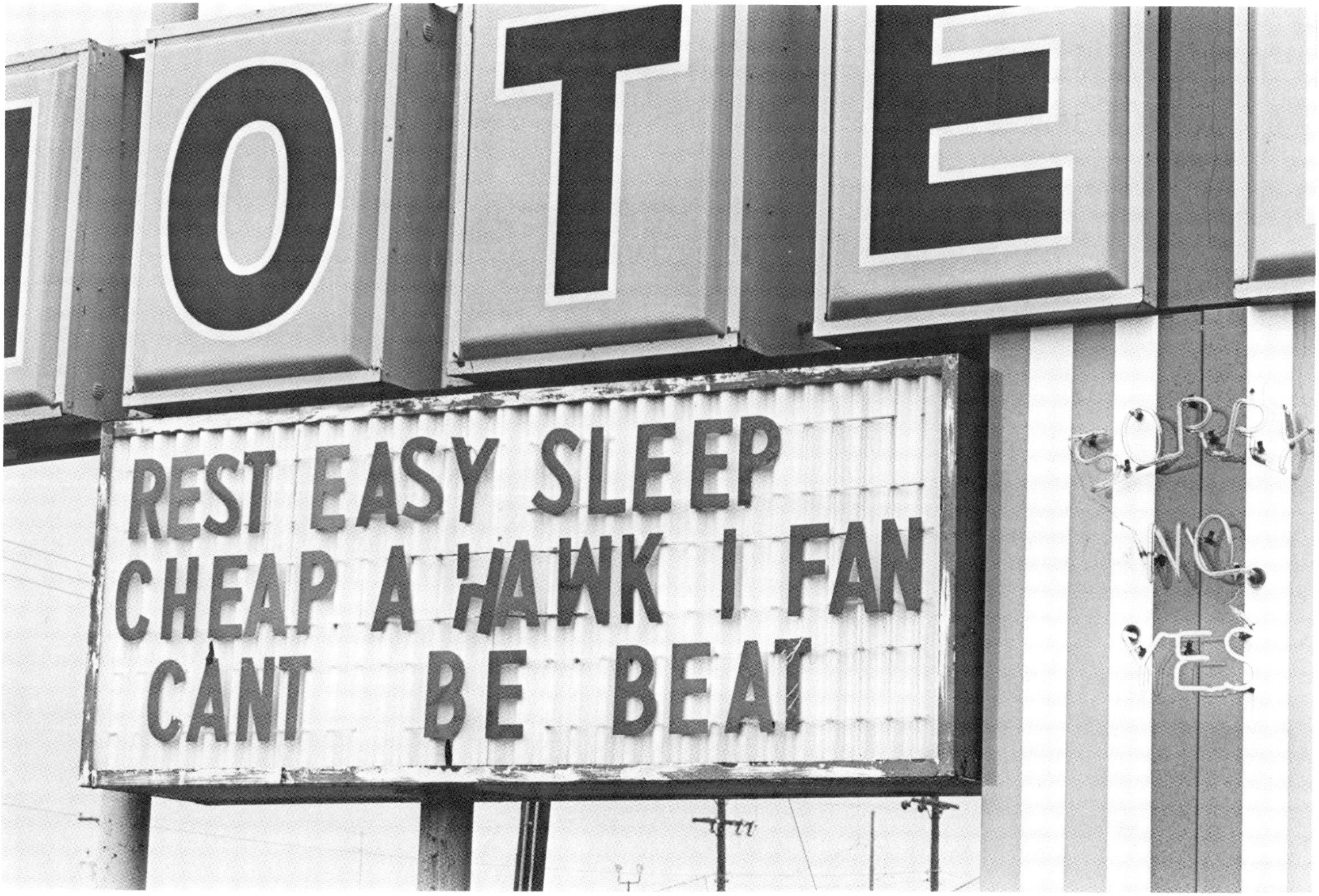
OTE
REST EASY SLEEP
CHEAP A HAWK I FAN
CANT BE BEAT
SORRY
NO
YES

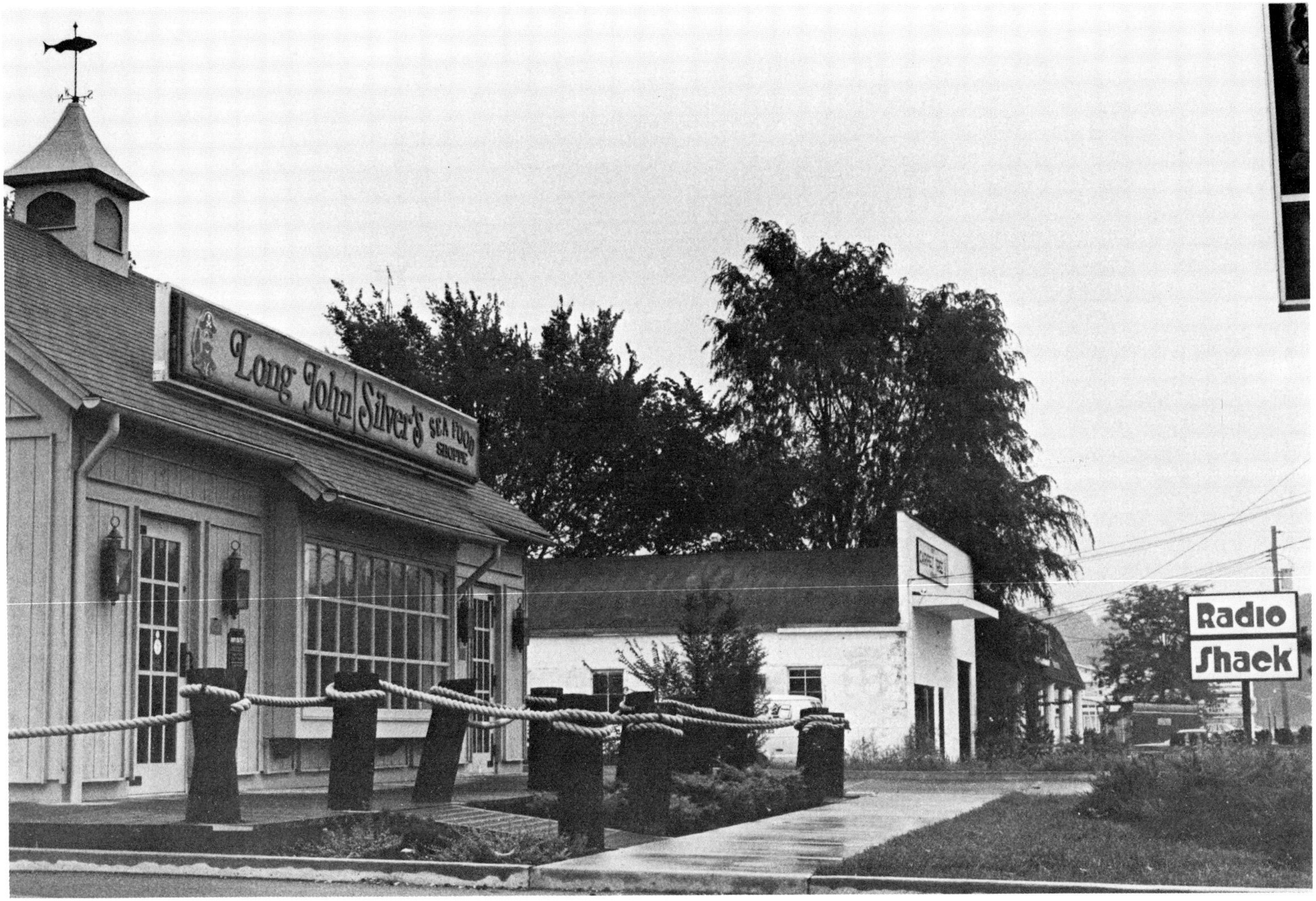
Long John Silver's
SEA FOOD
SHOPPE
Radio
Shack

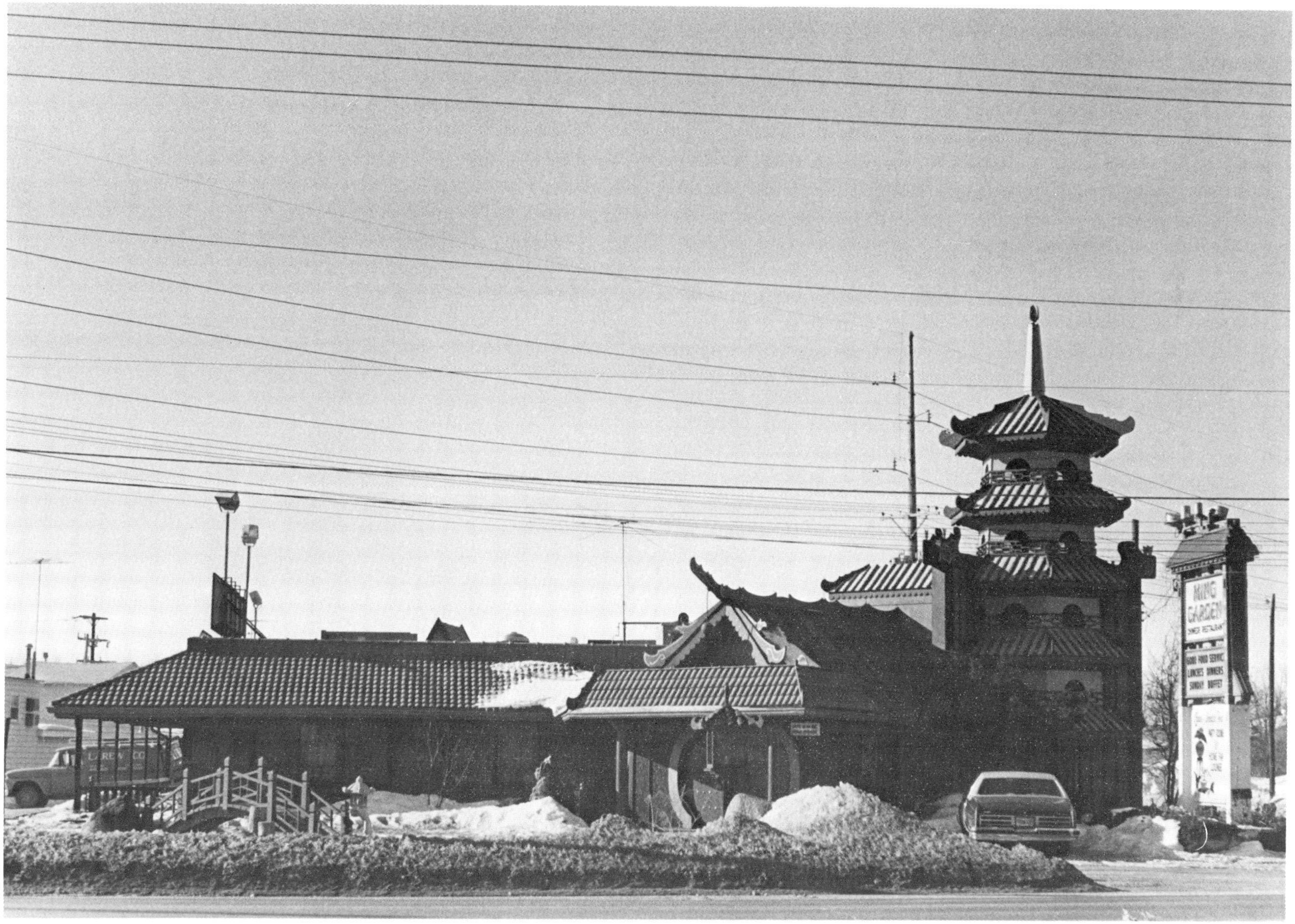
MING
GARDEN

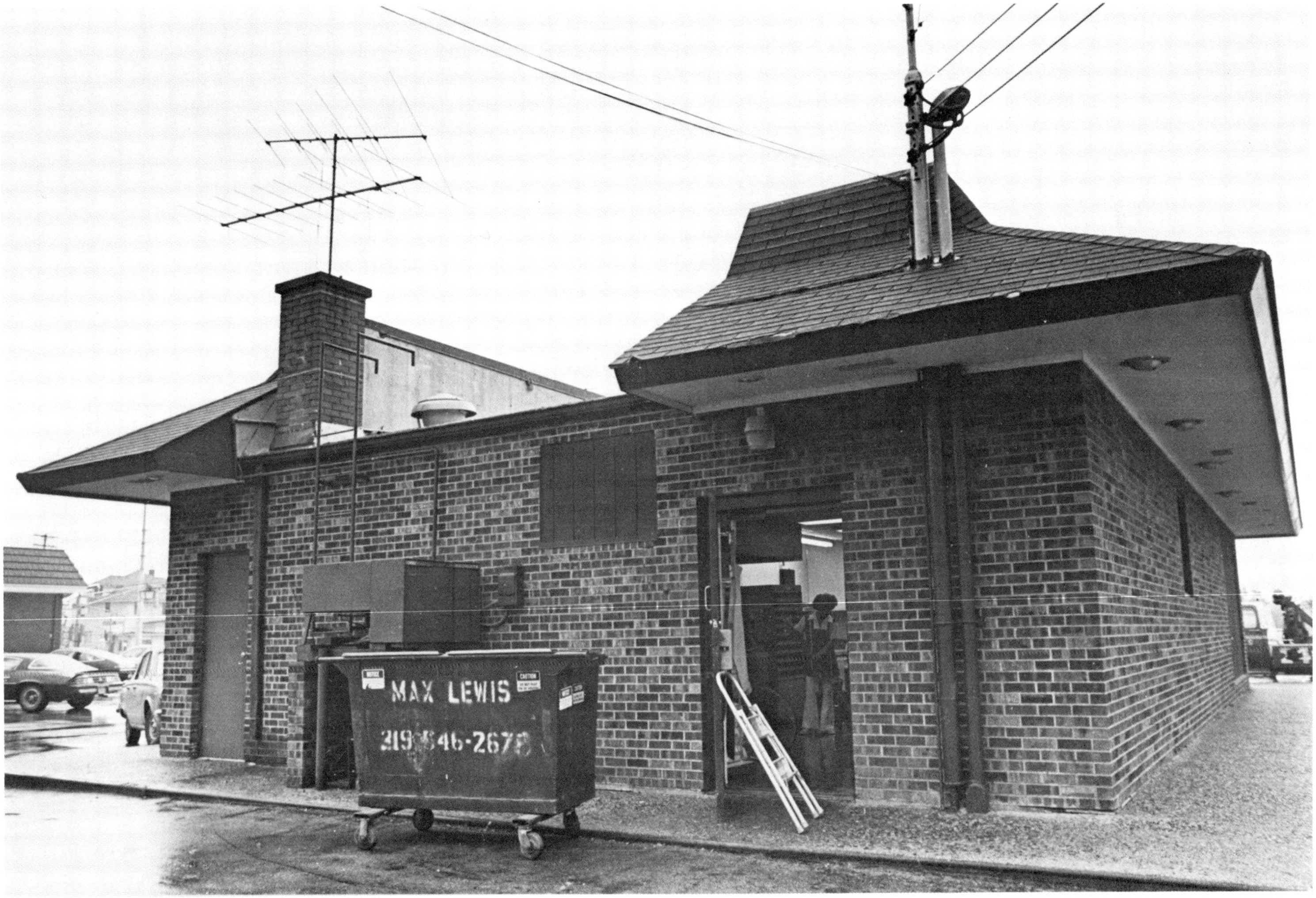
MAX LEWIS

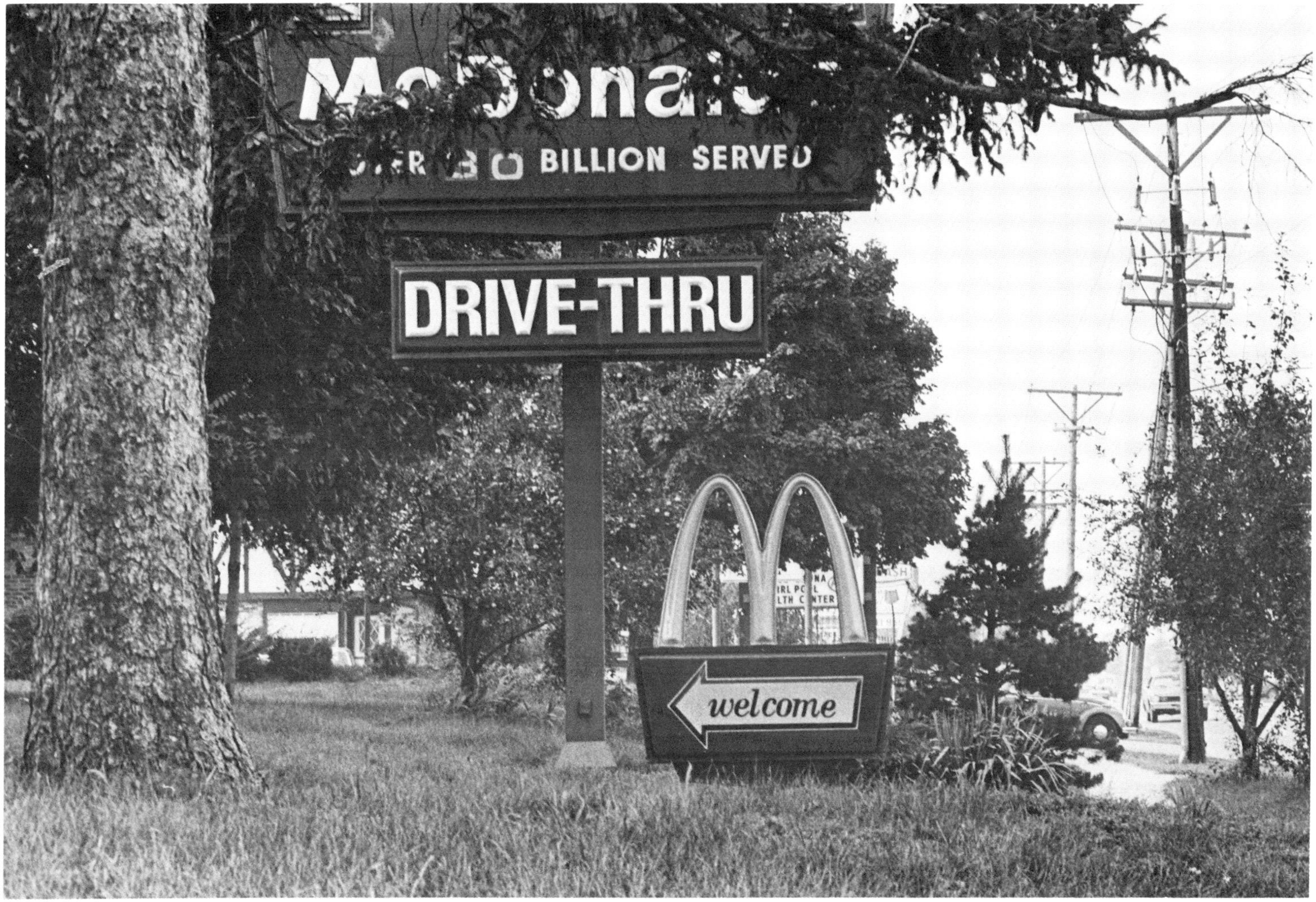
BILLION SERVED
DRIVE-THRU
welcome

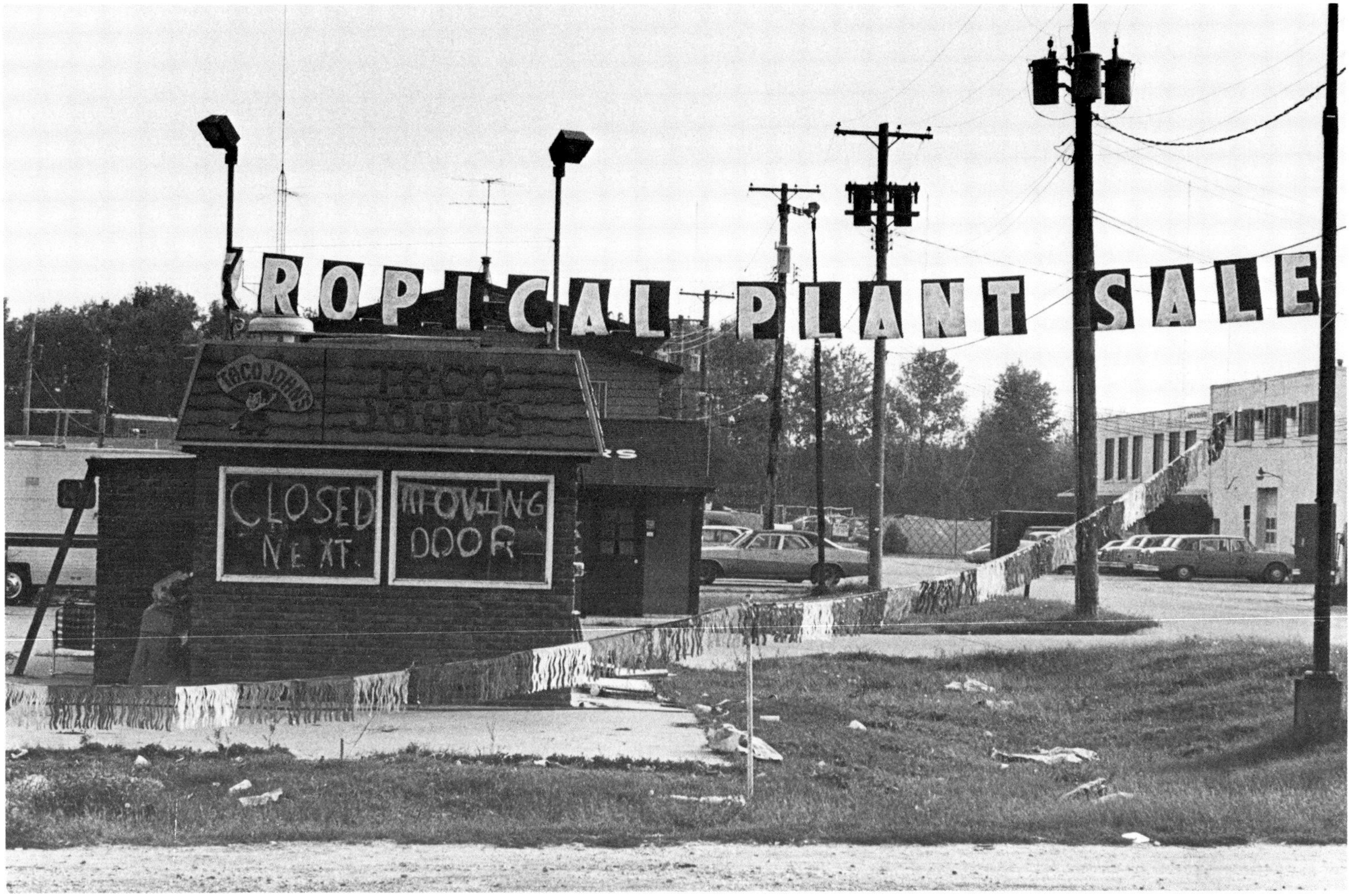
ROPICAL PLANT SALE
TACO JOHN'S
CLOSED NEXT
MOVING DOOR

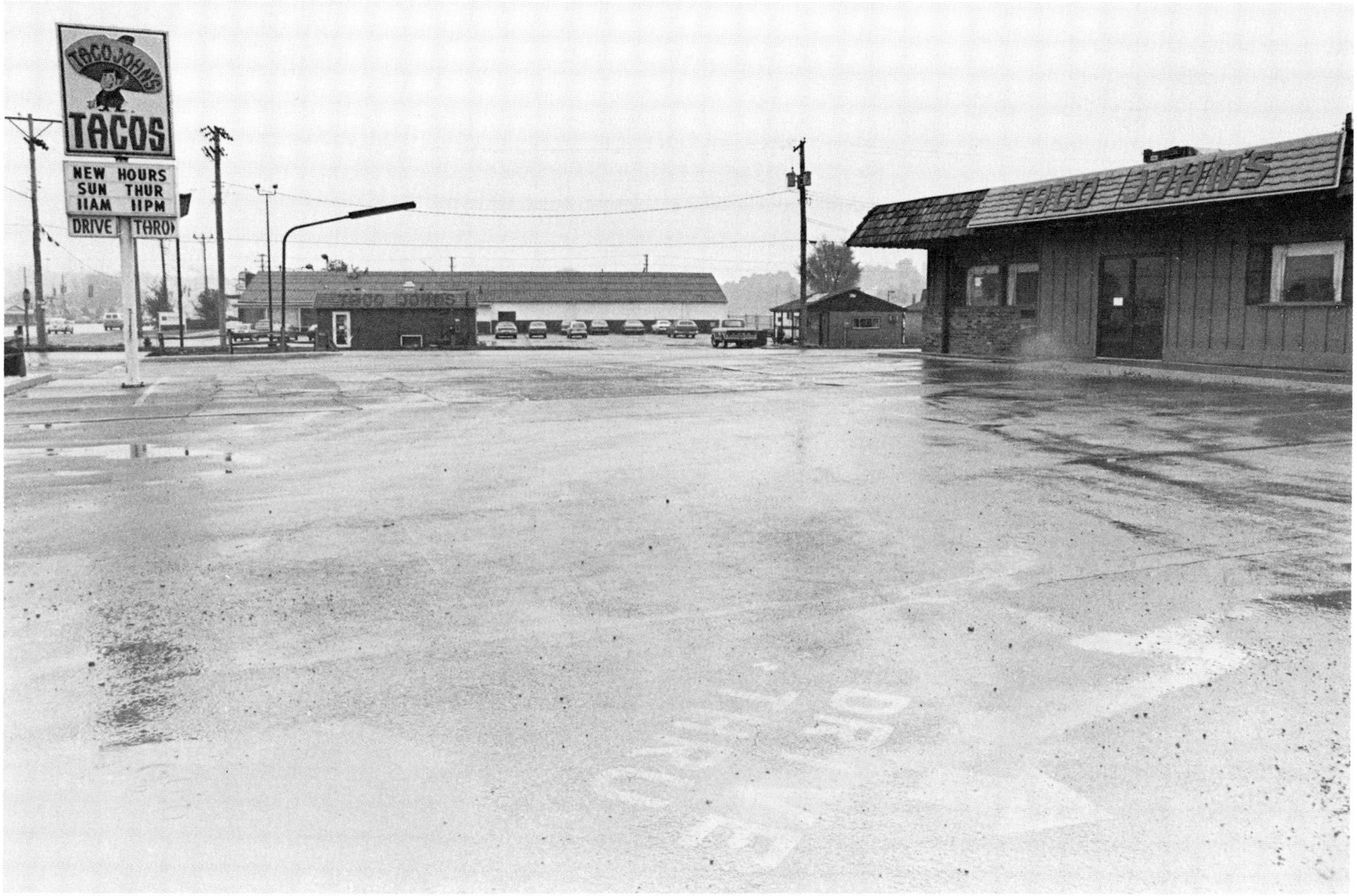
TACO JOHN'S
TACOS
NEW HOURS
SUN THUR
11AM 11PM
DRIVE
TACO JOHN'S

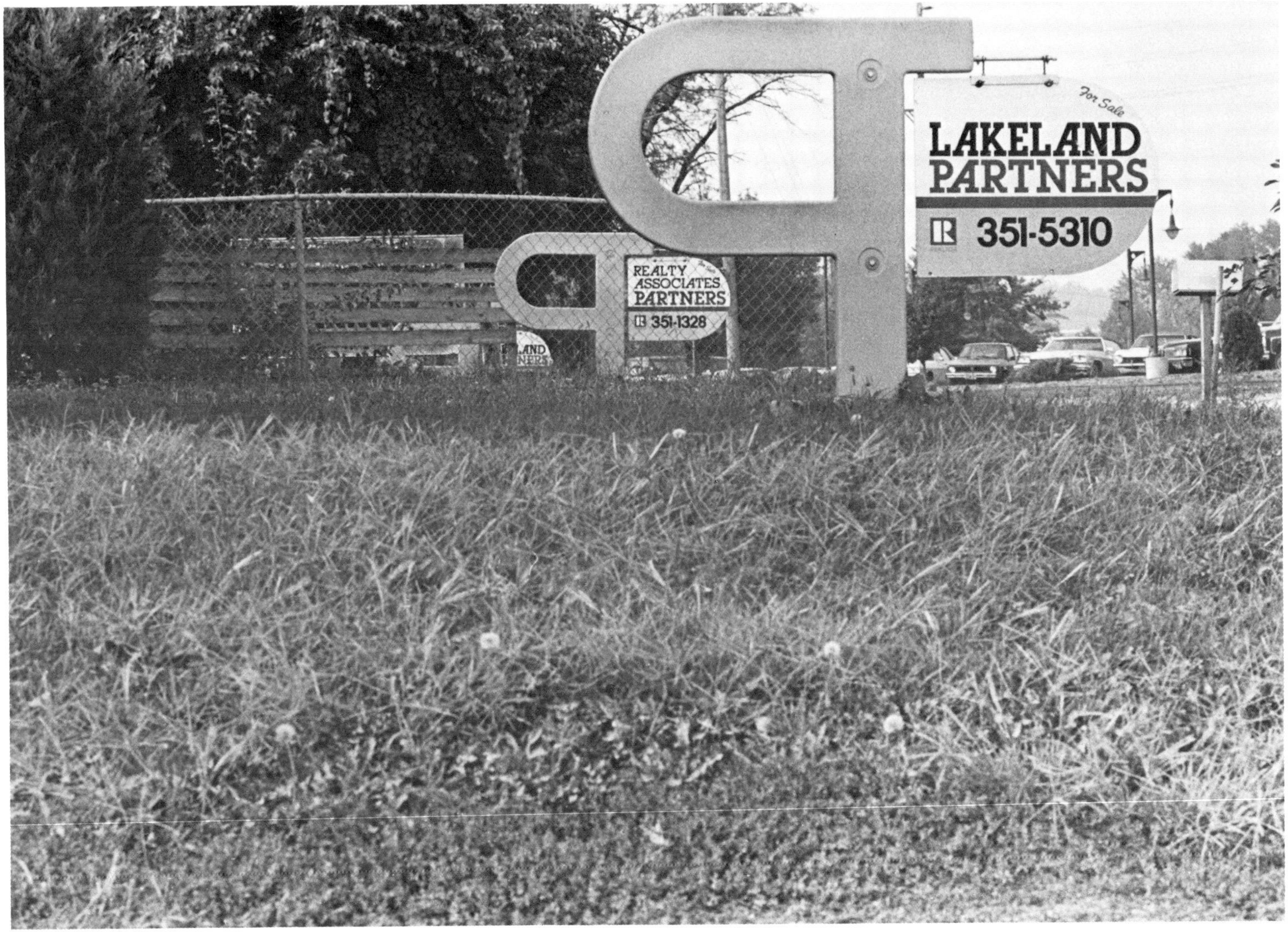
For Sale
LAKELAND
PARTNERS
351-5310
REALTY
ASSOCIATES
PARTNERS
351-1328

ne of the most conventional of wisdoms is that "you have to be from my town—or state or neighborhood—to know what it's really like," and this is as true in the Midwest as anywhere else. Between the Appalachian and Rocky Mountains are broad, blocky states bounded by muddy rivers and lines ruled in the nineteenth century. Most of their citizens live in cities and market towns, but the landscape is predominantly rural. It is an area that Americans more often travel through than visit. While other regions evoke a rich if less than accurate image, the Midwest is more of a mystery. People from the Coasts routinely confuse one midwestern state with another and find it hard to believe that it would matter.

Iowa City is uniquely a professional's town. Its largest property owner and employer is the University of Iowa, and other businesses are there because of it. Most of the retail, service, and housing industry is supported by university students, employees, and their kin, who constitute about 60 percent of the 50,000 inhabitants. Three hospitals (University, Mercy, and the VA), the American College Testing Program, and a division of Westinghouse Learning Corporation depend on the university for training, staff, or contracts. There are major manufacturers (Sheller-Globe, Owens Brush, Procter and Gamble, and Thomas and Betts) as well as some large shipping and construction firms, but they are fairly isolated, geographically and socially, from the center of town. There is no distinguishable boundary between the university and downtown Iowa City. "Old Cap," a gold-domed monument that once housed the entire university, is the official symbol for both. Although the university does not pay local property taxes, its allies tend to control city government.

City life follows the university calendar. The ebb and flow of some 20,000 students mark the seasons more clearly than any equinox. When school is in session, streets, apartments, and stores are filled with harried adolescents, but in the summer or over Christmas break the town returns to its older, settled, German and Bohemian core. If you are ever at a loss for conversation in any part of Iowa City, you can always bring up "the Hawks." University football, wrestling, and basketball teams are a local preoccupation and big business. Among fans of the performing arts, the same can be said of Hancher Auditorium.

By Iowa standards it is an unusual city, unusually educated, liberal, wealthy, and white collar. It is a temporary home for people of more diverse origins and tastes than any place around it. Writers and fine artists, people with handicaps or unconventional sexual preferences, crafts people, members of ethnic minorities, recent immigrants, and activists make Iowa City a haven in middle America. Even when compared to other college towns in the Midwest, such as Ames, which houses Iowa State University, Iowa City seems liberal, cosmopolitan.

It is a city, then, distinguished on the one hand by socioeconomic homogeneity and on the other by cultural diversity. It is both oppressively bourgeois and proudly tolerant of varying personal histories and tastes. If you meet someone from Iowa City, it is a good bet that he or she is young (or "young-minded") and upwardly mobile. References to books, films, professionals, or recollections of "my trip to the Coast" would not be out of the ordinary. At the same time, such persons would accent things they are uniquely "into": "I'm a Herzog freak," or "If you think that's weird, you should meet my friend." Hours are spent trading tales of "freaks" and "weirdness" that are assumed to be heroic. If your own life seems dull, you can at least be around others that do not.

Jobs around town that might ordinarily belong to members of a working class, distinct at least in their educational opportunities, are often grabbed by B.A.'s, M.A.'s, or Ph.D.'s. This is a way, quite apart from the sheer economic power of the university, that the social topography is flattened. Bus drivers, laborers, and clerks include university graduates who, in order to stay in Iowa City, have suspended their dreams of upward mobility. They may spend two or ten years thriving on local lore—the stories of awesome parties, protests, gambling, drug deals, eccentric celebrities, and street people.

Surely, as with most questions of taste, Iowa Citians would claim no single image of their town. But insofar as there is a typical image, it is one emphasizing diversity. Iowa City is great because it is "weird," "culturally rich," or, in the words of *Time* magazine, "the Athens of the Midwest."

But there are also those who find it less than great. Their view is less common in town, but it is common enough outside it. Chiefly on surrounding farms or in smaller towns, critics concentrate on the socioeconomic side of Iowa City. To them, all its weirdness signals only the shenanigans of so many spoiled brats. What can you expect from people who know more about school books or pushing paper for state checks than an honest day's work? Outsiders complain of their encounters with Iowa City bureaucrats and self-styled "experts," of drugs, immorality, and snobbery.

This is not, I think, a result of anti-intellectualism or intolerance but of a fundamental difference in attention. For Iowa City boosters, individual life style is the key. A fine community has people "into" as many different things as possible. But for its detractors, this standard is unreal-

istic if not parasitic. Labor, particularly agricultural and manufacturing labor, is the key. It is the realistic mix of productive activities, not leisure tastes, that makes a fine community. Charges of intolerance, then, can be hurled in both directions, toward Iowa City for its bourgeois decadence and outside Iowa City for its cultural depravity.

These are, of course, great abstractions. There is, in fact, no typical resident and no key. People do not deduce each of their opinions from some cosmic view of life or public rule. But I think these abstractions, particularly the tension between socioeconomic homogeneity and cultural diversity, make some sense of more particular, real situations that residents face.

For example, when faced with the prospect of a new subdivision, urban renewal, park, or restoration project, citizens argue how such a change would fit their image of a home place. Is it, in the land-use planner's jargon, "compatible"? Such arguments are effectively settled through complex financial and political agency, but citizens continue their debate long after they can have much direct effect. Yet, in continuing their debate new political and landscape ideals are crafted or old ones affirmed. The "lessons of history" are drawn.

An urban renewal project recently completed in Iowa City provides a clear example of this process. More than a decade ago, local business and government leaders took advantage of federal funds and bonding options to "revitalize" the central business district. Blocks of ailing Victorian commercial structures were razed to make way for a pedestrian mall, an enclosed shopping center, and a pair of parking towers, the whole integrated about public transit facilities, clay bricks, oak trim, and greenery. The project was controversial from the outset. A myriad of lawsuits between citizen groups, investors, contractors, and government agencies held up construction for years. As usual, the outcome was determined less by citizen debate than by the deliberation of business and government executives and the courts.

The new downtown has been completed, but the public verdict is pending. After its honeymoon period, will the new downtown still draw customers past suburban malls? Will officials identified with the project receive continued public support? Will revenue bonds for similar projects be approved and purchased in the future? *Should* they? In short, is "nucleated commercial development"—so popular today yet so costly in natural and human resources—a good thing?

Experts are consulted to answer this question by projecting the present landscape into the future, but it might also be answered by attending more carefully to the present and immediate past. Is "the malling of America" a proper application of the lessons of its own history? That history is, of course, complex and varied. Taken together, renewal projects are directed at a host of irrationalities and injustices in American life, but each is a response to more particular problems and opportunities. The problem in Iowa City, as in many other locales, is commercial sprawl. Residents point to booming, razzle-dazzle ventures on the urban periphery to justify the new downtown. The lesson is simple: since sprawl was a mistake, nucleate development to correct it.

Iowa City's model mistake is its neighbor, the city of Coralville. Not surprisingly, its makeup is quite different. It is more socially diverse and culturally flat. The same Toyotas and Volvos that clog Iowa City streets pass through Coralville, but there they are seasoned with Ford wagons, old Mercs, Jeeps, and pickups. The only institution for the arts in town is a defunct drive-in theater that specialized in Walt Disney and Johnny Wadd. The town has grown less from native veins than the silt in passing currents. Even the town's name came from fossil corals deposited when it was a Devonian rest stop, 350,000 years ago. It has had its share of notable citizens, but its only claim to national fame came when the Mormons camped there in 1856–57. More than a thousand emigrants got off the train in Iowa City, the end of the line, and spent a month in Coralville (then called Clark's or Coral Mills) readying for the "Mormon Trek" by foot and handcart to Great Salt Lake. In 1873, Coralville was enough of an independent entity to incorporate, but since then it has followed the familiar story of a small town turning peripheral community.

Most of the old-timers in Coralville tie local history to the surrounding waterways and farmland. Through the 1930s, commercial activity concentrated about the bridge and power dam near the confluence of Clear Creek and the Iowa River. The intersection of what is now First Avenue and Fifth Street was a nucleus for mills and retail and service establishments, representing the only town center Coralville has known within its legal borders. Resident so-called "pioneers," many of whom are still prominent in commercial and civic affairs, link their perceptions, for good or ill, to a break with that past commencing in the 1940s and accelerating ever since.

As commercial activity shifted from the mills and local trade to the booming traffic on "old Highway 6" (formerly Iowa's main east-west highway, then routed through Coralville on Fifth Street and south on First Avenue), the town maintained a slightly less active and concentrated business district as well as a modest rate of growth. Yet, as traffic increased, as Iowa City grew, and as development funds increased, the Iowa Department of Transpor-

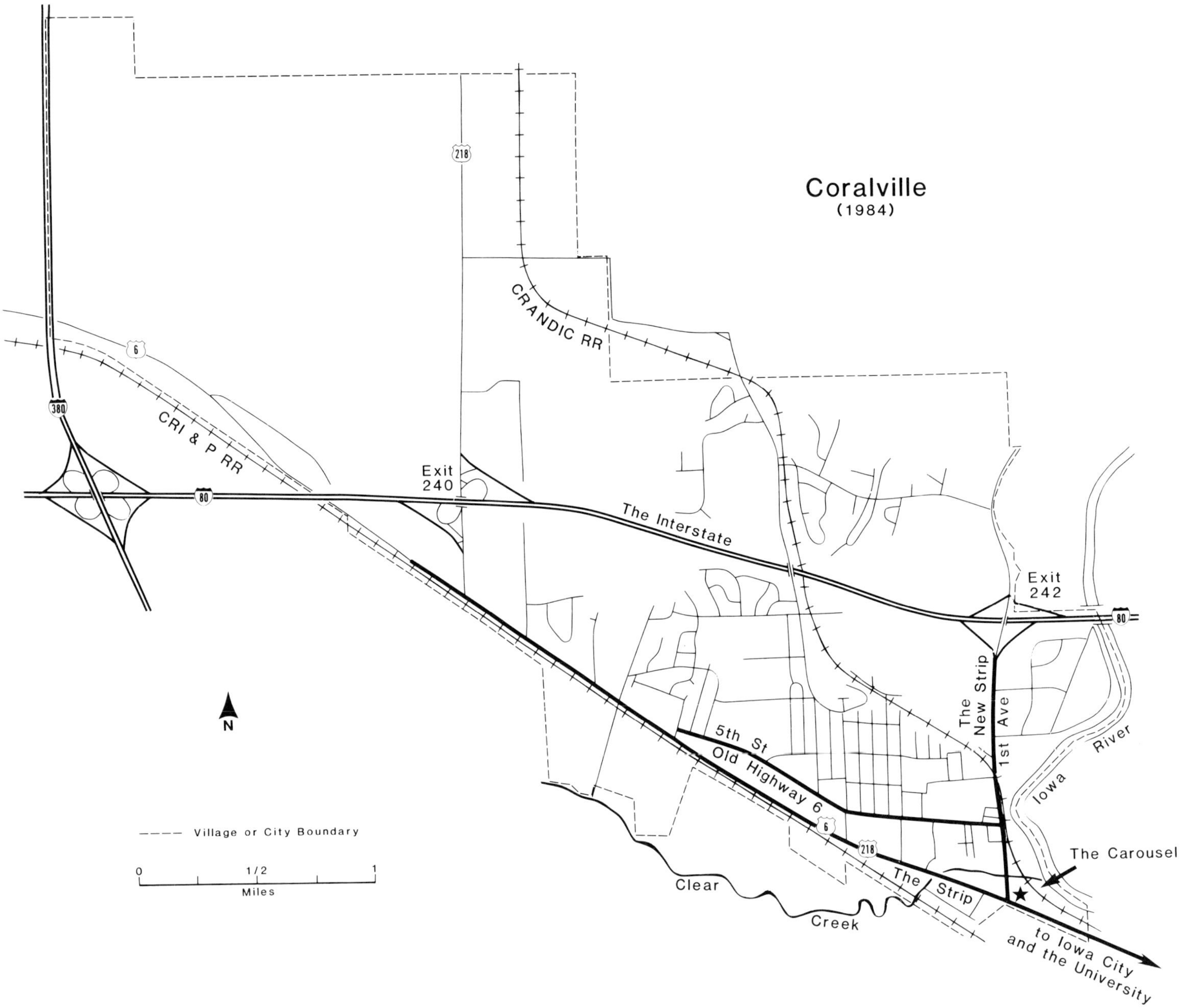
Coralville
(1984)
218
CRANDIC RR
6
380
CRI & P RR
Exit
240
80
The Interstate
Exit
242
80
The New Strip
1st Ave
5th St
Old Highway 6
6
218
The Strip
Iowa River
The Carousel
Clear
Creek
to Iowa City and the University
N
Village or City Boundary
0
1/2
1
Miles

tation and local entrepreneurs moved to relocate Highway 6. The choice of low, wet land to the south not only straightened the route but also moved it away from the center of town. In the mid-1950s, prior to the passage of limited-access legislation in Iowa, the relocation was completed. Local investors began to haul landfill to develop roadside commercial lots.

The central figure in this transition was Virgil Bowers. He is still called a "pioneer" in town, and stories of his escapades abound. Between club meetings, bowling tournaments, and real estate ventures, he is a hard man to get a hold of, but I managed to tape-record some of his reminiscences.

I graduated from high school in 1928, and started farming because I was going to raise enough money to go to college. I wanted to be an architect. But I made so much money the first year or two after school, . . . I made more than a lot of them. I bought a lot of equipment, in fact, a full line. I was one of those kids who was always crazy for equipment, out there watching it. I bought a binder, and my dad had a thresher, and then I bought an old tractor. Of course, then you didn't cultivate or anything with a tractor. They weren't built for it. They were designed just to plow and disc and harrow. The rest you did with horses. I was also doing some excavating and grading and running a sawmill next to where the Green Pepper restaurant is now. A jack-of-all-trades, I think you'd say.

But then the Depression hit. Corn dropped to eighteen cents a bushel, and a lot of people couldn't keep it going. That's when the Blacks lost their farm. The men died before I knew anything about them. There was just a couple, three women. Their cousin, Charlie Gould, was farming it for them, but the bank took it. I didn't have any money, either, but I had a lot of equipment, so I was able to get a loan. See, Charlie had a brother who was on the state highway commission, so we knew that High-

way 6 was going to be moved out there. There was a lot of planning for it, because they'd have to raise the elevation quite a bit, along the north side where the creek bed is, as much as fifteen or twenty feet.

So I bought it for $75 an acre, a hundred in Iowa City and fifty-five right where the new highway was going in Coralville. The Dennises, Halls, and some others had ground out there, too, but they never made anything out of it. Actually, I think the bank thought I'd put in a big crop and raise it all for them. They sold it to me without any money, thinking they'd get it right back, anyway. But the thing of it was we had a drought right after the Depression, and they had it a lot worse down around Fairfield and that area. The corn prices went boom!

The really funny part of it was that the dew was heavy in the little places I had. And I bought a team of mules only two or three years old, too young to work for a whole day. My dad had a bronco that was just tougher than whang leather. I'd plow corn with one mule as a partner and then trade mules each half-day. I couldn't stand them. They couldn't pull a lot, so I thought, "Well, I'll just plow my corn, scratch it more times, and keep the weeds down." See? With the drought we had, it was perfect, because it didn't stir up the bottom of the ground at all. All the dew took. You don't realize how much corn will take in dew anyway, and it's all low ground. Well, I had eighty bushel corn, and the price boomed. I paid for the whole farm in two years, most of it the first year. I thought it was wonderful.

I was farming, and Charlie was ready to retire, anyway. I worked it out so that the Blacks got the house with a little bit of ground, Charlie got some ground out by Tiffin one way or another (he worked for me for a while), and I got the rest of it. I knew the highway was coming through, so I'd planned then to sell a lot of it. Actually, I had a good many years before it did go through.

Of course, things were really different back then. You didn't need any permits. You just went ahead and did it. There were no city sewers or anything. Actually, we used to get special rates from Light and Power, because they wanted us to use them. But we had to fight the banks for a long time. The only way you could get money was to do something, have it done, and then get the money. You couldn't borrow ahead of time. Now, you want to finance things before you start. You don't even want to attempt it without the financing, but then it was a different proposition. Everybody was working on credit. Especially right after the Depression, it was not uncommon just to have a lot on the books. Twenty-five or thirty thousand dollars wasn't anything, even though money was worth a good many times what it is now. It was better to have something coming than not to have anything at all. I did a lot of work for beef or labor and such. All that trading on credit made for quite a bit of bookkeeping, but everybody paid eventually. It was just a matter of working back and forth.

At the time we didn't know anything about frontage roads or anything like that, and besides it needed a lot of fill. There was swamp and quicksand on the north side. You would never pick a place like that for a big project like a mall or something. It would have been too costly. Nothing would ever have been done if it hadn't been done individually.

It's hard to believe how much fill it took. We did a lot of it ourselves, more than half, I'd say. We'd use all the cheap dirt we could. If we were digging a basement somewhere and had dirt left over, we'd just haul it and dump it. It was a dumping ground for anybody with dirt they couldn't use. So it would be only fifty cents or a dollar a load. We hauled a good many thousand yards from the quarry, too, but we even got help there. A lot of times they'd strip and even load for us. Sometimes they'd even let us use their trucks.

I sold all of it a little at a time, the last of it around 1960. I bought it for almost nothing, so anything I got was just something to do. I didn't do it like a lot of people. Even

though I sold it for several thousand an acre, it still wasn't anything great, because the biggest end of it was labor, fill, trucking, or something. All turns into labor one way or another. Just making a living is what it was.

Almost all of it I sold to people I knew. They'd come and talk, and we'd work something out. I'd usually do some of the contracting. I didn't deal with corporations, just people around town I'd been trading with. Like, I built the Standard station. I was going to run it myself, but I bumped into Dean Carpenter who ran a station out on First Avenue. I thought, "There's the other station, and I've been trading with him, he bought a house from me . . . I'll do him a favor." It took a lot of fill, and I decided to ask Dean if he wanted it. But actually it was helping a big corporation because he sold it. And I thought I was helping him. See? I don't know whether it's rented now or who owns it or what.

But anyway, a lot of them have changed hands now. All together it was almost like a shopping center after it started developing. It was the best place for trade, the place. Anybody on the highway had a pretty good business. People driving by—that's where the trade was, and it grew from that. One would draw another, and pretty soon they were all there! The way prices are now, fact is I can't see how they can ever make money off it. Maybe they can! I hope they do. I don't like to see anybody go broke.

Virgil documents the origin of what became known, amidst some controversy, as "the Coralville Strip" or simply "the Strip." His memory may have twisted a detail here and there as I may have in the editing, but the most striking feature of his story is its color, accenting the frontier climate of Coralville's growth. Maybe that is only to be expected given his audience, a university professor, and the surrounding hoopla over the new downtown and the Coralville "mistake." Instead of the professional planners, bureaucrats, aesthetes, and financiers of Iowa City, we hear of Depression survivors with their roots in husbandry and machinery. To hear Virgil tell it, he qualified for the job not because he had capital or "taste" but because he had the first Caterpillar front-loader in town. The ingredients were inside information, kinship, friendship, hard work, and luck. The Strip evolved with simplicity, individual enterprise, and community spirit like the boom towns of yesteryear. It was not planned, just something that happened as plain folks struggled for a living.

It is next to impossible to verify Virgil's story, if only because so many of his contemporaries have departed and county and Department of Transportation records are hopelessly complex. His roadside lots were never numbered, and their history would require a title search for each. But other pioneers endorse his overall view.

For example, through the 1940s, everyone agrees, there was "really nothing" west of the Iowa City line where old Highway 6 veered down First Avenue toward Fifth Street. The only business on the bend was a gas station with slot machines, poker games, and whiskey for confidants. In 1949, Ermal Loghry, who had been working in the Princess Buffet in Iowa City, took over the bend to start Loghry's Drive-In with his family. He recalls, "There wasn't anybody out here to speak of from the corner on. Across the street was a big hole in the ground. In fact, we used to keep a fire extinguisher handy because it seemed like there was always a car going off in the ditch over there. We'd run out to see if we could help." The only local services on old Highway 6 were a couple of motels, the Pine Edge and Duncan Court; a fruit stand; and a restaurant, the Wagon Wheel. Ermal remembers well when the road was straightened because he had to close up for a couple of months in 1952 and take a job cooking for a restaurant in Cedar Rapids. But when he reopened, his business took off beyond his wildest expectations. As his nickname attests, "Add-a-room" Loghry could barely keep up with the growth. Through the 1950s and 1960s, he kept building onto the drive-in until it became an ele-

gant, full-service restaurant. He also acquired a new hotel next door, the Hawkeye Lodge.

In those decades the Strip brought to Coralville great commercial opportunities, expanding services, and a healthy tax base, but it also brought serious problems. Haphazard development attracted capital, traffic jams, and accidents; the old town hub withered; and Iowa City employees flocked to less expensive and newly convenient residential developments on Coralville's north and west sides. Between 1960 and 1970, the population of Coralville more than doubled, making it the eighth-fastest growing town in Iowa and anticipating its future as a "bedroom" and "kitchen" for Iowa City. Since the special census of 1974, the population has grown from about 6,600 to 8,000 and continues to grow. The majority now live in rental property and are associated in one way or another with the university or its hospital. The average residential tenure is about three years, making it, as some put it, "a city of transients."

When Interstate 80 was completed on the north side of Coralville in the late 1960s, the town's development was tied even more strongly to auto-oriented commerce. Interstate 80 is the most direct coast-to-coast route in the United States and carries more traffic in a year than any other highway in the nation. Since Highway 6, as it was realigned, parallels the interstate between Exits 240 and 242, it has become an infamous rest stop. In fact, its purpose is blatantly advertised. A Coralville committee collects about $10,000 per year to rent a billboard by each exit. They announce the volume of services that travelers can expect along the Strip as well as First Avenue (sometimes called "the new strip") which connects Highway 6 and the interstate at Exit 242.

You do not have to be from the Midwest to know what to expect. The Coralville Strip, like others across the nation, is dominated by national chains that make it a modular pit stop. Insofar as there is a unique environment or culture surrounding it, you do not have to learn it. Increasingly controlled operations and mass marketing guarantee that, whether you are in Idaho or Ohio, know or care, you can quickly find a burger with special sauce, a twleve-by-fourteen room, and ten dollars' worth of no-lead.

Businesses come and go, but the Coralville Strip consistently includes a couple of dozen restaurants, more than a dozen motels and about the same number of gas stations, a couple of banks, car dealerships, grocery stores, small shops, and a new, 120,000-plus square-foot retail mall (with more footage on the way). In all, there are over a hundred businesses, many of which are nationally known, such as Burger King, Best Western, Mobil, Toyota, and Radio Shack. Others you might not recognize because they serve purely local needs like agricultural equipment, because they are essentially regional franchises like Taco John's, or because they are one-of-a-kind like Robison's Furniture or Diamond Mil's bar. Even the mix of standard and parochial names may be regarded as typical. Surely their services, arrangement, and design are familiar. This is a strip.

Depending upon your experience, you might consider it representative. For example, a Los Angeles native whom I questioned in Iowa City found the Coralville Strip "cute," a miniature version of what she knew at home. And an Iowa native wrote me from the West Coast to say, "Los Angeles is the Coralville Strip writ large." Unfortunately, there is little way to accredit such judgments. Because strips overlap standard census categories and because, as I have argued, we define them visually or symbolically, the Coralville Strip must serve as an illustration rather than a representative of the American strip. The surrounding grain elevators and cornfields, the Iowa icons on marquees, and the magnificent sky above suggest that this strip could not be simply transported to another site. Frankly, I doubt that any place could. Nevertheless, this strip is not remarkably atypical, a fact that many advertisers stress and harried customers demand.

A sample of some initial reactions to the Coralville Strip suggests just how typical it is:

There's nothing really unusual here. I guess the only thing is—now that I think about it—it just doesn't seem like Iowa. It's more like what you'd see in Detroit.—Salesman at a drive-up pay telephone

I just came in last night. They took my sister to the University Hospital. She's had another stroke, and this time it looks pretty bad. We'll just have to pray and wait.

I got a room a couple of doors down, just the closest place I can find. I'll probably spend all my time at the hospital, so it doesn't much matter.—Woman having coffee and a doughnut while she waits for the hospital van

I had a breakdown on the interstate. They're supposed to get me another rig in the morning. They've got it set up so I crash here for the night.—Trucker checking into a motel

"We're all here for the game."
"Are you a Hawk fan?"
(Chorus of "booo"s and "Go, Hoosiers!")
"We took out a whole block of rooms here."
"Yeah, there'll be some partying tonight!"
—Crowd of Indiana alumni at a motel bar

God, this place is just full of franchises, plastic and neon. I mean, how many burger joints do you need in a town?

I guess it's good business, though. I wouldn't mind having one. They sure do a hell of a business, and, from what I understand, any idiot could do it.—Young sales representative on his way out of a fast-food restaurant

We're on our way to Colorado—have some family around Denver. I try to hit the Standard stations because I've got a card with them. I don't have to carry much cash, and I can keep tabs on my expenses.—Man filling up his car with a camper in tow while the kids dash to the rest rooms at a service station

This is just your basic American shit. You see the same crap all over the place. If you take this place and blow it up, you've got New Jersey. In fact, they probably ought to blow it all up and start over. If it weren't for the damned automobile, we wouldn't have this sort of crap. That was the big mistake.

You know, this is a town in itself! I first thought it was part of Iowa City, you know, just sort of a raunchy part of it. But they've got their own police, buses, and all that. God, can you imagine?!—Conventioneer in a bar

Reactions such as these show the variety one might expect in a public place. Outsiders come with gaiety or misfortune. They stop because it is near Iowa City or because it is anyplace for food, fuel, and shelter. With individual style and experience they improvise on Blake and Venturi themes.

More sophisticated impressions could be expected from residents, if only because they live near the Strip and the new downtown. These places are well-recognized symbols of the social and cultural difference between Coralville and Iowa City. The difference may, in fact, be slight, but it is heartfelt. When a member of the new Metropolitan Planning Commission (later renamed and atrophied) simply made public reference to the Strip,

members of the Coralville City Council threatened to secede from the organization. The Strip has been a sore point in disputes over regional transportation and comprehensive plans, school consolidations, zoning and building codes, and citizen action campaigns. In 1976, for example, Donna Epley organized a committee of the Association for Better Coralville to beautify the Strip. With little on its side except local volunteers, an instructor of landscape design from Cedar Rapids, and pastoral ideology, "Goal: Green" was frustrated. But whenever questions of community taste arise, as in the perennial battles over outdoor advertising, "the ABC crowd" makes its presence known. Local feelings about the Strip, then, run deep, and they have social, economic, and political import.

Since university professors were among the authorities who supported Iowa City's alternative to the Strip, I hoped they could help me understand its meaning. One of the first things I did was to call on faculty at the university who were supposed to have "related interests." I queried fifty professors representing nearly every division of the humanities and social sciences: "What, in your professional wisdom, is the origin and significance of a place like the Strip?" Their answers were standard in form but diverse in content. "There really isn't anything on strips, per se," they said, "but we do know it all comes down to . . . X." Unfortunately, "X" ranged from the importance of auto transit or retail marketing to the ravages of corporate capitalism and the decline of Western civilization. It was a pet peeve in academic garb.

The literature they recommended was just as disappointing. The American strip is a minor theme of interdisciplinary works on "larger" subjects (such as urban planning, suburbanization, or cultural geography) or, more commonly, the site of narrow case studies (as in spatial preferences, commercial architecture, transportation planning, or urban ecology). Whether they define the strip as "essentially" ecological, historical, or architectural, experts tend to start with the question, "How could such blight occur?" or "How can it be prevented?" They begin, then, with the conclusions of Peter Blake and that drunken conventioneer with little better justification. For example, I was excited to find one of the few theses ever devoted to a commercial strip. Barry Gordon reported "American cultural themes" on Erie Boulevard in Syracuse, New York. What did he find? Selfishness, conspicuous consumption, artificial glamour, and alienation. And how did he find them? By cruising the strip to see how it fit his stereotype of Americans.[1]

Wherever I turned for fresh, deep insights, I found the same consumer-oriented, symbolic projections that I originally feared. The lessons of history that observers draw from the strip say more about their taste than their subject. This is not just a problem of academic or barroom niceties, since in Iowa City, as elsewhere, these lessons figure in designs for the future. With massive quantities of capital, labor, and natural resources, planners and developers are working to correct a "mistake" they have barely begun to understand.

I then decided to document how this could happen, and it seemed like an ominous task. Unlike water quality or noise pollution, human perspectives on land use are notoriously difficult to measure, especially if a sense of context is to be preserved. Local planners complained to me of the inadequacy of their own attempts at public accountability, survey research, and open hearings. Similarly, elected officials lamented the weight they must give to people who ring the phone off the wall. Often, in effect, citizens with limited interest in "the bigger picture," alternative futures, or the past speak for the community.

Through intensive fieldwork I hoped to help. I spent more than three years talking with hundreds of community leaders, students, workers, and consumers. I followed them about their daily routines. They led me on tours of local commerce, through narratives of its past, and projections for its future. In miles of tape and reams of notes, I recorded their impressions of the Strip and its function in the community. Eventually, I hoped, my findings could ground the folklore surrounding the Strip in what I presumed were the complex tastes and activities of its public.

What I found, however, was simplicity. There were, of course, many people who were apathetic, but most seemed to be plainly for or against the Strip for obvious reasons. All the controversy surrounding the place seems to have pushed residents into two camps who, in fact, know their opposition well.

On one side, by far the more crowded, are those who find the Strip evil, embarrassing, or just a joke. Like Orange County or the state of New Jersey, it represents American commercialism gone wild. They view Coralville as little more than the Strip and a low-life suburb, a blight on the other side of the tracks. They stop there out of convenience or "necessity" and evaluate what they find in terms of their immediate consumer experience. They tend to assume that everyone, like themselves, is willing and able to move on when their stint in Iowa City is through. This particular strip is remarkable only because they are regularly exposed to it. What they see is ample evidence of environmental ignorance, arrogance, or simple bad taste among native Coralvillians.

This attitude is common on both sides of the tracks, but it is considered characteristic of "university people" or "Iowa City Types." Given the dominance of the university and its transient associates, this is hardly surprising. But even without the university, their attitude is understandable. Only Kroc or Venturi could find much architectural merit on the Strip. Daily commerce consumes tons of disposable place settings, fuel, and patience. Despite the notorious diligence of Coralville police, driving there can be dangerous. Most of the accidents, moving violations, and thefts in town occur along Highway 6 and First Avenue, where tens of thousands of cars travel each day.

But there is another side to consider. The Strip provides vital services and employment and a healthy share of local taxes. In fact, the mill rate often attracts to Coralville the very people who are its most severe critics. It is, I think, a happy irony that the taxes on those auto-oriented enterprises support the most effective public transit system in the state. The economic value of the Strip, among other things, lends Coralville boosters a ready defense.

They are actually a very small segment of the population, probably no more than two or three hundred, but their energy, position, and civic pride give them influence far in excess of their number. They dominate city politics and clubs. These so-called "True Coralvillians" define the spirit of their place. For them, it is a small town with a unique history, where friendly folks share continuing, common interests. They volunteer their time and patronage to neighbors. Thanks, in part, to the prosperity of the Strip, Coralville has integrity independent of its big-city neighbor.

The Chamber of Commerce, begun in 1953 at the Wagon Wheel, is the organizational base for boosters. Its regular Monday luncheons, now held at Loghry's restaurant, are sleepy affairs. Although there are about 150 members, meetings seldom draw more than 30. But again, their influence is significant. They sponsor ball teams, service awards, and community celebrations. They organize clean-up days, arts competitions, parks, and planting programs. They even contribute to the ABC despite its Iowa-City bent. It was the chamber that gave Coralville its slogan, "The Hub of Hospitality," in proud recognition of the Strip. The official city newspaper, the *Coralville Courier*, began as a publication of the Chamber of Commerce, and the two still share an office. In all they

stand for the alliance of business and community interests.

Many of the "pioneers," modern developers, and government officials belong to the chamber. When I asked the mayor to explain their role as a pressure group, he said, "They don't have to pressure me. I go to all the meetings." Of course, they do not always get their way. Probably their clearest defeat came in 1963, when the town voted to consolidate its schools with Iowa City. But in the more arcane world of capital improvements, zoning, and building codes, True Coralvillians are proud to have won more support for independent enterprise than Iowa City affords. For example, I attended a meeting of the chamber in 1980, where a member who was a banker and city councilman defended the latest compromise in the sign ordinance. Naturally, he emphasized its superiority over the Iowa City code. He began, "Now, I don't want to say anything against our good neighbors, but. . . ." An officer of the chamber interrupted, "Don't worry about that! You're among friends here!"

Iowa City Types characterize this alliance as a conflict of interest, but True Coralvillians disagree. Business and community interests are one and the same. Sure, the Strip may be a bit tacky, but so is Riverside Drive in Iowa City. We will just try to improve. Besides, who else but businessmen would serve the public, in effect, for twenty-five or thirty cents per hour? Coralville does not need expensive bureaucrats, just the common sense and good will of its citizens. If you do not like what you see, get involved! As a member of the chamber explained, "In Coralville we let it all hang out!"

There is a good deal of wisdom on both sides. Entrepreneurs and the public do share many interests. Cash that flows through town can be harnessed for community betterment. A government of volunteers is potentially cheaper and friendlier than disinterested bureaucrats. But it is always possible that a small circle of friends will just line their own pockets. Surely, both cities can be re-

spected for defending their integrity, but just as surely
they depend on each other. Moreover, the difference between developments in Iowa City and Coralville has more
to do with their past than with their modern spirit. The
Strip evolved on the fringe of town when independent entrepreneurs seized the opportunity of the moment. The
heart of Iowa City was planned in the nineteenth century,
when it was supposed to be the state capital. Each city
is politically organized in accordance with its scale. The
service economy of Iowa City may be more rationalized
simply because it is older and better financed. Property
values alone account for much of the concentration of
small businesses on the Strip and larger ones downtown.

Yet, whatever the facts of the situation, people on both
sides use the Strip as an instrument of symbolic warfare.
For Iowa City Types, it enshrines the chaos, waste, commercialism, and lumpen aesthetics of traditional land use.
For True Coralvillians, it is a memorial to freedom and
achievement in their small town. Similarly, on one side,
the new downtown represents a neat and rational alternative to commercial sprawl. On the other, it shows the
technocratic designs of a big-city bourgeoisie.

All of this is quite well known in town, as I suspect its
parallels are familiar elsewhere. People do not misunder-
stand each other so much as genuinely disagree, and I
can see merits and problems on both sides. What concerns me here is the proportions of the debate. People
use the Strip to justify whole ways of life, with little attention to the past or the present except for what it is supposed to represent. No place, I would argue, can bear
such a burden. As Constance Perin has explained, "The
metropolitan landscape is not a museum of contemporary
taste, but the theater of our social thought."[2] We have
heard from the patrons and the critics and know the set
well, but we have yet to hear from the players. We can
turn to the people who work on the Strip to gain an intimate view of the way of life it truly affords.

Chapter 3. The View from the Inside: The Flagship of the Strip

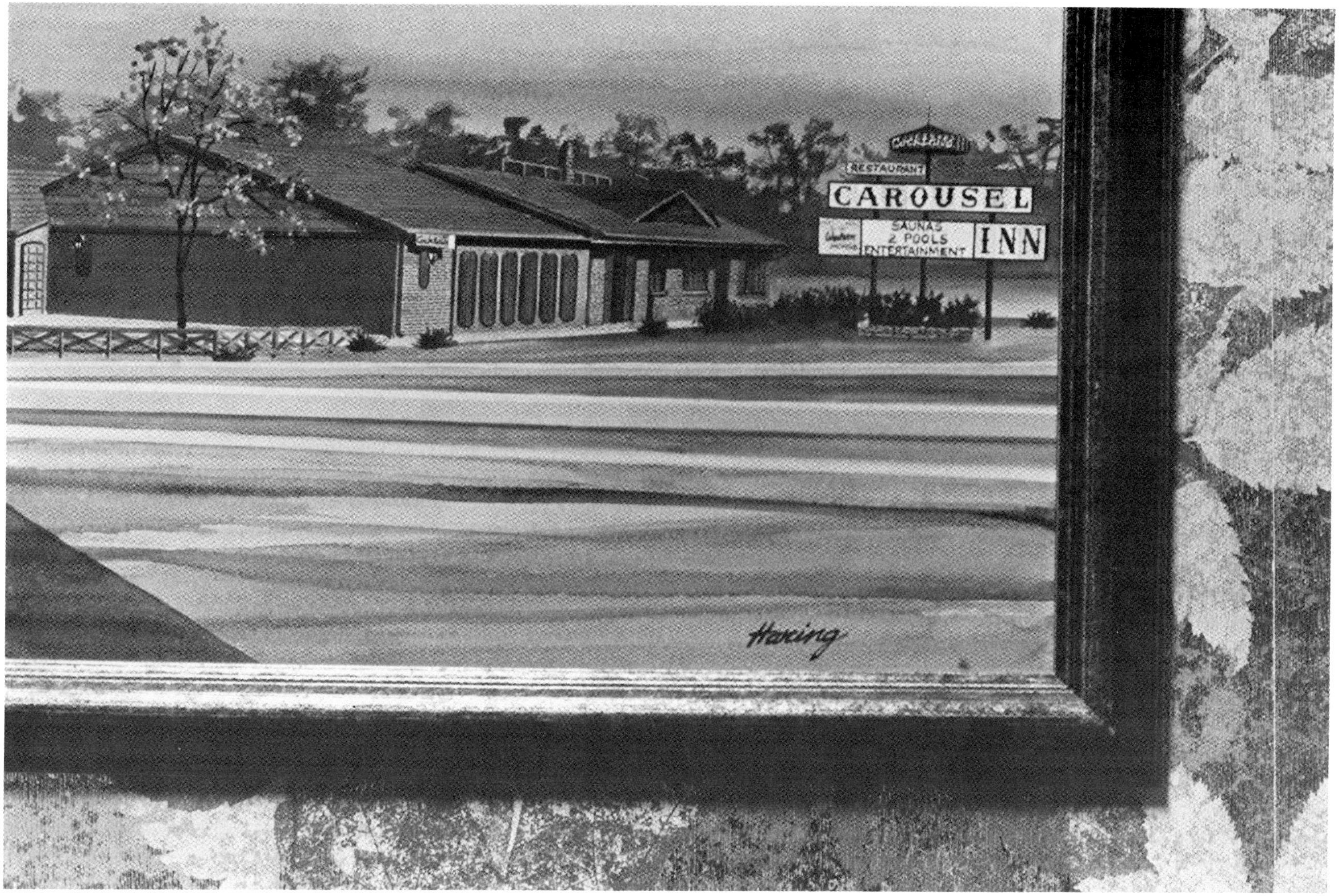
RESTAURANT
CAROUSEL
SAUNAS
2 POOLS
ENTERTAINMENT
INN
Haring

The way Americans read the strip testifies to the power of their imagination. They find evidence to inculpate or vindicate whole ways of life. Yet in the end, the evidence is no more substantial than their taste. I focus on everyday life along a particular strip to bring these readings a little closer to the ground. I choose the Coralville Strip both because it is near my home and because it is such a public concern. Maybe only tacitly elsewhere, but overtly around Iowa City, the strip figures in social and environmental policy.

Having pared my subject to a single illustration, I am still left with an overwhelming amount of material. Each site has a complex history that turns on hundreds of personalities. Since my focus is social life in its concreteness, I choose what might be called a "natural sample," a group of people who share a setting they call their own. It does not strictly represent the Strip but a slice of it whose particularity cannot (as I think it should not) be overlooked.[1]

The setting is the Carousel Inn on the corner of First Avenue and Highway 6. Together with Loghry's restaurant, the original "Carousel," it has been dubbed "the flagship of the Strip." It is an ordinary motel, vintage 1969–70, but it is luxurious by local standards. It boasts an array of recreational facilities and eighty-four oversized rooms. Each "chamber" is individually decorated on a "country-French theme" in a middle-American mode. The furnishings cost over one thousand dollars per room, and halls are painted by a part-time artist-in-residence. The clientele is as diverse as any to be found in town. The location, amenities, and rates ($20–$40 per night) make the Carousel a popular stop.

On paper, at least, it is independently owned and operated. The principal owner and president of the corporation is Dave Steckling. But the Carousel is part of a much more ornate corporate web. It is affiliated in one way or another with the whole leisure industry and with Best Western International in particular. Locally the Carousel is affiliated with Heritage Systems, a management, design, accounting, and supply firm that Steckling began to serve his investments. Heritage holdings now span several cities in the Midwest and include not only the Carousel but also the Alamo and the Cantebury Inn just a few doors down the Strip. The Carousel, then, is a hybrid of standard strip offerings, a cross between corporate mammoth and mom-and-pop mite.

At any given moment, there are between twenty and thirty people on the payroll: managers, maintenance men, desk clerks, laundry staff, and housekeepers. In 1979 and 1980, I spent an average of about one day per week getting to know them. As well as I could, I helped them work the books, move furniture, fold sheets, clean the rooms, and fill their breaks. All the while, we talked casually about almost everything: the Carousel, the Strip, family, friends, their past, and how it might all be different. They were amazingly generous with their time and attention. Many of them have long ago left for unknown parts, but they are all due my deep appreciation.

In each department there were one or two people who were particularly helpful. They had insights they were especially able and willing to share. I spent most of my time in the Carousel with them, and met them away from work, too. They became friends as well as informants. Their voices, edited from tapes and notes, dominate my presentation. They read my rendering of their lives in draft, and, I am proud to report, they said I got it right. Only a couple of names were changed for those who wanted to guard their privacy.

Getting "the truth" was less difficult than deciding which parts of it to preserve. There is far more to the Carousel and the lives of its staff than I could hope to learn in a couple of years, much less compress within a single book. One of the last questions I asked everyone was, "If I could say only one thing about you and this place, what should it be?" Their answers provided most of the organizing principles I needed. Nevertheless, there was no obvious principle that tied them all together.

For example, I originally hoped to introduce the staff through a moment at the Carousel that captured their spirit. But fortunately, for my taste, life defies such simplicity. Each moment gains its significance only in relationship to the characters who engage it and the other moments that surround it or that might have been. I could gather the staff under some tidy message like the lights in a publicity photo, but it would be little help, a curtain call before the performance. The only likely candidate would be the Christmas party. It is one of the few times everyone in Heritage assembles without posing for the public. But to understand its spirit requires a series of translations. Play replaces work. People ordinarily on the bottom of the hierarchy are pampered by those on the top. It represents a ritual reversal of workaday life.

I will not, then, offer a hunch to pursue or hypothesis to test. Instead, I simply ask you to accompany me inside the Carousel as it was, 1979–80, to learn of ways of life the strip affords.

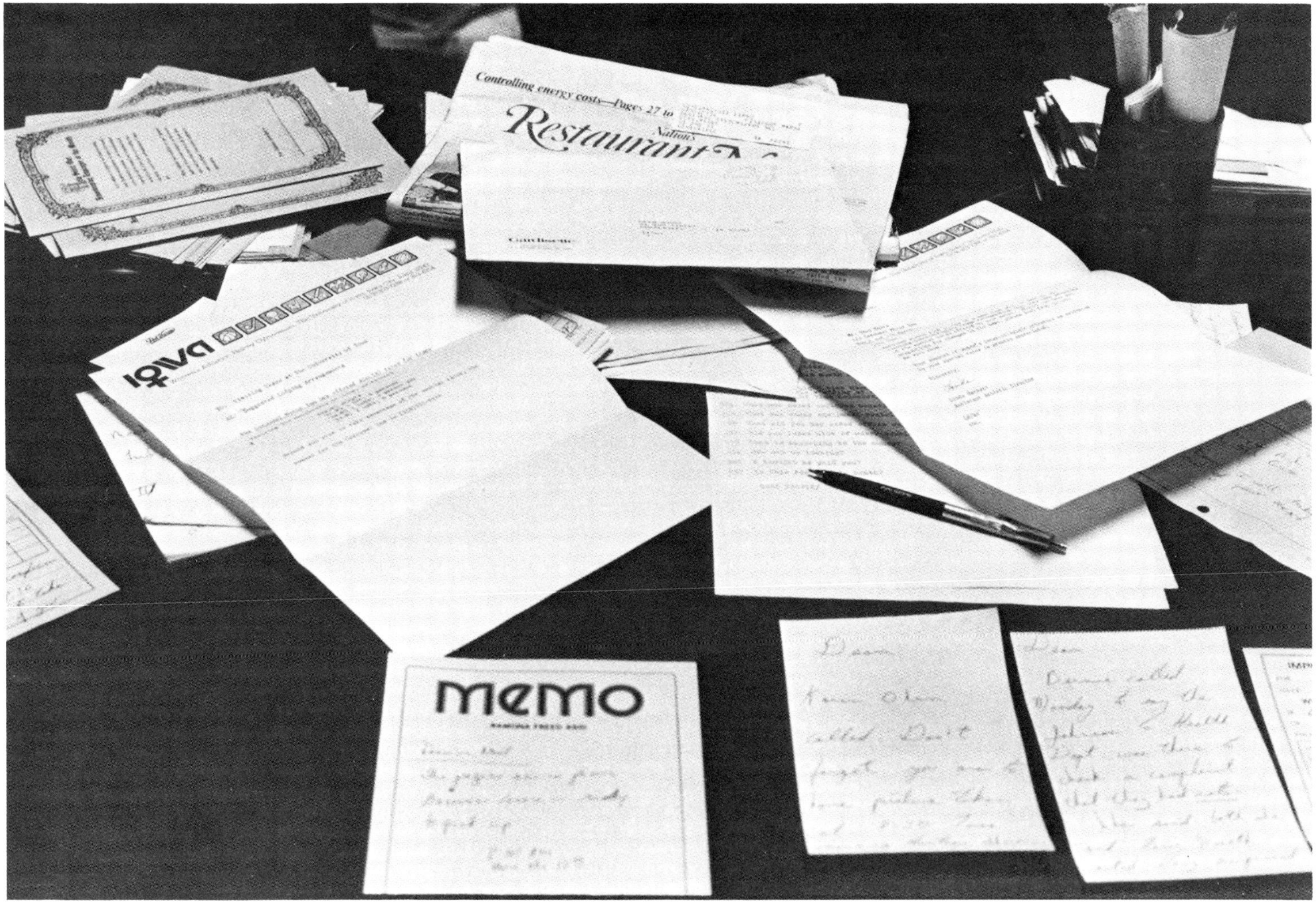
Controlling energy costs—Pages 27 to
Nation's
MEMO

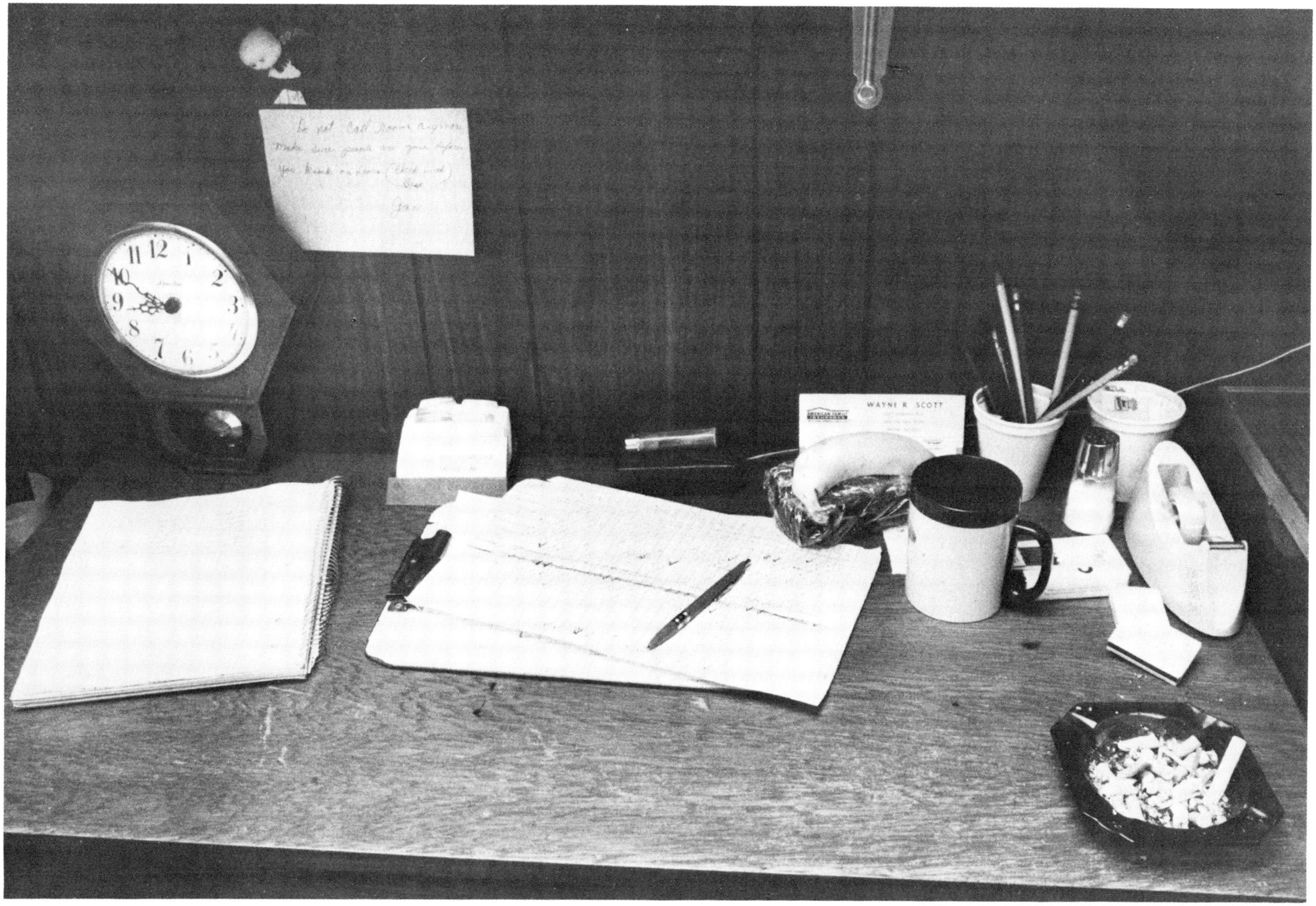
WAYNE R. SCOTT

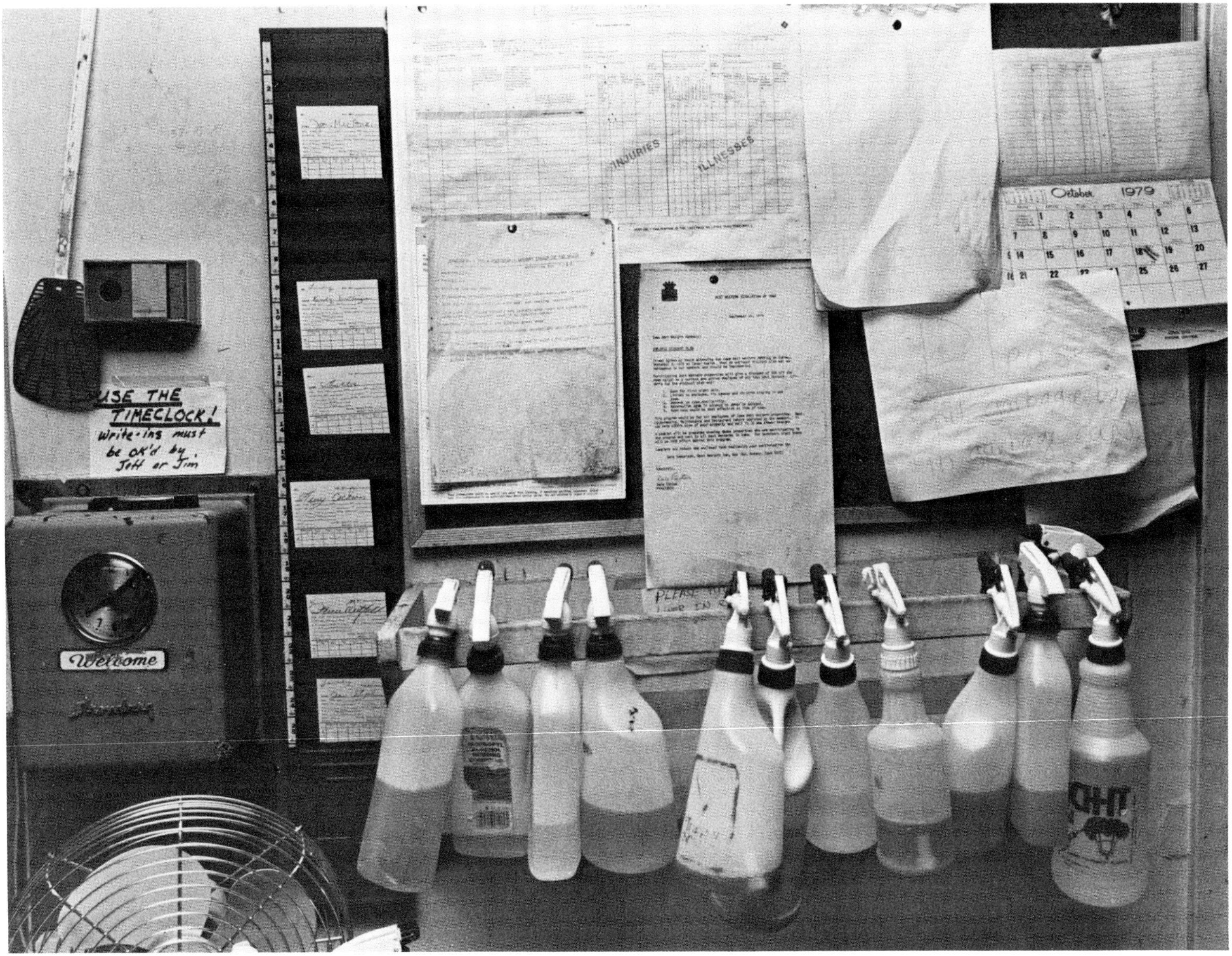
USE THE
TIMECLOCK!
Write-ins must
be OK'd by
Jeff or Jim
Welcome
INJURIES
ILLNESSES
October 1979

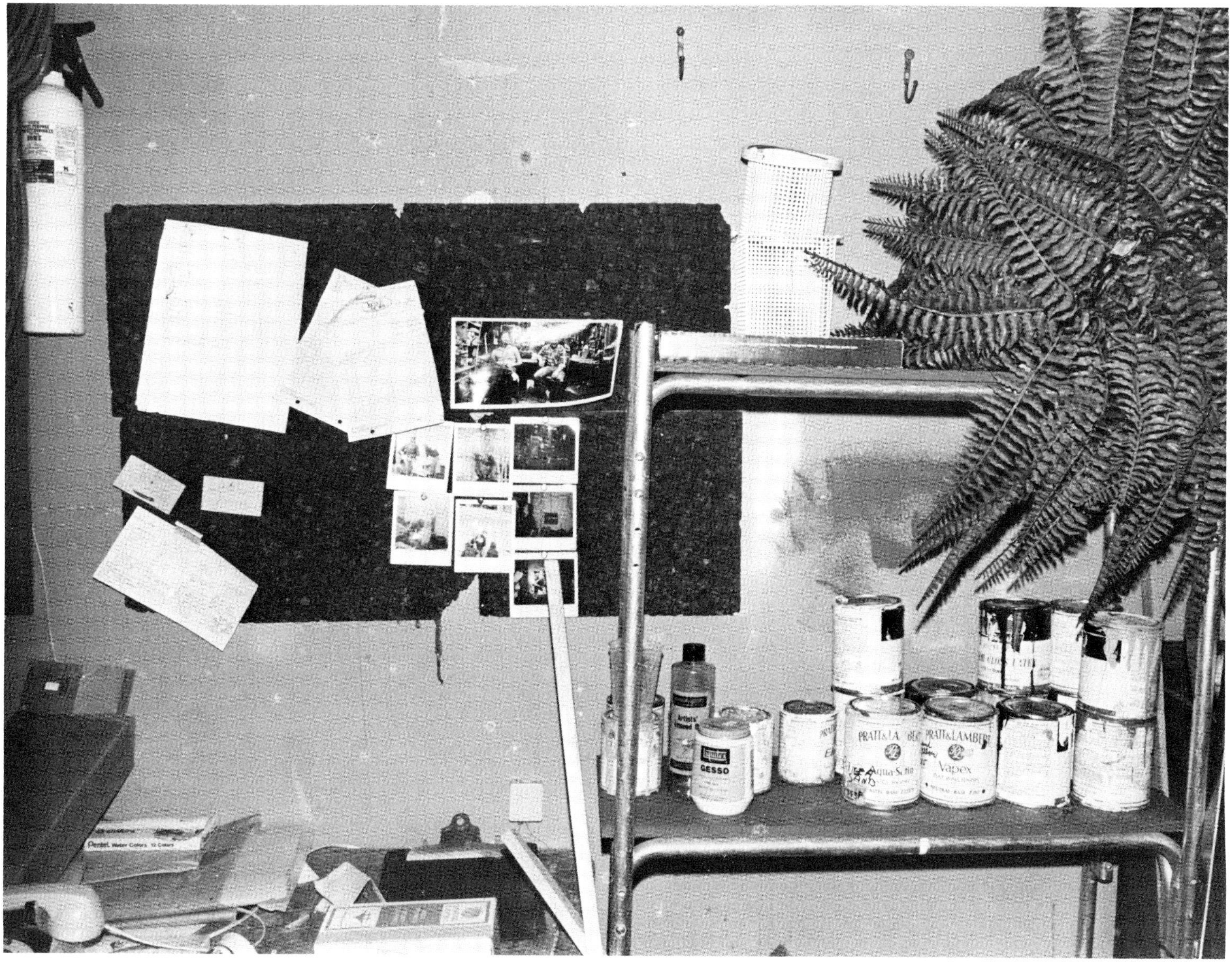
Pentel Water Colors 12 Colors
GESSO
PRATT&LAMBERT
Aqua-Satin
PRATT&LAMBERT
Vapex

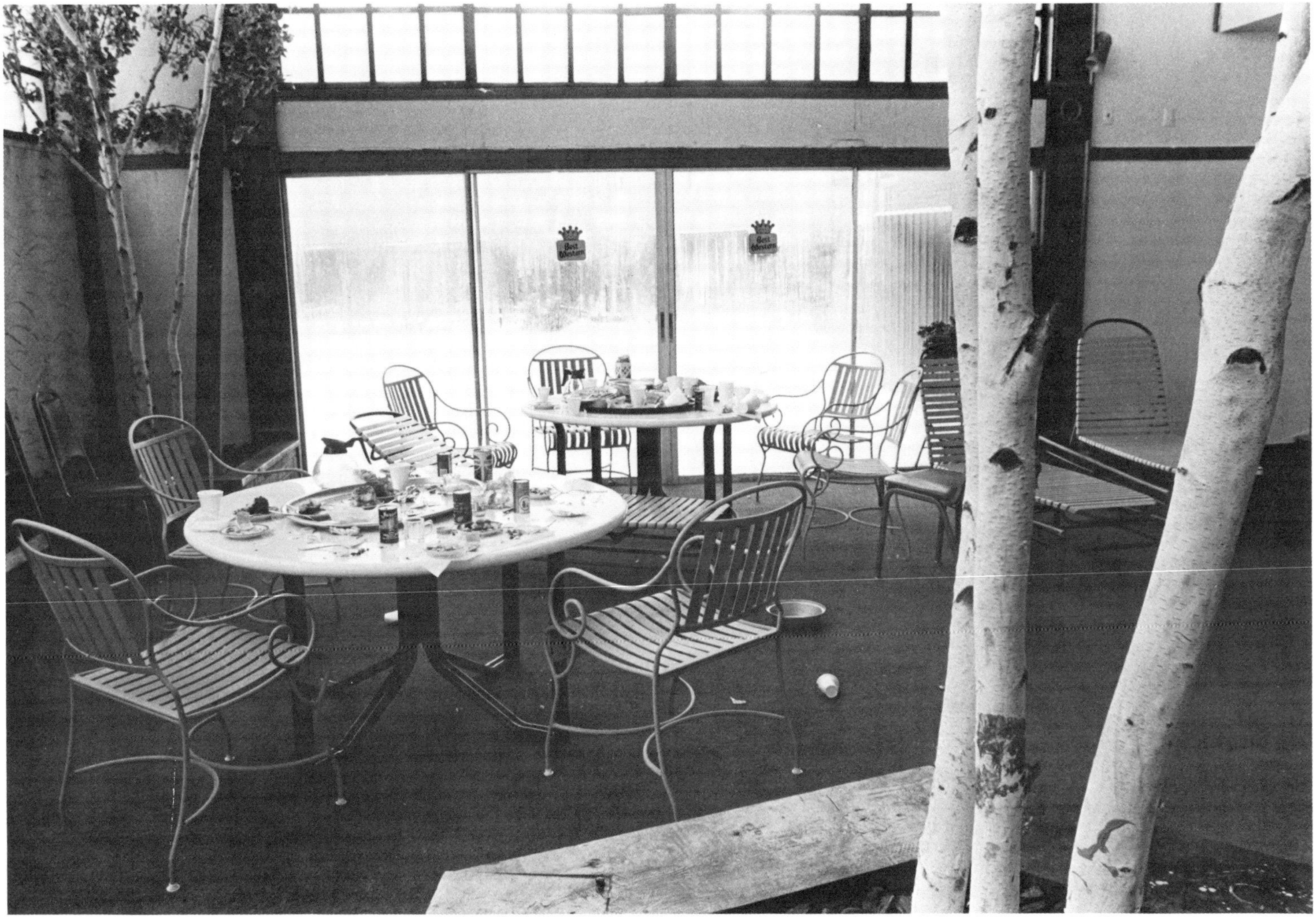

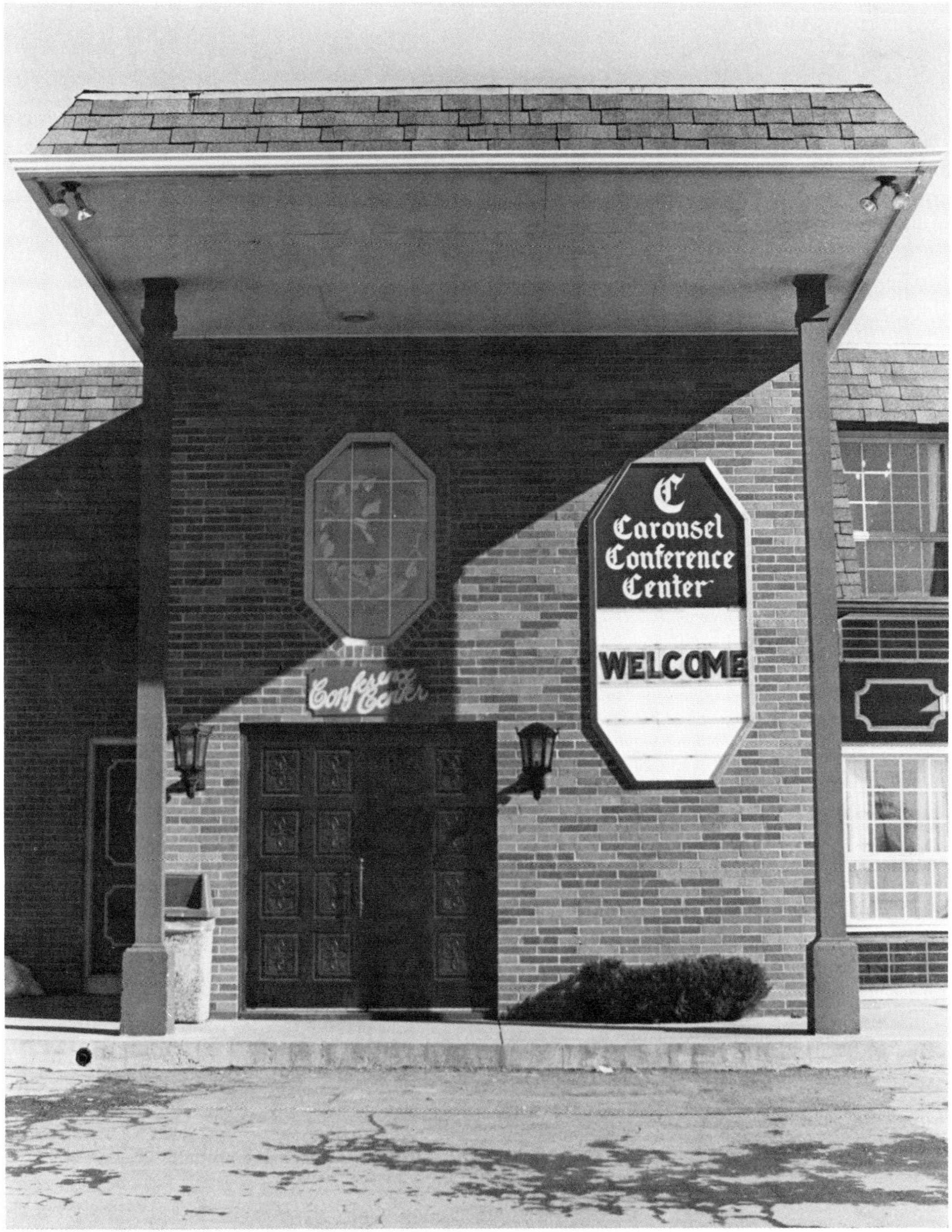
C
Carousel
Conference
Center
WELCOME

Kathy Yager – The Desk

A canopy perched two stories above the parking lot marks the entrance to the Carousel Inn. Beneath the canopy a large picture window separates the lobby from the out-of-doors, from the stream of cars starting and stopping for the corner light. If you look closely from the road, especially at night, you can see through the window, inside, see the desk and the upper torso of a clerk. But more commonly you see the light that the glass reflects from passing cars, electric signs, or the southerly sun. The last image you might catch before the door is your own reflection.

As you enter the Carousel, you step from concrete to carpet, and as the doors slowly close, the roar of traffic fades to a hum and then stops. If you look to your left, you might again catch your reflection, but this time in mirrors over an ornate, fireless hearth. And now you share your reflection with the leather-bound books that line the opposite wall. Memories of glare and motion on the Strip dissolve amidst pastels and plants, carpet, curtains, and upholstery. You are still on the Strip, but it is no longer a kinetic landscape. Just as these walls join with their neighbors to present an aggressively public face on one side, they enclose a more private, crafted space on the other.

For a guest spending the night, this contrast is simply expected. The interior is supposed to be an oasis in an otherwise desolate or hectic "real world." But for those whose workplace is the interior, such reactions are themselves curious. A desk clerk gets to watch them on a daily basis.

I think a lot of people get the wrong impression. Local

people have no cause to come here; so they have no idea. There are no sidewalks or anything. No one looks as they walk by, just a quick glance driving by in a car. Even the guests, when they first drive up, will say, "Oh, I didn't even notice you were there."

I guess it's the location, being here among the gas stations and the street lights and all that. I know because a lot of people say, "Oh, it looks so much nicer than you'd think, you know, from the outside."

These are the observations of Kathy Yager, a desk clerk on the day shift. She started working for the Carousel in 1974, when another employee, a girl friend, recommended her for the job. Kathy will not reveal her age or, for that matter, much of anything else that is "personal." Like other workers—like the guests—she draws a firm line between life within and life beyond these walls. But she does admit her ties with the community. She grew up in Coralville and graduated from district schools. For lunch she will often run home or visit with her mother in town. It if were not for her obvious maturity on the job or the presence of her teenage daughters on the weekend staff, you might guess she was still in her early twenties. After five years, she already has remarkable seniority, in fact, more than the managers.

I guess things just happened, and I just stayed longer and longer. . . . You don't get to really know very many people who work here because the turnover is so great.

For guests and managers, Kathy is the "face of the motel." A basic tenet in the industry is that a desk clerk, more than anyone else, determines the fortunes of an inn. She is supposed to be attractive, friendly, and efficient. Kathy has long tenure on the job because she has all these qualities.

She knows many of the guests by name, especially "the VIPs." These are members of a "club" that the manager began in 1978. Since the VIPs, generally businessmen, are a staple in the motel's trade, they earn special treatment. Their embossed club card allows for speedier check-in and entitles them to a discount, one dollar off the regular rate and every eleventh night free. Many of the VIPs also earn an engraved, golden nameplate on the door of their favorite room. Other plaques honor notables such as actors, dancers, or musicians who have stayed at the Carousel in conjunction with a university performance.

A more ornate system of special rates is tailored for others. Athletic teams, government representatives, conference participants, and an array of trucking and sales firms arrange discounts or pre-payment guarantees to allow for credit and late check-in. There is even a hospital rate for the friends and families of patients at the VA or University Hospital who stay at least five consecutive nights.

Such arrangements complicate record-keeping. The desk is jammed with file boxes, notebooks, cards, and papers in an elaborate code. A single set of initials, a number, or a color can indicate everything from a charge procedure to the time a housekeeper should be able to clean the room next Tuesday. Keeping all of this straight is one of the most significant and complex tasks performed at the desk. "To really understand what we do," Kathy explains, "you'll have to learn to talk motel." But most guests do not know or much care about "talking motel." Their needs must be met as if it were a simple matter. The personal treatment that is such a focus of a desk clerk's day is, for a guest, "the least I would expect."

Kathy has learned to distinguish businessmen, athletic recruits, truckers, and "hospital people" at a glance. She knows when a guest will welcome conversation or expect her to stick to business. A person's age, sex, clothing, or stride can tell her what file to pull, how strictly to arrange payment, or what room to suggest.

Few of the eighty-four rooms are alike. A room number by itself refers to a particular location and decor to be matched with particular tastes. Most rooms have two queen-size beds, but there are also rooms with king-size, "hospitality" (Murphy), round, and water beds. There are triples and suites, rooms with wet bars and sunken living areas, rooms poolside or on a balcony, rooms that are painted or papered or out for repair. Kathy knows, for example, to direct businessmen to one of the "down-and-outs" (the odd-numbered rooms between 105 and 141 except for 129). These are on the ground floor with doors directly to the parking lot. In handing out a key to 137, a down-and-out, she recognizes that "you probably have stuff to lug in and out."

A desk clerk must learn to anticipate not only the guest immediately before her but also those who registered yesterday and may register tomorrow. Rooms must be set aside for that VIP who "sometimes shows up early" or for a sports weekend or a conference. But it is always possible that some of the hospital people—like the one who has the VIP's favorite room—will need to stay longer than they thought. And then there are travelers who glance at their *Best Western Atlas* or *AAA Guide* and just show up.

The idea is to place each individual in "his" room, as if that were its sole purpose, while keeping the motel as full as possible. As the motel nears capacity, the chances of an "overbook" and a lobby full of irate guests rise dramatically. Given an average occupancy rate in the Carousel of over 80 percent (well above the industry-wide average of 60–70 percent), conflicts between guests' demands are not just possible; they are probable. Overbooks are the nightmare of every desk clerk. A bad guess here, an unexpected change in plans or a broken air conditioner there, and Kathy will spend the day absorbing curses. Calmly: "Would you like me to see if we have a room for you in our other Best Western?" She can only hope the Cantebury will help out.

Undoubtedly, balancing all these interests requires intelligence, care, and practice as well as the patience of a seasoned flak-catcher when things go wrong. It is a wonder to watch Kathy "put the rooms up on the board," as she does every morning between 7:15 and 8:00. She begins by removing papers representing "check-outs" and adding colored cards for "stay-overs" or rooms out of service on a vertical display with slots for numbered rooms. Then, armed with more color-coded cards for different lengths of stay, tabs for special room requests, registration slips, and books packed with abbreviated motel talk, she deals out the rooms. Every day she plays this 84-cornered bridge game. The board holds trump that must be played to cover every trick. But she is less a master than a matchmaker. Working the board means imaginatively wedding particular places and people in motion. Only guests could believe their match was made in heaven.

But the motel experience is crafted to encourage just such an illusion. Kathy is there to serve *you*. She silently, effortlessly translates lobby conversation into the motel talk that keeps the establishment in gear. Responsibilities to "other people" are effectively hidden from guests in the lobby. All of those files, ledgers, papers, and related paraphernalia are barricaded behind the false front of the desk, neatly out of view. The frenzy of wake-up calls, arrangements with the Heritage bus or cabs, laundry services, messages, postage, newspapers, reservations—all are handled through the switchboard insofar as possible. The intricacies of billing—taking "time and charges" for phone calls from the operator, making out slips for the restaurant or other services, sending in credit card invoices, making up deposits, working the drawer or the imprinter—are ideally completed in private. The most patently financial activities of the desk are performed on the night shift, from 11:00 to 7:00, when the clerk is actually an accountant. Since most guests use some sort of credit card, check-out involves the simple presentation of a "folio," that is, a bill.

Moreover, unless it is absolutely urgent, this switchboard and paperwork is suspended in a visitor's presence. A guest in the lobby claims Kathy's full, devoted attention, whatever the tenor of her personal and business day. Guests and management agree that the face of the motel is to be calm, friendly, consistent. Nothing in a desk clerk's manner should suggest the financial and emotional complexities that are her responsibility.

For Kathy, as for other workers in the motel and all along the Strip, being calm and friendly is natural, easy. But holding that pose so consistently is a challenge. Again, like others, Kathy does not speak of days as good or bad so much as more or less trying.

I was wondering what distinguishes good days and bad days. Like you said today was a "slow day?"

Today is a slow day. A lot of things go wrong and people are coming up to check out. Their TV doesn't work or the bed wasn't comfortable, no towels. . . .

And what about when it's not a slow day? Do any really stand out? Nice surprises like flowers or a bonus?

Yeah, wilted *flowers. Ha!*

No, I guess I have a short memory. I can't think of anything in particular.

We've had some overbooks. They really stand out. Those have been some of the bad days.

Mostly the bad days for me are when people complain about things wrong in the room, or they think the room charge is too high. They weren't pleased with the restaurant or the swimming pool or anything, *you know? A lot of times there is nothing to it and nothing you can do about it. Some are just going to complain, and some aren't.*

The better days are just when no one complains about anything.

The idea is to make it through the day, to give the guests that friendly face no matter how abusive they become. Kathy is glad that most of them are nice, especially the regulars. But "it only takes one or two to make it tough."

The face the motel presents beyond its glazed walls is difficult to keep on. It is a pose, a mask, not in the sense that it is phony but fixed, more like a serene death mask than a costume. The living face behind the mask is Kathy's. It is the one she makes up in the morning, sets during the day, and takes home at night.

Frank Deleon and Craig Poock—Managers

asically, I guess, there are two kinds of managers. Most of the old-timers are PR types. They're involved in the community, belong to all the clubs, sponsor this and that, know everybody by name. No matter how it goes, they'll smile and slap you on the back. If something screws up, a PR type will shrug his shoulders and say, "It'll all work out. Everything's going to be fine. Keep smiling!"

Ermal is like that. I guess I'm usually like that. You cultivate your business and figure that the details will pretty much take care of themselves.

The other kind is more of a detail man. "Keep on top of things," you know? Check for cobwebs in the light fixtures, keep your costs under control, watch your reports and stuff. If a problem comes up, you analyze it, set priorities, hop on the phone or whatever, and take care of it.

We're in a pretty good situation now. We've got Frank as the manager of the Carousel. He's from New York and a pretty good detail man. His assistant, Craig, is from California. He's more the laid-back, PR type. They really complement each other. —Dean Moore, General Manager of Operations, Heritage Systems, Inc.

Movement through the Carousel is coordinated at the desk. There, guests make reservations, registrations, payments, compliments, and complaints. In helping them and handling the switchboard, a desk clerk is the key link between the motel and the outside world. She is also a key link between workers inside the motel. The heads of housekeeping and maintenance plan their day with her advice. The timely movement of every sheet or fixture can be traced back to a record she made. As a manager put it, "The desk clerk is like the operating manager, more or less. If I ever want to know what's going on, that's who I'll ask. Really, they hear just about everything." In this respect, the desk is as much the nervous system of the motel as its face.

But the real gray matter is downstairs in the manager's office. Within limits defined by Heritage Systems, Best Western, and economic reality, a manager claims ultimate authority and responsibility for the Carousel. There are pressures from outside to deliver the perfect motel experience, from above to outperform the past and competitors, and from below to provide meaningful, rewarding work. If you are successful, you make everyone happy and earn a bonus. If you are not, you will not last very long. One manager estimates, "The average life of a manager is in more jeopardy than a pro football coach. On the average, I think, most of them last about a year." The Carousel and most motels (and football teams), in fact, have a better average, but not much.

Since 1976, Frank Deleon has been the manager of the inn. He and his office mate, Assistant Manager Craig Poock, are good friends. They are both young and hip though a bit of an odd couple—Frank, the detail man, dark, East Coast, ethnic, and Craig, the PR type, blonde, West Coast, all-American. If their office is the motel cortex, Frank is in the left hemisphere.

In the following monologue, built from conversations in the fall of 1979, Frank introduces himself and the Carousel from a manager's point of view.

About four years ago, I met Dean Moore. He was man-

ager of the Carousel at the time, but I met him out in Colorado. I was still going to Colorado State, but he said, "If you're around or coming through, drop by." Later I was on my way back to New York, and I did drop by. We got to talking, and I wound up coming back. I started in maintenance, moving tables around and stuff, but then in six months I was Dean's assistant manager.

I guess the main thing was working with Dean. The people in this organization, Heritage—this place, the Cantebury, the Alamo, the Pepper Tree—they are all pretty young. That's why I found it easy to just fit in with them. So there was Dean, and when I came, I thought it was a nice place. Of course, at the time I had no knowledge of motels at all. But as far as I could tell, it was nice, not just a run-of-the-mill place.

By "run-of-the-mill" I mean your basic roadside motel. The walls are thrown up with no thought really put into it. And the clientele is definitely different. Some people are just looking for the cheapest room they can get. They don't care about anything as long as there's a bed in the room. And there's a definite need for that. But there are also people that won't stay anywhere that doesn't have a pool and full-service restaurant. And, of course, there's eveything in between.

Some places just have a lot of imagination in them. When you're walking through the building, you feel like you're in a different land or something. Like, a lot of people come here from Des Moines or neighboring towns just to get away for the weekend. We go after that business, especially in the winter, offer them a good deal. We send them a letter introducing ourselves and saying, "Thank you for coming with us." And we give

them a little card as they check in. Not everyone can afford to fly to California or Florida, but they still want to get away. And you wouldn't want to get away to a place where you just had a room on a hallway.

When I check into a motel, I go in and look around. I notice every little thing, like if there's a hair in the tub. And, of course, I'll see how the desk clerk treats you. The way people treat you is really important. You have to have a nice, clean place and keep it that way, but the people can kill you. You know how it is, if you check into some motel and the guy makes you feel like he's doing you a favor. Or you call up when something is wrong, and they just say, "We'll get to it when we can get to it." People are walking through the halls, and you can tell they just hate their jobs. Someone asks a housekeeper for an extra bar of soap, and she barks, "No, I don't have any" . . . rather than, "Sure, here you go," happy and humming. They have to like their jobs. If they don't, people pick up on it.

What I can do as a manager is acknowledge their presence. If they want to talk about anything, talk to them. That's the most important thing. But you can't give them everything, either. I learned that. Like when I started, I tried to be "the nice guy." Everybody liked me. I was young and wasn't your run-of-the-mill person. But then you can get used, too. It's just the way people are. But they will respect you if you let them know when they're messing up. Everyone knows when they do, so you've just got to point it out to them. They expect it anyway.

I don't like to use the word "loose," but I think we have a relaxed atmosphere. Everyone knows they have to do their work, but, "Let's all get going and make it as easy as possible." I don't see anyone who thinks they're better than the next person or goes around saying things like, "You, do this!" or "You, go over there!" If someone doesn't make it to work or messes up, we step in and take care of it. I think people basically work together, and that's what we're really shooting for. I think it works.

The Carousel has a pretty good reputation. People comment on how the rooms are different, with living areas and beds unlike a normal room. People comment on the pool area and the hallways. They create a kind of theme that people mention, too. We're trying to go with the French theme throughout the building. It's hard to do, not just a matter of hanging up French banners. In everything we do, however little it may be, we try to tend toward that theme.

We've got a perfect location, right on the corner. We're the nearest full-service hotel to downtown Iowa City—the hospitals, the stadium, Hancher Auditorium. That's a big plus. We've got a whole big piece of 6/218, the major highway, as well as First Avenue, right on the way to the interstate. And our parking lot holds a lot of trucks. Sure, people don't like the Strip, sitting frustrated behind the wheel. But they accept it. They don't have much of a choice. I guess the Strip could be beautified up a bit. It just looks like a lot of buildings in a row. Some landscaping would help, like the flowers Rebecca planted for us around the sign out front. When those flowers are in full bloom, I think people will really look over and appreciate them. That's why I called Charlotte Larson over at the Coralville Courier, and she did an article on it. I did it for Rebecca, and I did it for the place, too.

There are more budget motels than full-service motels in this area, and I think everyone knows we're up in the top range of those places. Probably most people in Coralville have been here one time or another. When this building was built, it was the biggest one around, if I'm not mistaken, and it was brand new. They have had all kinds of receptions and parties. For people around here (I've talked to a lot of them) just having been here, it's not "that building" but "the place right down the street."

Of course, a lot of people who are traveling come here just because it is a Best Western. They go with a chain, stay in the same kind of place wherever they go. They'll get a hold of the Guide and follow that right along. Some of the Best Westerns are nicer than others, but all of them are basically clean. They are pretty strict that way. They come around twice a year and inspect the building and the rooms.

It is a chain, but the properties are privately owned and operated. It's basically just the name, a referral and reservation system. You're still owned by the individual, but you can call another Best Western, say in Des Moines, and have some kind of relationship. The advantage is that they don't have direct interference with management.

In our organization that's Heritage Operations. Dean is the general manager. I've known him for quite a while, and we get along fine. He was the one I worked with until I learned how the place actually runs. Neil Trott is the vice-president, a nice guy. He takes care of insurance and taxes, a lot of the paperwork, a lot of the building-on of the motels. Like, they built onto the Cantebury not too long ago. He takes care of that kind of thing.

We have meetings every other Tuesday, sometimes once a week, where we get together: "Okay, let's just talk about things." We might talk about some advertising gimmicks or promotions that someone saw along the line. For example, we were thinking of getting one of those big helium balloons, a huge one, and tying it up over the roof. It would cost some money but definitely turn a lot of eyes. The advantage is that we can do a lot of mutual things. You try something at one of the places, and if it works, you bring it to the others. That's how we got the double-decker bus for the motels. I guess the *idea came from one of the lodging magazines. It works out pretty well. We share things. If you run out of supplies and can't get them for a month, you can just go borrow them. So the relationship is a big advantage.*

That's also where we go over the monthly statements. Each of us has a bookkeeper, and we get all the materials to Heritage. Every month they prepare a statement of our net profits with a breakdown—how much we spent on housekeeping, supplies, and this and that. We'll go over that. Things that are out of line will show up on paper. It's more or less black-and-white. It comes down to "Are you making money or aren't you?" We get paid a percentage of what our place nets, but we don't really compete with each other. At least I've gone beyond that kind of thinking, because it's not worth it. We're in it together. They send us people when they're full, and we send them people when we're full. That makes money. Great. I think we get along pretty well.

Dave Steckling, the main owner, will also meet with us when he's here. He lives in California, and he flies in once every four or five months, I'd say, on the average. He's progressive as far as the ideas he likes to have in his motels, like carrying a theme. Something may sound like a wild idea, but he's usually for those kinds of things, because that's what works in this business. There are so many places to stay; why not stay in a place that's really neat, that you can tell people about, that's just completely different? But he'll mainly just talk with me or Dean. He'll come around to each property and see how it looks. If the place looks good and if it's making money, he's happy. If those two things are okay, basically everything is in line.

Once you're in the business, it's pretty clear what needs to be done. I learned with Dean, talked to people, and went to conventions. Like, the Iowa Hotel/Motel Association has a big annual convention, and Best Western has some. You can get a lot of ideas that way, but it takes time to get a real feel for how things run.

It's mainly a matter of getting someone that can head up each department—the desk people, maintenance people, housekeepers, auditors. If you see something that's wrong, you just go to one person. If you see a room that doesn't look up to par, you don't have to track down the particular housekeeper. Just go to the head of housekeeping and say, "Jill, there's a problem."

We'll have meetings with the housekeepers, the maintenance guys, and the desk people, so we can just talk. You tell them to be friendly, tell them they definitely have an effect: "You're the first people they meet and the last people they see." I tell them definitely to push to be friendly, but not in any particular sentences or anything. You know, if you make somebody say, "Hi, my name is Frank. How are you today?," it comes off like that. It doesn't work. I'd just ask how the guy is feeling, you know, "How was your trip? Are you tired?" You've got to get people to understand what you want from them and then to be themselves. If they're not that kind of person, they're not really right for the job. For example, anyone who is intimidated by people definitely couldn't be at the desk.

I spend a lot of my time trying to attract business. Like, if people are coming to Hancher Auditorium, they'll call up for some rooms. You really want to go after that. I'll go over to Hancher or get some names of groups that are comng in, then track down their address, and get a hold of them. "We'll give you the best rates we can" and this and that. If people call up to reserve a good amount of rooms or, say, a trucking outfit wants guarantees or credit, I'll take it rather than the desk people. We especially try to keep the Conference Center filled. We put together a stereo show not too long ago. We have a lot of classes that meet here—Dale Carnegie, Weight Watchers, Mary Kay Cosmetics—and a church group every Sunday.

Our job entails things like that, the advertising, going out to meet people. It's good to go to Chamber of Com-

merce meetings, though I don't get to go as much as I'd like. It's good to know what's going on in the community. But when there is a problem with the actual running of the motel, you've got to forget about everything else. If the rooms aren't getting cleaned or if no one is at the desk, what's the sense of doing anything? First, you have to keep the people and the place running smoothly, all the time! You can go off to get a stereo show in here, but then things go downhill real fast if you let them. You need those key people.

Housekeeping is a big complaint of mine in this particular area. You can't afford to pay any five or six dollars an hour to get a housekeeper. And they don't really expect it. You can offer them decent money, but I think they're basically interested in work conditions. There are a lot of motels in this town, and you can get a job housekeeping anywhere. But in some of the places it's just: "Here you go. Do what you want. We don't really care about you, because you're not that important anyway." So it's a constant battle to keep the ladies happy.

You get some that are happy, doing real well for you—showing up, cleaning the rooms right, friendly people—and then the university enters the picture. Everybody has applied for a job there, got their names on a long sheet. Then, one day someone at the University Personnel Office says, "Oh, Mary's gone today. Here's the next name on the list." They call a housekeeper and say, "We need you Tuesday." Then she comes to me and says, "Hey, I like it here and everything, but they've offered me $5.50 an hour. I've got to go." "Well, geez, could you give us two weeks' notice?" "No, they said I have to be there Tuesday." It's not very fair to local businesses. They should at least tell them, "Give your previous employer two weeks," instead of, "Be here Tuesday or I'll call the next name." That's happened to me a few times, and it's really discouraging. Housekeeping is the hardest job to fill.

Of course, sometimes the guests are the ones you

have to watch. If someone wants a block of rooms, guarantees, or credit, now I ask them to send some money. Otherwise you can get burned. If they're serious about it, it's no big thing either. There's nothing like holding twenty rooms and then getting a call in the morning, "We don't want them." Or one guy comes and says, "That's it! The rest of the people aren't coming," when you know you could have sold those rooms.

Then there's the building, too. It is nine years old now, so sometimes things just go. Like, I was here when a water heater for half the building went out, and we were full. People were all over the place saying, "Hey! what's this? No hot water?"

Probably the worst thing was when we had a convention scheduled here with one of those big lab companies. They sent out all their bids to have people flown in from California. They had these people come and measure the rooms before they decided it was okay. They flew in all this equipment, and we had to get electricians from Cedar Rapids to set it up.

I leave the night before, and about half of it is all set up. I come in the next morning at 7:30 and see this stuff going out again in boxes. I run around till I find the guy, and he says, "It's too small. We're moving it to Cedar Rapids." I said, "What do you mean, 'It's too small'? I had one of your guys come down here and say it was fine!" That kind of thing can throw you for a loop. I have all these rooms that are guaranteed for three nights, and half of them are leaving without a word. So then I have to get the money out of them, and they don't want to pay. That was a mess.

Then, on the other hand, everything can just go fine, no problems. All of a sudden you fill up on a Monday or Tuesday night. You look into it and find out there's some huge event at the university. We haven't done anything, and they just come flocking in for rooms. Sometimes I come in, and you can just feel it. Everything is running real smooth. People are happy and humming. But it's *important for me to always come in and just walk through the halls to say "Hi" to everybody. I know there have been days when I come and feel, not depressed, but washed out. I lumber around: "Hi." "How are you doing?" "Fine." Keep walking. People start to go, "Wha?!" You kind of rub off on people.*

The Hancher groups are really a lot of fun to get. They're good for the place. People talk about it. The San Francisco Ballet was here, The Wiz, *and* Little Feat. *The help gets all, "Wow! Emmylou Harris is right down the hall!" You know? So it's great! I know a lot of people just go through the halls to look at those names on the plaques.*

We try to keep the atmosphere here relaxed, just people working together. If you ask me how I feel about this building and what's important, I think that's what it is.

"Relaxed" is the right word. The atmosphere is the pride of the Carousel and Heritage management and a goodly share of the staff. In fact, up and down the Strip, with notable exceptions, workers ungrudgingly join together to provide a service. Many of them are refugees from the disciplined drudgery of industrial or agricultural labor that they know from their parents' experience or their own or from occupational lore. In motels, gas stations, restaurants, or the like, work is so varied that individuals must still largely pace themselves. Each hour may bring new demands, but there are always free moments to chat, grab a smoke or some coffee, or head for the john. The work gets done because people feel they owe it to themselves, their coworkers, and the public.

Anyone who is irresponsible or emotionally down is just not "with it." Frank is right: the atmosphere is relaxed but not loose. There is unrelenting pressure to be cheerful and efficient and *naturally* so. Troubles at home, distaste for workmates, benefits, routines, or the public must slip out of mind. Most people at least one time or another

are in the curious position of struggling to relax.

The pressures on management are particularly intense. You cannot force employees to be "happy and humming," but your fortunes depend on it. One increasingly popular option is to impose disciplined pleasantries. Workers chant, "Have a nice day," "Have it your way." They resemble grinning zombies, but you will not get customer complaints. Another option, the relaxed Carousel approach, is to appoint managers the spiritual leaders of the workplace. Their manner must be so spontaneously, so genuinely right that they inspire a following.

Frank seems to be holding up well. As long as his attention is fixed on procedures, he is "happy and humming." But Craig is having more trouble. He seems to be reeling from a sort of culture shock, anxiously waiting for his attitude to right itself. His frustration is hardly unusual on the Strip. If you are not happy and humming in the absence of rigid or alien commands, you can easily believe there is something wrong with *you*—you do not have "the right attitude," or you are not "right for the job." Craig can only hope that he will come around and attribute his frustration to the peculiarities of personal history.

Dean Moore is the one who hired me. He was friends with a good friend of mine who knew that I was getting a little frustrated in Los Angeles. He knew that I thought I wasn't making the kind of money that I was putting my energy out for. So, Dean called me one day and said, "Well, are you interested in coming back here and checking out the No-tell/Hotel scene?" (That's what I call it.) And I go, "I don't know. . . . I'll fly back and see."

So, I flew back, checked it out—this was in March of 1979. And I liked it! I liked the company, liked all the youth, the young energy—Dean, Frank, Neil, Charlie Bringle over at the Cantebury, Dave Steckling, the owner of the company. I was particularly impressed with Dave. He's got that California energy. He's really open, looking for new ideas all the time, looking for new trends from all over the country and trying to apply them back here.

But I'm having to go through some pretty heavy changes. I had a production company in L.A. I had a couple of rock bands that I booked around the area and was trying, you know, to make that million dollars, trying to crack the record market. And I was working on a movie, a rock opera that should be out soon. It's a New Wave–type situation, ultra-violent, interesting.

My partner is still out there now, co-producing, definitely in on ideas. He's doing great. He's got an office on Sunset Boulevard and one in Carmel. He's got a publishing company now, and he's taken over all the responsibilities for the movie. So, he's doing well. He keeps calling me up and saying, "When are you going to come back out? I need you." I say, "Well, no. I'm sorry. I committed myself." I tell him that I made a commitment to this place and that I'm going to hold to it.

But it's been heavy—from living right in the city to living out in the country—it was like . . . poof! And the older people around here aren't nearly as aware as the older people out there. I mean, California people are more trendy, trying to get in on what's happening, whereas here, I think, the older people are more into, "Well, this is the way it is; this is the way it has been; this is the way it's going to be." . . . which is fine . . . for Iowa. It can't get too outrageous. There can only be one California, I guess.

To hear Craig tell it, things ought to work out. He likes the job and his co-workers. If he puts California behind him and learns to deal with the old folks, he will come to fit in. At least now he can say why the adjustment seems so difficult.

His understanding was given a surprise test in November when Frank quit and left him in charge. Heritage expected the change for several weeks, but I learned of it with the rest of the Carousel staff on the day it happened. I strolled downstairs to discover Craig at Frank's desk

finishing a conversation with a friend from a building supply store down the Strip.

"So, did you finish painting yet?"

"No, I still haven't painted that one pink corner."

"It's still there?!"

"Yeah, I've got to get that taken care of one of these days. We tried some paint that we got for the Crown Room. When we bought it, the stuff looked great. But when we put it on the wall, oooooh! Jesus! It was sickening. So I gave it to my housekeepers to paint the laundry room with."

"They're going to be real happy about that!"

"Yeah, that stuff is wicked. Say, have you got any Christmas lights out there? I've got to get a bunch more Christmas stuff."

"I don't think we do, but we might. I'll have to let you know at winter Softball League. You're up for that, aren't you? Got your snowmobile suit, gloves, and all? By February it will probably be sixty below with the wind-chill factor."

"Yeah, that should be something. Look, I've got to talk with this guy."

"Okay, I'm out of here. And Frank? What happened to him? Moved on, huh?"

"Yeah, He's still around town. He's just kicking back. 'Deprogramming,' he calls it."

So, after three years, even Frank had enough. Walks through the hallways to get everyone happy and humming had become trying. All that attention to detail helped the days to pass, but with them went parts of Frank he was no longer willing to give. Craig, who already found it hard to lose himself in detail, would have an even tougher time. But he was determined.

When the demands of detail started to get to him, like many in the Carousel he found comfort imagining how much worse it might be in a Holiday Inn: "They are strictly straight format. Room 105 is the same as 242. All the walls are white; the beds are just so; everything is standardized. They have videotapes on everything. Like, for housekeepers: 'Take three steps to the right, make two swipes with a cloth. . . .' You walk into a Holiday Inn in Mississippi and one in Wisconsin, and except for the personnel structure, they're exactly the same." At the Carousel, a displaced, New Wave producer might still fit in.

Craig counted himself especially lucky to be Frank's last-minute replacement at a Management Development Program held in Phoenix in November 1979. His trip was sponsored by Heritage Systems, but the rest of the thirty-odd participants hailed from Best Westerns scattered throughout the country. They got to see some showcase properties, share problems, talk about solutions, play a little golf, and get drunk together back at the hotel. Most of their time was spent in classes run by Best Western representatives. They heard about legislation that might affect their business, such as proposals to shorten the work week or refigure overtime. But most of the attention was on management procedures, everything from energy conservation and incentive programs to day-care and morning devotionals for employees. There were slick handouts on worker psychology and handling complaints. There were videotapes, too, but, Craig emphasized, they were not simply directives. They would watch a videotape and then discuss how it might apply to their situation.

When Craig returned to Coralville, he was genuinely excited. He did not learn much about meshing his past or personality with the old folks in Iowa. In fact, most of the other participants were fairly settled couples, co-managers with ma at the desk and pa in maintenance. He felt out of place in Phoenix, too, but he learned that details might be the answer.

One of the handouts he especially liked was for the front desk: "See, G.U.E.S.T.? *G*reet the guest within five seconds. *U*se the guest's name twice. *E*xtend *Best Western Travel Guide* reservations. *S*how room location. That's logical, right? 'This is where it's at.' And then the last point is kind of here or there. *T*elephone the guests as soon as they get in the room. Like, call up and say, 'Is everything all right? Is your room okay?' We try to use this, but we usually don't telephone the guests, because there's not that much time we can, and they might feel a little harassed. But I think it's a great idea."

In his few months on the job, Craig had begun to discover the lure of detail and its promotion. The service sector of the economy is progressively rationalized, not because of the strip or evil corporations, but because of sound lessons drawn earlier in the industrial sector. Regular, rationalized procedures increase productivity, profits, and consumer satisfaction. They work. Just as importantly, they promise a way for managers to handle the responsibilities and personal alienation they encounter. But for that purpose they do not seem to work anywhere near so well. Only the most "hard-core detail men" persist. Frank did not, and I still had my doubts about Craig.

The last time I saw him on the job was the day of the Christmas party. It was one of those frigid Iowa nights with a driving wind, when a water line in a second-floor ceiling decided to blow. The pressure blasted paint off doors and walls, flooding everything below. Fortunately, it was a slow night. All but a skeleton crew whooped it up at the Cantebury, but Craig spent the night like a little Dutch boy holding back the North Sea. At 2:00 a.m. I left him sweating over a wet vac and wondering who would pay for the damage: "God, I wish I were back in California."

Brad Gardner and Mike Allen – Maintenance Men

While outsiders cruising the Strip bemoan commercial clutter, insiders boast a workplace that is, or at least promises to be, uniquely relaxed. The division of labor is still primitive enough to accommodate personal styles and talents. There is a chance to fit in, to meet new people, to chat, and to plan a bit of your day, opportunities that are increasingly rare in the occupational world as a whole. In job-hunting it helps if you bowl or play softball in a city league, a sort of Chamber of Commerce for the working class, but the grapevine and classifieds are reliable. Students, dropouts, and working mothers can drift in and out of work with few credentials or contacts. Given a high turnover, especially in this college town, there is even the possibility of rapid advancement for those with the right attitude and persistence. Heritage Systems has made a special effort to promote members of its own ranks. It is no wonder, then, that the Strip is a haven for workers who are unable or unwilling to submit to the rationalized drudgery of desk, factory, or farm work.

But a relaxed atmosphere has its costs, most obviously in wages. Chain restaurants, for example, employ more than 10 percent of all the minimum-wage earners in the United States. Almost everyone at the Carousel starts at the minimum and stays there for at least six months, which is close to average tenure. Pay raises, though high for the area, are not scheduled and seldom exceed forty cents per hour per year. It is nearly impossible to collect overtime, and only the supervisory staff can earn a bonus or significant fringe benefits.

Furthermore, a relaxed atmosphere is costly to owners. In the short run it is more efficient to discipline employees in a profitable organization than reorganize for each employee. Moreover, customers, like the transients who frequent the Strip, will demand service that is at least predictable. As the American economy falters, especially the automobile-related leisure industry, and as consumers make more exacting demands, the pressures to rationalize these services increase. Even the Carousel, with its devotion to a relaxed atmosphere, inches its way toward detail men and inflexible procedures. Guests who demand a dependably perfect motel experience help thrust industrial organization into the workplace. For Kathy, Frank, Craig, and others, work on the Strip is becoming less an alternative than just another job and a low-paying one at that.

But there is still good reason to work there. In fact, many people sacrifice better pay for variety and human contact on the roadside. The ability to personalize a desk or a locker, to trade stories at the time clock, or to craft some personal flair into the routine are deeply prized freedoms.

Almost every establishment boasts one or two "characters" who push their liberties to the limit. They insist that management take them seriously but only barely so. They are the outlaws, jesters, and good old boys, the James Deans and Bruce Springsteens of the roadside. They comprise a roving subculture of young men with such special talents—ace welders, cooks, mechanics—that they can demand a position in their own style no matter where they are. From co-workers they may attract some jealousy, but more often, if they pull their weight, they win admiration. Like mythic cowboys or renegade truckers they are heroic reminders that productivity and personal expression can coexist.

Even without setting foot in a motel you might guess where to find the characters. They certainly would not be in management or behind the desk, where the public demands grinning chameleons. Nor would you find them in housekeeping, where each maid meticulously scours room after room in her section. A character needs space to roam and challenge for his wits. If you were to look to maintenance, you would be on the right track.

In the Carousel, two or three men are responsible for the upkeep of the entire facility, inside and out. It is they who cruise around town for supplies in the company pickup. Only heavy construction, snow removal, and landscaping are contracted out. Routine trash and pool care open and close the day, but the rest of the time they are painters, truckers, mechanics, carpenters, gardeners, masons, electricians, plumbers, laborers, or whatever else the moment demands. Since, too, there is little telling how things will hold up, they more or less arrange their own hours. Sometimes a job demands a team; at others a lone ranger will suffice.

Anyone on the staff who sees a problem can note it on a list kept at the front desk, but the crew usually set their own agenda, depending on their mood as much as the problems at hand. Each of them will put in at least eight hours for six or seven days then take a couple of days off, maybe more if the hunting is good. But they are effectively on twenty-four-hour call. In a crisis, like a breakdown in the plumbing or electrical system, maintenance becomes the Carousel SWAT team. They may at any time be almost anywhere doing almost anything of untold importance, a fact which alone causes staff to

think twice before adding to the maintenance list. A complaint about damaged carpet or a light bulb has to seem petty. The crew do not take directives so much as entertain requests.

In general they are uniquely free of supervision. Their work is too varied to be routinized and too far backstage for attitudes to matter. Managers monitor their performance by surveying the facility, the maintenance list, monthly breakdowns, and customer complaints. For the most part, as long as the property is kept up at reasonable cost, the crew's independence is unchallenged.

But a truly serious challenge comes with the semi-annual inspection by outside officials. "Best Western guns," armed with cameras and an eye for detail, pay a surprise visit to the motel every few months. As far as the guns are concerned, an inspection helps owners assess their property and the chain, its consistency. They score every public area and a sample of rooms on a thousand-point checklist. For example, they count the hangers in the closets and logos in the rooms. But the maintenance crew are hardly worried about Best Western. The Carousel is obviously well above minimum standards. But an inspector's score is an incontestable measure of how well their independence is deserved.

Hunting season, moods, and characters aside, inspection must be taken seriously. Between official correspondence and well-placed informants, the crew arrange at least two weeks' warning for a "surprise" visit. Using old checklists they prepare rooms for "random" selection and, in fact, rehearse the whole business before the guns arrive. Through careful preparation they consistently score well into the 900s. In 1979, for example, the Carousel earned a 940—not bad, even compared to the Cantebury with a 960, considerably newer rooms, and a bigger crew. Should management start talking attitudes or procedures, maintenance has a ready defense: "Hey, man, 940! We do our work. Don't mess!"

So, they get to strut a bit of their stuff. While other employees march in from the bus or the family car, a maintenance man is just as likely to come screaming in aboard a custom Harley or a pickup packed with greasy tools, old cans, girlie magazines, shotguns, and shells. If recently reminded—very recently—he may be wearing a Best Western uniform, but everything else, from his boots to his hat, will show that he is still his own man.

For about a year Brad Gardner and Mike Allen have been the Carousel maintenance men and designated characters. Brad left better-paying but irregular work laying carpet when Frank Deleon, then manager of the Carousel and softball teammate, invited him to replace the old head of maintenance. Mike, who had been working in a feed store, started about the same time in the motel Conference Center, arranging tables, chairs, and whatnot "for everyone from Dale Carnegie to the Past High Priestesses of the Mystic Nile." They grew up together, going to school, haying, playing ball, and sharing mischief with the other kids in Wellman, a farm town southwest of Iowa City. So, when the boys got together in maintenance, they formed a spirited twosome.

Their arrival each morning could qualify as an entrance. In fact, a few of the housekeepers hang around the time clock just to catch their act. They await a bawdy joke or a hunting yarn, complete with well-timed winks or maybe a limp for dramatic effect. Even the time cards show appropriate style. Cards filed on the wall by the clock read "Kathy Yager," "Tammy Freeman," and so on in tidy script except for a coffee-stained pair near the bottom where "Brad" and "Mike" are scrawled. In the relaxed atmosphere of the Carousel, it is Brad and Mike who chart the stratosphere. Their performance around co-

workers announces they are far more than organizational components.

But they mean no disrespect. They recognize that the owner, Dave Steckling, is due a good day's work, even though they doubt they would know him on sight. Their relationship with managers has been "more like friends than boss-to-worker." Managers even deserve some sympathy, since "they take so much bullshit, just having to act friendly to people who can be such utter assholes." There are similar feelings for the desk: "You couldn't pay me enough to smile all day at those people."

It is an understandable attitude, since the guests who most affect maintenance are misfits and malcontents. The crew takes enough pride in their work to consider vandalism a personal affront. For example, nearly everything around the swimming pool is indestructible, synthetic, and too big to move, but one Monday morning Brad and Mike found evidence of a weekend bash in the pool. Deck chairs, beer cans, and plastic plants littered the bottom. Even the sole real tree in the area was ruthlessly pruned: "Wouldn't you know it—the only live thing in there, and they had to break it." Anyone who must be civil to such folks deserves loyal support.

The maintenance men have special regard for the housekeepers. In part it is enlightened self-interest. Mike explains: "One of the first things Brad told me when I started working here was, 'Keep the housekeepers happy, and it'll make life easier for you. Start to give them shit, and it will just make it harder.' They can do it, too, with little, nit-picky things. Like, you'll be working on something you've been on all day, tired and dirty, and one of them will waddle up to you—'My vacuum cleaner doesn't work right,' 'I can't get a light bulb out,' or some other trivial thing. If you get along with them, they'll work around it or take care of it themselves."

But the housekeepers also win heartfelt sympathy: "Nobody could like cleaning twelve pots and making twenty beds a day, every day, including Christmas and

New Year's. It's hard work, I mean physically hard even compared to ours, and you've got to be meticulous in everything you do. I could see doing it for five or six bucks a room, *maybe*, but they're paid shit and don't get any bonus. Nobody could ever like that. They're just in it for the money or because they don't have any choice. Once in a while we'll get a real good housekeeper, but she'll usually find something better and quit. And who could blame her? You just have to get burned out real quick."

Like all good tricksters, then, Brad and Mike ham it up for others as much as themselves: "Sure, we kid around with almost everybody. It's just got to help them through the day." For example, after Brad takes a swim "to work on the pool light"—"the damned thing seems to act up every few days (ha!)"—he travels the halls to towel his hair and foster knowing grins. Their antics provide both a momentary release and a recurrent reminder of individuality and solidarity in the workplace.

Between performances, Brad and Mike scurry here and there to keep the motel in shape. Regular duties, beyond the pools and the trash, range from changing the marquee to setting up and tearing down conference rooms in banquet, theater, or classroom style. Irregularly, they could be doing almost anything. Their favorites are new projects, like installing a heart-shaped tub, that require improvisation. They have picked up enough skills on the job to handle routine air conditioner and television repairs. But the bulk of their duties are far from novel or glamorous: "We check the maintenance list and take care of that . . . usually . . . at least serious things like a plugged-up toilet. Televisions are kind of serious but not near as much as an air conditioner or a heater. A lot of the time people just don't know enough to flip the switch on the wall as well as the one on the set. Other things, like lights, aren't too high on the agenda. We'll usually leave them to the afternoon when the people are out of the rooms. Towel racks and curtains fall down; lights, telephones, and TVs won't work; drawers are broken;

chairs are broken. Just imagine anything that can go wrong in a room, and it will. Between the usual shit, running around for supplies, fixing stuff people trash, and getting ready for inspection, the two of us keep busy."

The shop, which doubles as the maintenance hide-out and game room, is tucked behind the whirlpool in the basement. The door is flat black except for the words "Keep Out" painted in massive white letters. Like Uncle Walt's tool shed it is usually a shambles and always about as far away from the official country-French theme as you can get (though maybe not so far from what you would find in rural France): "Frank and Dean are always on us about the shop looking messy. You know: 'If your shop looks nice, the whole building looks nice.' But it's what's in here that makes the outside look good. We know where everything is at. Say you're racing against time to get something fixed and need a certain tool; we want it where we left it. It may look like a mess, but otherwise everything gets screwed up. Besides, it's a shop. It's not supposed to look nice all the time. This is our little place here, and no one else should even be in here for any reason at all." Still, after repeated complaints, Brad and Mike sorted some of the heaps of tools and spare parts ("mostly stuff we never use") into jerry-rigged compartments. Motorcycle, hunting, and other magazines for "men's entertainment" were neatly stacked in an out-of-the-way place.

But around this semblance of order are enough props and "art works" to suit Spanky and the gang. Small pictures of deer, fox, and pheasant are targets for projectiles of infinite variety, most often fired from a hydraulic toilet plunger. A paint bucket tacked to the wall serves as a basketball hoop, and space on the floor is reserved for a sort of box-soccer. The walls are splattered with small white globules from the latest fire extinguisher fight or a baseball game: "The batter sits over here, and if you hit one of those wads of paper when they're wet, the stuff just goes everywhere. We usually bat with an old broom handle, but we've run low on them. Whoever loses usu-ally breaks it."

You can imagine why the management might get on them a bit. When a mouse is spotted in the Crown Room, could they be convinced to set a simple trap or put out some d-CON? No, the hunt is on! Shouts echo down the hall, "Over here . . . he's under there!," as BBs rapid-fire from an air rifle called "the annihilator," the M–16 of pest control.

Between their antics, the motorcycles and attire, the shop, the games, the magazines, and the mysterious "agenda," management is always on them a bit. In case inspection scores should fall, Brad and Mike toy with a second line of defense: "The manager runs the place, but let Mike and I not come in just three days and see what it's like. Once we went on strike for three or four days, and this place was a mess. It's not because we're all that good at what we do, but because we've been here long enough to know the little tricks. Like the circuit breakers are in boxes all throughout the building. We barely know where certain things are. We're the *only* ones who know where the circuit breaker is for all the televisions. One little breaker shuts down all those TV sets!"

For the moment, though, management and mainte-nance ally in the motel mission. Despite warnings from ground control, Brad and Mike probe the far reaches of the atmosphere. A gallery of co-workers anxiously awaits reports of just how relaxed it is. For Brad, all systems are go: "This is the lowest paying job I've ever had, but it's the best. We have a lot of room to move. It's not as if there's somebody always watching you, and it's not a certain schedule every day, either. Like, you can pick out your day, do something different. We kind of do what we like, because we've got the responsibility. As long as we get things done, as long as we stay good, there's just a lot of freedom."

Dave Steckling—Founder, Principal Owner, and President of the Corporation

There are only a few self-made millionaires in the inn-keeping industry under 40 . . . fewer yet from Iowa. Dave Steckling, 38, of Iowa City, is one of them. And he's one of the most interesting millionaires in any industry.

His earliest goal was to be a millionaire by age 30. He reached it. Now, eight years later he holds controlling interest in four thriving motels, three restaurant-lounges, an office building and some apartments. And from the looks of things there's a lot more in store for this growing little empire.—Gordon Kopulos, "Dave Steckling—Motel Entrepreneur," *Motel/Motor Inn Journal*, March 1977, p. 8.

I was born in Wisconsin in 1939, lived there until I was twelve. My parents were in the grocery business. In fact, my father had been in it since he was little, and my grandfather before that. But at that time, the late '40s, my aunt and uncle, Elmer Prochnow, took over a small cabin court here in Iowa. It was called the Shady Park, now the Park Motel, out near the interchange on Highway 6 and 218 in the west end of Coralville. They ran that court business for a few years and convinced my parents to try it, too. My father was in his forties and had never tried anything else, but he took a fling at the motel business. And he did pretty well at it.

So they sold the grocery business to buy the Oak Grove Motel, which was nearby. Again, it was a cabin court of about eighteen units. They ran the Oak Grove from about 1949 to 1952, while my aunt and uncle ran the Shady Park. Around then my aunt and uncle decided that they needed something closer in and more up-to-date. In the lodging industry they always say, "There are three things that are important, and those three things are location, location, location." Location basically means that you want to be next door to a university or a hospital, right across from a major airport or an industrial area, right next to a big shopping area or an interstate. In other words, you want every means of transportation, every form of downtown life or whatever, as many places that draw business as possible. And at that time the Oak Grove and the Shady Park were just a long ways out, too far from the university, the hospital, and downtown Iowa City. Also, cabin courts were a thing of the past. So they bought a very small facility, only eight to ten units, called Dunkin's Motor Court, now the Alamo here on Highway 6. Of course, this was way before the interstate. Highway 6 still ran down Fifth Street, and the highway in front of the Alamo was three or four feet lower than it is now. This was long before the Strip.

My aunt and uncle added some additional rooms, bringing it up to about twelve units, ran it for about a year, and convinced my parents to go into a partnership together. This must have been around 1953. I was in my early teens. At that time they enlarged the motel together to bring it up to twenty-six units, and it was run that way for many years.

So I was brought up in the business. The Oak Grove had a huge lawn, about five acres. At twelve years old, I was the one mowing that nearly every week. I was making beds, cleaning the floors, cleaning the bathrooms, dusting the furniture from twelve on (that was one of my jobs during the summer months), plus a lot of maintenance, repair, a constant something to do. And I learned some things about construction, running the front desk, all the things to do and not to do . . . supposedly. We lived right there, in a house that was part of the motel. At the Oak Grove there was a good-sized two-story house, and at the Alamo a good-sized one-story house.

To me it seemed ordinary. I can't think of any real negatives. I didn't mind helping out. I didn't think much of it, other than that was what I was supposed to do; so I did it. I spent most of my time with farm kids, and so, when I wasn't doing things around the motel, I was out helping do whatever farm chores had to be done, playing in the haymow, or whatever it might be.

During that time I was trying to decide what I wanted to do. First, I thought I'd be an architect. I had done a lot of drafting in courses at City High School, and I really thought architecture was a fascinating field. But the University of Iowa didn't offer much in architecture, so I decided on another field that interested me, "double E," electrical engineering. I took the first year of it at Iowa, nineteen hours the first semester. I started at 7:30 in the morning and went till 5:20 at night. It was one hell of a schedule. I became convinced then, too, that there was something more important to me than electrical engineering.

At that time I had one criterion. It probably wasn't a very good one, but I thought money was the absolute, ultimate goal. One of the friends I was running around with had a father who was a dentist. He was very successful. I liked the money he was making and became convinced that I ought to go into dentistry. So I switched fields completely. I had two years of pre-dentistry, was accepted to the College of Dentistry, and did two years of that. Then I spent some time in California, including about a year of school, and then back to Iowa for the final two years. It was a seven-year process before I finally graduated in 1963. I graduated from high school in '56, so I was only seventeen when I got into college. That may have been a mistake, because I didn't really

know what I wanted to do. That is why I switched from field to field to field. I picked up courses in general science and psychology and business and physical education and a little bit of everything along the way. And I had done a number of other things. I had worked at the Alamo some. I worked at Green Giant, up on a farm in Ripon, Wisconsin. I worked for the Iowa City school district one summer, moving furniture around so they could really clean the floors.

Anyway, about the time I graduated from the university, my parents wanted to sell the Alamo. They were willing to sell it to me on a basis of the going market price but on a low down payment. I had some money put aside, and I bought it.

The first year or so things went really well. I always kept saying, "Well, it must be the location; it isn't me." But I had done so many things to the motel, new furniture, just on and on, things that my parents didn't do. They weren't all that necessary. It was good enough, but I thought it had to be better. I always kept trying to improve it. We were the first motel in the Iowa City area to put in color TV.

After owning it about two years, business was good enough that I was approached by the man who owned the Carousel Restaurant, Ermal Loghry. He wanted to know if I wanted to build a motel adjoining the restaurant. I told him I would consider it, but at that point I wanted to enlarge the Alamo from the twenty-six units that it had been for a number of years to forty-some. So I started doing that and got the money lined up. My uncle and father were a great help. They really helped push me to get the building built, doing a lot of things ourselves. We did a lot of the general rough-in work, some of the electrical, plumbing, and hot-water heating, all the insulating and painting. So again, I got a pretty good experience of what it takes to get a building built from beginning to end.

I was working so many hours that one day—at that

time I liked T-birds and always wore the seat belt—I re-call sitting in the dining-room chair reaching for the seat belt. I was just dead, wiped out. I was living in a kind of suite in the motel, getting up at 7:00 in the morning to open the desk for the regular desk people who came in at 8:00. Then I'd go out and do construction work on the motel addition until 5:30 or so. Since the office closed at 11:00, I'd get up during the night to rent rooms from 11:00 to 7:00. It was just . . . not the greatest life. But it didn't really bother me, because i realized I was making money. That was my goal, and I think I still have that goal. In fact, I'm sure I do. Being a millionaire was really important to me, but now I was doing it in an area I en-joyed, instead of dentistry. That would have been the worst mistake I ever made. I would get the dental maga-zine each month, and a month later get the next, without the first ever being opened. I guess you've got to go through those things, and then you realize that, hey, it's not for me.

After we completed the addition in '66, '67, some-where in there, I moved into Iowa City, eventually acquir-ing a house. About that time, too, while I was manager and owner of the Alamo, I started playing the stock mar-ket. I was playing the market in 1968, right at the peak, day-trading forty, fifty thousand dollars of stock a day. That's about all the money I had in it, but I was back and forth—buying, selling, buying, selling. I made the bro-kers a lot of money, and for a while did pretty well myself. I was really into it. I would go down about 8:30 in the morning and read the Wall Street Journal. By 9:00, when the market was ready to open, I knew exactly what I was going to buy or sell for that day. I'd watch the tape for a while, see what's happening, and when conditions were right, I'd buy. In fact, many days I bought much more than I had money to cover, but I had enough stuff going. I would buy up to $120,000 worth of stocks and get them sold off again before the end of the day, so I could cover it, and I'd still be okay. For a while I was really en-joying it, and I'd say I made pretty good money. But eventually it became work, because I was there from 8:30 until the market closed at 3:00. The stockbroker would bring me lunch because I was afraid to miss any-thing on the tape. So I finally decided, "Hey, what was fun is now work." It was time to get out of that.

About that period of time I was approached again on the Carousel. I decided to go ahead with the first phase of construction. We got that going in 1969. Then, about '70 I got bored with that. I decided I could run things from a distance, move to California for a while and run everything from there. I've spent most of my time in Cali-fornia ever since.

My father had a completely different philosophy of operations. He always felt that nobody could run an op-eration as well as he could. He was even afraid to go out of town for a vacation, because he wouldn't know what happened the two weeks that he was gone. And there's a plus in that. The guest coming in feels that he's relat-ing to the owner. That's a real plus. When you come into a restaurant or a cocktail lounge or a motel, and the owner shakes your hand, you say, "Well, I'm dealing with the top guy!" You're on friendly terms; the owner greets you by name. If there's something wrong with your room, you shrug your shoulders and let it go by. But I think that limits you, too. If you're going to be in a travel industry, I think you'd better know what the rest of the world is doing.

Obviously, I've gone to the other extreme and say, "Bye! I'm going to move to wherever I feel like moving." If I decide I want to live in California or in Europe for a while, I'm going to do it. I know there are good people that can run things in my absence. I still have to be telling them, maybe every week or two weeks, "You've got to do this; you've got to do that, or else. . . ." But basically I know that a well-run company doesn't need the top indi-vidual there all the time.

But it's funny, when you're running an operation the

way we run it, as an unknown entity. Just to cite an example, one of my friends from New York called the Carousel. He told the girl at the desk, "I want to talk to Dave Steckling." She looked through the room file and said, "Sorry, he's not registered here." When he informed her that I happen to be the principal owner and president of the corporation, she said, "Oh. Oh, really?" I guess it's just a philosophical difference.

About six months after I moved to California, I went to Europe for a month. During that period of time, '70, '71, I was starting construction on the next part of the Carousel. Then I kind of outgrew that, wanted something to do, so then there was the Cantebury. We started construction in 1972 and finished the first part of it in '73. So far it's had three phases. The second phase put on another fifty-some units, and the third phase twenty more. Right now we're planning another forty to fifty units. We also have the Cantebury in Muscatine. That's a hundred-plus-unit property we built in two phases. We have a supper club restaurant in Des Moines, a Country Kitchen in Wisconsin, and we're building another one up there. Right now we're buying a fraternity house. We're also getting funding to tear down the oldest part of the Alamo, the west end of the building, and put in thirty additional units. The Carousel complex I want to completely redo. So, we don't sit still. We like to keep things going.

I think the only time we made mistakes was when we tried to grow in an area we're not good in, not knowledgeable. For example, we got involved in Paul Revere's Pizza; now we're trying to get uninvolved. It wasn't the growth vehicle I thought it was going to be. Basically the lodging industry is what I know and like. Some of the others I've gotten to understand, but I've either become bored with them or whatever. My interest isn't there.

I guess I've developed a philosophy that everybody needs to be good at something in life, whatever that

something is. I don't care if their only capability is digging ditches, or their capability is being president, or whatever else. You need to be good at something. And if somebody's chosen, let's say, the lodging field, they need to try to excel in that area. I guess that's the best way to try to show people where your own head is.

On Quality

In the lodging industry there are five criteria of things that are important. One of them is the quality of the product. Another one is cleanliness. The third one is service, including the desk and how well they handle it. And you've got to have fair prices and good decor. Those are the five items, and you've got to have all five of them, and you've got to do all five well. You might get by with a weakness in one or two areas, a little bit, but the better you can do on all five, the better you'll be.

I think everybody is looking for a good experience, whatever that might be, at a rate they can afford to pay. To me, obviously, a good experience looks different than the typical Holiday Inn or Howard Johnson's or any other facility that offers an average room and an average restaurant and that's about it. I guess I believe in a total experience. You need to offer people more. We were the first motel in the Iowa City area to offer color TV, an indoor pool, men's and women's saunas, whirlpools, rooms with over-sized and water beds, sunken living areas, wet bars, fireplaces. All these amenities cost money to put in; so you've got to weigh the cost of any amenity versus what you can charge for rates.

We do nearly all of our own design work. You've got

to understand what's happening in California, New York, the rest of the world. It's not that I look for models; it's more of a subconscious thing. Like, I remember at one time being impressed by the first Hyatt Regency in Atlanta. The lobby is something like twenty-three stories high with the rooms around the outside. That was impressive. Actually, I tend to go the other way, try to make every inch of space count. I figure, "We're paying taxes on it; I'll be damned if I just have it sitting there doing nothing!" But I think it takes seeing a lot of things and seeing some of them make it. Even in things that are supposed to be the "best" vehicle for whatever they're trying to do, I always see, "Well, if they would do this and this, it would be a much better situation." If I were to redesign our motels right now, I could see a lot of things I'd do differently.

There has been a change in the lodging industry as a whole. If you were still building motels like the Oak Grove or the one-story part of the Alamo, you'd be building something obsolete. Outside corridors, one-story motels, these are a thing of the past for several reasons. People do want to park right beside their door. That part is important, but you have a tremendous energy-loss problem with a building one-story and one-room deep. Every room is losing energy through the roof, the front, and the back. So the next step forward would be to set rooms back-to-back with the plumbing chase down the middle. Another step down the road, like the Capri, is to move the hallway in, a design concept so you can get from the motel room to the lobby or the coffee shop or whatever without having to go outside on a really cold or hot day. The next growth potential would be the Holiday Inn—two-story, back-to-back, again the outside corridors (which in this climate is a mistake). So motels basically evolved from the cabin court like the Blue Top, Oak Grove, or Shady Park to the Alamo or Hawkeye Lodge to the Capri to the Holiday Inn. And the next most viable thing after that is what we're doing at the Carousel and Cantebury—central hallway, two-story, as much outdoor parking as possible. So that is one of the places where the lodging industry is today.

There's another trend again back towards the high-rise hotels. As an example, we worked on the new downtown hotel planned in Iowa City, seeing whether we could put together a viable proposal. I would like to be part of it. It could be a flagship type of property, which would be nice. But economically it just doesn't make sense. There's no way that we could figure out to come up with a room rate that we could justify. And you have to have both; you have to have people staying there and paying the bills. When I first looked at it, we thought we were talking about a thirty-some-dollar room rate, and then, boy, every time we'd go back and look at costs, it kept getting higher and higher and higher. By the time the consumer was out of there, by the time he'd paid for the city parking ramp (allocation fees, I think worked out to about four dollars a day), paid his room rent and everything else, we were looking at forty-some dollars. We began to question whether the traveler coming to the Iowa City market was going to be able to pay those rates. Yes, there will be some who will, but we just couldn't justify the whole facility. We didn't want to build something that was "good for the grandchildren." It's got to be good for our generation, or don't bother to do it!

The Midwest is always slower on everything, slower to adapt. That's both good and bad. The Coasts go to the extremes, both ways. Iowa is more right down the middle, middle-class, very conservative in philosophy. So there are things like high-rise hotels that can be tried. They will make it in big cities. They will probably make it in big cities in Iowa, make it in Des Moines, but probably won't make it here. Down the road a way—I don't know how far—when Iowa City has experienced a lot more growth, et cetera, et cetera, then maybe they'll be viable. Right now, I can't see that they are.

I wish we were more progressive. There's something I find frustrating in Coralville right now. I'm not sure how much Iowa City is really different than Coralville. There are definitely some imagined differences, but with the university there, that alone has helped push or drag Iowa City into being a better place. We've got to keep up with Iowa City and hopefully surpass it, and that's going to take some doing. Beautification out there on the Coralville Strip, First Avenue, and Fifth Street is the most obvious of things that need to be done. The power poles are a real detriment. We ought to bury the power lines, plant more trees, and just improve the buildings we do have. I know I keep pushing and pushing, and I have some support, but I'd like to see more people within the community saying, "We really need to do something! Let's go out and do it!" I guess I am concerned that we do move forward with the city of Coralville, or we will be a second-rate city. Over the years, the Coralville Strip maybe has looked a little bit on the junky side, and this is one reason I believe it's so important that we take some positive steps to dispel that image.

I think people have reached the point where they've had enough plastic. I don't mean just "plastic" in terms of actual plastic but of the artificial. They want something authentic. I guess I'd cite something like Disneyland with the authenticity of some of their buildings. And they certainly have been successful. This is another reason to travel. If you're going to do something, like the Canterbury with the English Tudor theme or the Carousel with the country French, you'd better see England and France, get some idea of what it was like in the 1500s, 1600s, 1700s, 1800s, so you have some idea of what you're trying to do. I'm not saying you have to document everything down to the way it used to be. But the more you can give people a hint of something they can't experience today at the typical Holiday Inn, the better off you're going to be.

I see the 1980s as being a decade of quality. People will be more and more conscious of getting value received for the dollar. I think they will tend to buy less, particularly of the shoddy American merchandise that's been turned out over the years. The things that will sell will be the quality consumer products, those that may cost a little bit more but last a longer period of time so they justify their cost. And I think the same thing may be true in the lodging industry. I'm not talking about spending twice as much for a room or whatever, but the more you can offer a good, quality, total experience, the better off you'll be.

John Allen—Artist-in-Residence

The French theme and lush amenities of the Carousel are intended to provide a total experience that is "authentic" in a curious way. The Strip has been and remains a site for intense, auto-oriented commerce, but now consumers demand that it wear a coherent disguise. A simple bed, some fuel, or a meal are no longer enough. They await transport to another place and time. Surround pavement with greenery, they say; give us antiques, weathered boards, and cobblestone; bury power lines—as if the whole emerged immaculate in Hesperides. It may appear to be a movement "back to the earth," but it is an earth that never existed, the Disney version. In place of crude functions, plastic, and workaday life, progressive entrepreneurs like Dave Steckling promise genuine experience that is genuinely unreal. Quality is an authentic fantasy.

Appearances to the contrary, it is far from immaculate in origin. The Carousel did not arrive via Air France or time machine. Dave Steckling scoured the globe and capital markets for materials. The daily toil and shenanigans of men and women lie behind every amenity. Any imperfection is merely a smudge from their hands at work.

Most of the interior walls of the Carousel were originally rolled with white paint. Here and there frames were tacked around patches of velveteen wallpaper. There were ample allusions to French elegance, but why not go for the quality, the authentic, total experience that no budget motel could match?

These were among the thoughts of Dean Moore in 1976 or thereabouts, when he was managing the Carousel and an old schoolmate, John Allen, dropped by the office. Like Brad and Mike, John had been doing odd jobs around Wellman, at the moment a little masonry with his uncle. He was looking for another job, any kind of job, but the motel could use his special talents. He had lettered signs for neighbors since high school and studied painting and sculpture at the university. He even took a couple of courses in French. So, for five dollars an hour, the Carousel acquired a part-time artist-in-residence.

John greets most things in life with a bemused if not sardonic air, himself included: "I always kind of giggle at the people that come in here, see the murals and stuff, and think this is such a *great* place. People like the Pittsburgh Ballet Company have said, 'Oh! Isn't this nice!' But if you look a little closer, that's all it takes. . . . I don't consider myself a fine artist, you know. I'm just a painter, a sign painter. I like to do things fast—get it done and get the money."

Still, some of his work is truly impressive and shows increasingly fine detail. On admiring his first mural for the Carousel, a cameo over the pool, I asked him how he learned to do such a thing.

How to paint on a wall? What's to know? There aren't any basic rules as far as painting on a wall goes. No problem, as long as you can reach up there.

For sure, you have to have a design on a piece of paper. You just grid it off, blow the sections up on the wall, and then fill in the sections. I learned to do it in elementary school, I guess. You learn to draw, and, you know, "You're better than anybody else"; so that's what you do. I don't really remember where I learned it.

That is just the logo of the place. It's on all the

pamphlets, all the Best Western stuff. I don't like the face at all. It's too fat. The chin's too large. It looked better from up there. Once you get far away, it enlarges itself some way. They wanted it done fast, so I did it in just like three days.

Signs

After the logo, they needed a bunch of signs made. Their placards, telling where the rooms are, kept getting ripped off. Everybody wanted to take one home and put it up on their bedroom wall. So they took them all down, patched the holes, and told me to paint every sign in here. That took quite a while.

They wanted everything in French. I'd just look it up and then ask around: "Can you pronounce it, and does it look French?" People know. You can't have anything too spectacular. Ask the maintenance department. Ha!

The capital letters come out of a lettering book. Other than that, it's just plain writing. It's my hand. I put little flowers on the doors, around the walls, and on the bottom of the pool. They came from something like Enjoy Your Flowers. *I like to find models and improve on them rather than just start from nothing.*

It's all pretty boring to me. They're just something you do in twenty minutes. Murals take weeks, and they're a lot more fun. But there's a lot of money in signs. Everybody wants a sign painted.

Murals

They have so much blank wall around here; they just wanted something to fill it up. They had a few extra bucks and said, "Go ahead—paint a mural on it." I said, "What do you want?" And they said, "Oh, something French. . . ." So I said, "Okay!" They keep saying, "Here's another big wall; paint a mural on it." I don't even show them sketches, and they're satisfied. White walls

abound in this place, and if it were up to me, there would be a mural everywhere.

I usually make a sketch from pictures in the Art Library or my old French books. I took two semesters of French in college for the language requirement. I didn't like it at all, though, so I don't remember much of anything. Last September, 1979, Dean and I went over to France for a couple of weeks. We tried to communicate. We tried! We got around quite a bit in a van that Steckling left parked in Amsterdam. We had to stop hundreds of times for directions, and that's where we met a lot of people. Great fun! I can't really say it affected the way I look at the murals, though. I just feel more wholesome about doing it. It's nice to have an understanding of what everything is really like over there. But I usually work from photographs anyway.

They're black-and-white, so I have to choose the colors. Most of them are pastels, mainly because I use latex, regular wall paint. Most pastels are latex, and most latexes are pastel. It's easy to work with, dries fast, and you don't need a base like you do with enamel. Plus, I think the lighter stuff goes well with all the tourists that come through from Nebraska and Iowa. They think it's a really great place to stay, "staying at the Carousel Inn!"

I get the main colors premixed at a paint store. When I need another color, I just mix it myself. They say never to mix premixed paints, but it works fine. I don't know why they say it. I mix some of them right on the wall. I use two coats, so it holds better. It even washes up pretty well, as long as nobody hits it with Magic Marker.

There's really nothing to it. Like, for the store fronts around the pool, put in elongated windows and French

doors. For the village scene—I've seen a lot of little vil-
lages—what's to it, you know? Just put a few peaks on
the roofs, mountains back behind, a lake in front, add
a few clouds. Or in the Crown Room—that was kind of
inspired. They had a great big farm group coming in. So
I painted some furrowed fields and some green stuff. (I
don't know if they noticed. They were real busy talking
about growing things.) The big one by the entrance
came from Paul Klee [the Swiss painter and graphic art-
ist, 1879–1940]. I've never really studied him at all, but
I really like his stuff. I used his drawings for things like
hats and positions. I just needed some French-looking
women, some bright colors and swirly patterns along
where you walk. It doesn't mean anything.

That was hard, though, just to get up there. Climbing
the ladder over and over really got to be a drag. It was
a month's work, but it probably took about two months
since I don't work all the time. Working by the front desk
or an exit is just horrible, people coming and going, put-
ting their two cents in. Otherwise you can set up with a
rock station on all day. It's nice when you can take your
time on something, and there's nobody coming up every
day wanting it finished. Once you're up there, though,
you just want to get it done and down off the ladder.

As John describes his work, he pauses here and there to
point out a color or pattern change left in haste or to admire a few details. Small gestures betray some of the
care that is obvious in his murals but that he is unlikely to
admit. It is simply not worth investing much pride. In the
end the idea is to make a few bucks and please an in-
scrutable public.

When guests pass by him teetering on a ladder, their
comments ("Almost done? How about a lighter green?")
are just annoying. They obviously have not spent enough
time with John or his work to offer anything very gratify-
ing or insightful. When Hermione Gingold visited the Carousel, he heard that she could only shout, "Oh, horrid!
Horrid!" A few people have even phoned the desk to report "some guy marking up the walls." Most guests seem
to be overcome by the mystique: "'Oh, an artist at work!
An artist at work!' over and over again." Except for the
ribbing he welcomes from maintenance, John would prefer to paint in private.

He is stunned when his work attracts any serious attention. He was especially taken by the reaction of his co-
workers at a Christmas party a couple of years ago: "I
was half-done with a mural on the back wall of the Crown
Room, and they decided to have the Heritage bash down
there. I left my paints under a table, and . . . you know
how it is. Everybody got drunk and threw paint all over the
walls. But not that wall! That amazed me."

He more or less assumes that his work is merely a line
in someone else's score. The theme may be a little silly,
but that is the responsibility of the management: "They
have their own ideas. They're not going to consult somebody outside like me. I'm not here every day. It's their job
to make sure things look good. They think they can do
the job, and they're making money."

Sometimes he is just asked to match the colors in a
carpet, but he has had some bizarre requests, too: "I was
in the middle of doing a French village down in the Conference Center, but they had a big dinner coming in for
all the people who donate more than five hundred dollars

to the University Athletic Department. So the management wanted a hawk over there, on the wall I was painting. I put a big 'Herky the hawk' in the corner, and they covered the rest with an Iowa banner. Scratch away some of the paint, and you can see it!" For the most part, though, John is glad to be left alone.

The Carousel sells its guests a room and an authentic alternative to workaday life. But an outsider's escape can depend on an insider's confinement. While patrons search the Strip for a well-appointed entrance, John Allen among others keeps his eyes on the exit.

This place is about as weird as anyplace, I guess, but you get your fill of it real fast. It's not the people working here. I mean, they aren't drab and stupid. They all are on the ball. They're fun. It's just the place, being in the same walls every day. I hate being in the same place. Don't you? I don't think too many people like their jobs. They do what they can do.

I'm set up pretty well here. I don't put in that much time. I just want to get it done fast, so I can make a buck off the thing and never have the management feel ripped off, either. See, motels can't spend an overabundance on this kind of stuff, frills. I think I'm worth more than five dollars an hour, but, you know, why press it? I don't want to be on any hard terms with the management.

My usual check for two weeks' work is like two hundred dollars, but I think that's reasonable, because I can come and go whenever I please, come in and work at night if I have to. You know, how many people have a job like this, even for a short time?

Dean Moore—General Manager of Heritage Operations

never thought this would happen, that I'd be doing this game. You have to do it. At home I just wear jeans and stuff, and then put on a suit and tie for work. It's just a game.

I'm an officer in the Chamber of Commerce and all that. I like that—going over to Happy Joe's Pizza and hearing about everybody's grandchildren.

But I have to worry about my image. In this book, how are you going to make the Carousel look? I want you to tell the truth, and I know we're not perfect, but this is business. People sometimes don't want to hear the truth, or they'll take things out of context. Will I look like a jerk? Will people still want to come to the Carousel? I don't want some housekeeper's husband or cousin or somebody telling her. 'You work in that place?!' You know? Or someone else in the Chamber might read what you write, even if they're wrong, and think I'm responsible. I just don't want anybody to get hurt.

Hell, we've talked about this before. I guess it will be all right. Just make sure you talk about my dog, Jack. He's a Coralville celebrity. Every morning he has breakfast at Randall's. All the neighbors know him. He used to ride on the roof of my MG.

I first came across Dean Moore's name in newspaper articles on the Coralville Sign Committee in the late 1970s. About twenty members—merchants representing roadside food, lodging, and retail establishments and one optometrist, Doc Kennedy—make annual donations to maintain a billboard on city property visible from the interstate highway. Just east of the main Coralville exit, it directs motorists to the umpteen motel rooms, gas stations, restaurants, and stores that can be found on or around the Strip. On page 1 the *Coralville Courier* for February 22, 1979, featured Dean's appeal for donations as chairman of the Sign Committee:

All businesses benefit from the sign. Studies have shown that every dollar spent in Coralville "turnsover" up to 20 times. For example, a dollar spent in a motel will pay wages for an employee who will eat, buy groceries, medicines, pay rent, or partake of any one of the hundred things that the Coralville community has to offer.

Iowa City reporters also wrote about the sign when it engendered a dispute with the Iowa Department of Transportation in 1978. Since passage of the Highway Beautification Act in 1965, a major victory for Lady Bird Johnson, billboard restrictions have been attached to federal funds for interstate programs. The Iowa DOT, charged with enforcing those restrictions, informed the city of Coralville in January 1978 that the billboard on its property was illegal and had to be removed. Advertising could appear on the interstate only if a business specifically served motorists and was located just off the ramp. The state would construct modest blue signs before each exit and rent space for standard-sized logos, but traditional shoulder billboards were outlawed with few exceptions. To the delight of the Sign Committee, the City Council decided, in the mayor's words, "to dig in its heels." The council directed its attorney, Bruce Washburn, to do whatever might be necessary to keep the sign. The city argued that it should be permissible under federal and state law. It did not bear the names of any specific business and was really an on-premise sign for the city as

a whole. After eight months of correspondence asserting and refuting interpretations of the law, the Iowa DOT agreed that the Coralville sign could remain, since it was "directional" or "informational" rather than "commercial."

Apparently it was not really much of a battle. Representatives of the DOT initially came on strong, but that is only to be expected. They could always lower their demands. They might challenge a business here or there, but they would accommodate municipalities as long as federal funds were not jeopardized. The principals agree that negotiations were generally amiable. But in this legal skirmish citizens saw symbolic warfare. Cynics, Iowa City Types, followed the story as yet another example of aggressive commercialism in Coralville. The city had become a Strip annex. Boosters, on the other hand, delighted in their victory over outside interference. For once, practical reason was triumphant, even if they had to endorse some silly terminology.

Knowing that Dean Moore was chairman of the Sign Committee as well as general manager of operations for Heritage Systems, a company with extensive Strip holdings, I suspected that he would be a model booster—an established, middle-aged, True Coralvillian. Generally that would not be a bad guess.

The first hint that it was bad came in an entirely different setting. I had been working one or two days a week as a hired hand on a neighbor's farm on the other side of Iowa City. It was, I thought, a combination exercise and Iowa-orientation program. One day, while helping to sort cattle, I learned that the full-time crew all knew Dean and his extended family. Nearly all of them had grown up with Dean on mom and dad's farm in this conservative, closely knit community. Theirs is a world of hard work and kin only lightly seasoned with images of the outside from the media, travels to cattle shows around the Midwest, and an occasional venture to Colorado or the Wisconsin Dells. It is a decidedly normal American life, where the only weirdos are life-style anarchists from the East or the

university, who must, unfortunately, be tolerated, and the Amish. Unlike the Amish in nearby Amana, who can at least be admired for capitalizing on romantic tourists, the Old Order Amish around Kalona, south of Iowa City, are often considered masochists. They are nice enough people, easily idealized, but "you have to be crazy to live the way they do." Amish and mainstream farmers have to pay the same banks for the same high-priced land and compete with the same Soviet, Canadian, and Latin American producers, but with radically different technology. Once you have driven a combine it is pretty hard to imagine choosing to pick a couple of hundred acres of corn one ear at a time or hand-tying sheaves of oats for a 1928 thrasher.

So, most farm boys in my and, as it turns out, Dean's old neighborhood, Sharon Center, are expected to steer a fairly straight course between the cosmopolitan decadence of Iowa City and the back-breaking traditionalism of Amish Kalona. All of this was simply presumed in a remark by one of the hands, "I never did understand why Dean didn't take on his father's farm." Our guesses about his motivation were interrupted by some uncooperative Alabama Holsteins, but in any case it was clear that Dean fit neither the stock farm boy nor the booster image. He could not be very old, established, or Coralvillian.

I then bet he could teach me a lot. He had passed well beyond the margins of strip life. His job kept him running between roadside motels and restaurants scattered about Iowa and Wisconsin. Most of his days were spent at the Heritage Systems office or one of their three motels—the Carousel, the Cantebury, and the Alamo—off the Coralville Strip.

A Life Story

Anyway, I just told you how I got into what I do. I was wondering if you could just tell me

The whole story?

Yeah, just briefly, what you've been up to. I know you grew up near Sharon Center and consider yourself a "Sharon Center boy," right? You grew up on a farm, right?

Yeah, I was strictly farm—used to getting up at seven in the morning, going out and choring, catching the bus at eight-thirty to school, coming home, working—working every Saturday and Sunday and every night.

By the way, I heard that you kids would get hassled if you rode the bus into the city. Did you?

Yeah, yeah. It was always the low-ranked kids that were the farmers.

But first I went to Middleburg. It's a one-room school down about four miles outside of Kalona. We had one teacher and eight grades. I rode a horse to school and all that, but I was the only kid that wasn't Amish. I was the only kid that didn't get my hair cut with a bowl around my head. I didn't wear suspenders and that type of thing. And that was a pretty good deal.

But then I remember going to city school, Mid-Prairie in Kalona. That was a "city school." All the kids were swearing. This was in third and fourth grade, and they knew about swear words and stuff like that. That was pretty hard to handle.

Well, I started off bad, 'cause I didn't learn how to read in the one-room school. The Amish don't really start teaching till third grade. The Mid-Prairie kids knew their ABCs and how to read and this and that. So I copied, so I didn't seem like the dumb person of the class. To save face I was always trying to be the big guy, the leader of the class. You know how the apple syndrome is when you're a little kid. But I had to go through summer school, and all through school I was lucky to get C's. But I could copy. I probably could still take a test at the university and do a good job without going to any classes. That's how I went through college. I didn't buy a book in college. But I didn't really care. I never was into the books.

You see, I was either supposed to be a farmer or a baseball player. That was pretty much the way I was brought up. And I didn't want to be a farmer; so, it had to be a baseball player. I got drafted by the Cincinnati Reds out of high school.

Really?

Yeah. What happened was that Bob Otis from Montreal was watching me. Then I was asked to go to Norway to a try-out camp. I think, just because I really wanted it so bad, they gave me an opportunity.

They told me that I had to go to Ellsworth College, and that way I could get up my grades and go to a Big Ten school or some big school. It was Arizona at the time. They wanted me to go to Flagstaff and do my minor league stuff through school. That's what they try to do now. So, I'd signed a letter of intent, and they got me into Ellsworth so it was free. That was the deal.

Would you say that you were poor?

No, we were probably . . .

I mean—I don't want to know how much money you had—just . . .

Yeah, we were probably poor, but I never knew it. I didn't know we were poor at all. I thought we were very well-to-do. My father came up here from Tennessee, and he was a "hillbilly." My mother was disowned from her family 'cause she married a "hillbilly," a "no-good-for-nothing" and this and that. At least that's the way I understand it. My dad just worked all the time. We had to rent all through school. I didn't realize that my folks were always working hard to keep us clothed and have everything we wanted at Christmas. But they did.

But it wasn't a sad case, either.

So what happened next? You did two years?

In two years I graduated from Ellsworth with retail marketing. I had been an R.A., and then I was supposed to go to Arizona.

An "R.A."?

Yeah, a resident advisor in the dorms. That was how I got money to go to school free. They rigged all this stuff up. I wasn't supposed to get financial aid because my folks only had two kids and they owned a farm. But a farmer doesn't have that much cash. He puts it all back in the farm. My folks were just buying a farm the year I went to college. So it looked on paper like they were worth something, but they didn't have nothing. I couldn't get government aid, but baseball swung that around.

See, Ellsworth is a school where they get all the scruds that want to play Big Ten sports, all the black guys from every city and raunchy hole in the country. They send them to Ellsworth, this little faraway, out-of-the-way place where they can rape the farmers' daughters and this and that and get by with it. You have a good time. You don't have to go to classes yet get good

enough grades to go to a Big Ten school and play for one season. That's the way I look at Ellsworth.

So, we had a good time. I had the floor with all the black guys. There were about six of us that were white. And we were just as wild, and we all had a great time. When I was an R.A., that's when I learned about managing people. I think that's how I got into it, how I got to really enjoy it. You'd tell them, "Hey! Come on! It's two o'clock in the morning. We're trying to sleep!" but they'd be your best friends.

So, what about Arizona. Did you go?

No, I never made it. I spent money on sports cars and this and that and started as a desk clerk at the Cantebury Inn. (Moving faster than you thought, huh?) That was '75. I came home in the summer of '75.

God, that wasn't that long ago, then.

Yeah. A lot of things have happened to me real fast.

So, I came home and had to get a job. My dad couldn't afford to have me working on the farm for the summer and make enough money to go to school in the fall, to pay for my way down to Arizona, much less fun times.

So I got a job for Barton Construction, working on oil roads, running a grader. It was pretty great for the farm kid, and they liked it. They loved it. They get them real cheap, minimum wage for construction. I think I made three dollars and twenty-some cents. But I was just a student and a farm kid that didn't know any better. I thought it was fantastic money. So I ran this grader for Barton Construction, and I worked at the hospital on weekends for Gary Grout, head of the radiology department, on transferring film. He was my cousin and a coach of the softball team that I was playing on. I had to make a lot of money to get to college.

Well, I bought a foreign car, a little Fiat, and it just ate me to death; you know? Everything was going wrong.

Say, is this okay? Should I just keep talking or what? I've never done this before.

Yeah. This is fine. My life is so boring in comparison.

No! No, I think everybody's got the neatest life in the world, according to themselves; you know? You wouldn't change a thing, no matter if you did everything fucked up.

Anyway, on the grader we'd start at seven and get done at six-thirty. You know how you sit on the machine half the day and don't run it, and you just sit around and smoke joints, read, and write letters and this and that? And then you run it for another three hours and get paid for eleven hours? So, that was sort of a good deal, but it was boring. I couldn't stand it—no one to talk to. I learned how to juggle, did everything out there with clods and stuff, but I hated it. I wanted to play baseball. I wanted to go down to Arizona, have the sun, the mountains, and play baseball, just have a good time. I wasn't into anything like this. I'd had two years of partying, and I wanted more.

Well, I had a softball game this one weekend, but I was supposed to be working weekends, hauling this film back and forth. Gary Grout and I wanted to play, but I'd lose my job if I did. So, Gary Grout says, "Play! I'll give you a full-time job at the hospital."

You know, I was working with these dirty-mouthed old men, construction guys. I hated it. It was like—no ambition other than to drink beer when they got done. I couldn't handle it. You weren't learning anything. It was crazy. And at that time I was trying to get my Christian life straightened out. So I'm reading the Moody Monthly Magazines out of the Bible Institute in Chicago and all this other stuff about the Bible. And well, you just sit out there, and you're lonely, and it's crazy and weird. So I thought this was great: play softball and get to work at the hospital, take sandwiches and cigarettes to the nurses; right? That's all I did. I was making about the same amount of money and having a good time doing it.

But in the meantime, I'm spending all my money on this stupid car. It was August, and I still didn't have enough money for college. They were going to pay for my tuition and books, but I had to live some way. And I had to have a good time, you know. I didn't even have money to get there. Thinking of moving somewhere and not having the bucks at that time was just out of reach. Now I'd love to try and do it.

So, I realized that I needed more money and took a job at the Cantebury as a desk clerk from three to eleven. (Now we're moving along.) I'd get done at the hospital from seven to one in the afternoon, take a nap, and then go to the Cantebury and work the desk. That was a lot of fun—visiting with people, seeing a lot of good-looking chicks, and this and that. But the working thing got old real quick then, too.

Is there any story behind how you ended up getting the desk job in particular?

Yeah, there is. I moved to town and was living with two guys in a small apartment on Church Street. The guy Mike and I moved in with (I didn't realize he was such a jerk, but he had a place and we needed one), he was one of these guys that, you know, had "drive"—just almost the thing I'm hating about myself now. He was all that stuff.

What do you mean?

You know, he'd get the fancy shoes. "You've got to put on the show for everybody." "You've got to drive to make money." And you get sick of that, too. You've got to come back to earth now and then. But he was all that. He was a junior that way! He was only nineteen years old at the time, and he'd never done anything else.

Well, he was out at the Highlander Inn and he knew Neil Trott, who was vice-president of Heritage Systems. He knew Neil because they met at a Hotel/Motel Asso-

ciation meeting. So he thought he'd be with the big guy, you know. He's only a desk clerk out at the Highlander and he met this guy—accidentally! But he says, "Hey! I'm good friends with him. I'll call him up and see if he can't get you a job." Ha! Can you imagine? That's where this guy was coming from.

So he called Neil. I go down and have an interview with Neil, and I've got to wear a suit and tie. (Hate that stuff.) So I go in and visit with him, tell him that I'd like to be the motel manager, and I want to get rich.

You know, my whole life I always wanted to have a lot of money because I always wanted to be a baseball player and have the money, have the sportscars, drive around, see the country, be a bum if you want but not have to worry about money. So . . .

IF you make it.

If you make it. Yeah, really! Well, I grew up with this dream, right, this big outlandish dream of being a major league baseball player and having a lot of money. And I believed it! All the way up to college! But I've always wanted to have the cash, to fly somewhere if I wanted to or . . . you know.

Anyway, I wanted to make a lot of money, and I like dealing with people, so I thought this might be a good possibility to stay. The big story was I'd be able to be manager of the Carousel Inn soon, because someone probably would be leaving soon. They had no one ready, and they needed some new assistants to come into the company.

Yeah. Did you know what the managerial scene is in hotels?

No! Hell, no! I was a farm kid! I didn't know anything about hotels! I just wanted a job.

So Neil says, "We might have a job. I'll check the desk, see if they have an opening. If you want to be a desk clerk, you could start there, and you'd have your maintenance man. . . ."

Nothing! Didn't sound like anything great at all. But big me, I believed anything and thought, "Oh, yeah. You can do anything!" Right?

So I am the desk clerk, desk clerk for a month, and all of a sudden I'm desk supervisor, 'cause the desk supervisor quit. I worked the night shift full-time and for the hospital full-time for a long time. Then, a couple of months after that, everybody quit in front of me, right away. So, everything just fell in my lap.

You know, it was working pretty good. There wasn't much competition to it because none of them were really into it. Most desk clerks aren't. So, I'm desk clerk, stealing toilet paper to stay alive, making two-ten an hour, thinking I'm going to be a millionaire in a couple of days. As desk supervisor I got two and a quarter. At that time it was shit wages. Now it's shit wages but two and a quarter!? I put in fifty hours a week. And I was maintenance man. And then the manager at the Carousel quit. Mitch Jensen was manager of the Cantebury, Bill Dixon was the assistant, and I was the desk clerk. So Mitch took the job at the Carousel, Bill took over the Cantebury, and Mitch needed an assistant and someone to help him at the Carousel. So, I went down to the Carousel.

This was only like three months after I started, and then, three months later, Mitch Jensen quit. I'm the assistant at the Carousel doing all this dumb stuff—maintenance work to the Conference Center—anything he didn't want to do, and he didn't want to do nothing. He was running the Alamo, too, so I was his assistant for those two places. He quits three months later, and. . . . I don't know. I'm just a punk kid that worked maintenance and the desk. Here I am managing two places! Gosh!

We had a stupid system where, if you made more money or didn't lose as much as you did last year that month, you made bonus. So what Mitch Jensen was doing was not reporting the bills that he got that month to come off of his statement. So he made bonus every month. It got to the point where: "Hey, it's going to show up. I'd better quit." So he quits, and I'm stuck there with all these bills! And the Alamo! That place! And the whirlpool doesn't work. No whirlpool. It was shitty, a lot shittier than it is now.

So, we did a lot of work at the Carousel. It was on the warning thing for Best Western. Rick Schmidt ran it down the hole, and then Mitch Jensen tried, but all he did was. . . . No, he didn't try. He just painted a lot and didn't report the bills, made bonus, and quit.

Is that a standard thing for managers to do?

That was at that time. People are getting wiser and putting them on different types of bonus systems, but still . . . like a chef in a restaurant can. If he's on bonus for his food cost or something like that, he'll not report half the food they got that month or have their inventory low at the end of the month. His food cost will come out real good. Anyway, it's pretty much of a thing. If you screw up, they run it down. You know, most people are honest, but everybody's got to feed their own face, too. If they're going to quit, why not stay on a couple of months? They make their big bonus money for the last two months, and then they're gone. But that doesn't happen any more with us. It hasn't happened for a couple of years.

Anyway, I got Frank in then, Frank Deleon. You know Frank? Do you want me to go through that whole spectrum, too, about Frank?

Part of it. You can go over it real quick, though.

Well, I met Frank skiing in Colorado. We were at Randy Porter's house. I didn't know Frank at all. We were all just getting loaded and met this guy who played the harmonica. Well, a year later, I'm in my apartment, and somebody comes knocking at the door, and says, "Dean?" And I said, "Yeah. Am I supposed to know you?" It was Frank. It was raining like hell, and he was

riding back to New York. I had something going on that night, and I didn't really have room in my place to put him up. I was living in a little office that I turned into an apartment. We built it, a loft bedroom with rough cedar, pretty nice, but no room.

So, I put Frank in over at the Alamo, and he stayed for two or three days. We got to be great friends. And I says, "Hey, if you don't get to go back to school, call me. I need an assistant. Look at this bullshit!"

So, what do I get but this letter a couple of months later. Frank's interested in coming out. I was so disorganized at the time, doing a terrible job at the Carousel. Geez, I got this mess on my hands. What am I going to do? I got a little Mexican running around fixing up the stuff, a drunk as a maintenance man. And they keep talking me into keeping him! I couldn't fire them, you know. Geeez! I call my folks and say, "Hey. I've never asked you guys to help me with anything, but what am I going to do?!!" You know? That kind of thing.

Well, Frank comes. He'd been on the road for a while, and he's got his act together. So, he takes over the Conference Center. Frank is the type of guy who knows what's right and what's wrong. He's traveled around, just a real good guy, a close friend. He doesn't care if we get fired or what happens. We were both into it. We thought we'd get the Carousel going, and then we'd get Steckling to help us buy a place on the West Coast. So, we were going to blow everybody away with a great job.

What did you have to do to the place to make it a good job?

Oh, bring in the French feeling, make it more professional with desk clerks wearing a tie, calling the rooms "chambers," getting an image or a theme. Ours was a country-French theme. So, we had to wallpaper all the rooms, redo all the linen, recarpet the whole place. We painted the outside, redid the pool area and the conference rooms. Most of the whole place was repapered *and recarpeted. Now it's getting old again, but it was all new then.*

Who were you doing it for? Who did you want to impress?

Dave Steckling. He's the main owner. He owns at least fifty-one percent of the company. He's the guy I work for.

And you just sort of assumed that he would think a lot of what you were doing?

Yeah. I knew he would. He'd have to. If you're right, you're right; if you're not, you're not. And, if I would have done a shitty job, then I had no right to be there.

Yeah, but he kept on all those people who you thought were doing a shitty job before.

Yeah, but he was letting the Carousel slide. They were working on the Cantebury. They were growing and letting this one slide. And there were problems between him and Ermal. (This has been a real touchy issue. You'd probably get a different story from different people. But you might as well know the truth, at least as I see it.)

See, Dave Steckling was a young guy. He wanted to be a dentist, but he got into the Alamo. He got in rather cheap, I guess, because a relative owned it. I guess he didn't want to look in other people's mouths for the rest of his life. Being intelligent and wanting to live free, he wanted to do a lot. And he did it all. He wanted to be a millionaire by the age of thirty, retire at thirty-five, and move to California. He could run things from there. His goal was to get someone good underneath him to do it all, and he could just sort of manage it from out there.

So Steckling got some money together, and Ermal Loghry owned a little hamburger shop, a greasy spoon on the corner. That's what it was. It wasn't much I guess, from what a lot of older people tell me. But he was good. He's been good to the community. He's donated to everything. He kept a good PR image. And I think Er-

mal's a real nice man at heart. I think he has the same goal, but he never made it. I don't know what his problem was. Everybody's got their faults. I do dumb things, too; so I can't say. Anyway, Ermal's a great guy.

So he owns that whole corner. It's a prime spot. It should be a great big hub—if you can imagine, the hotel, added onto, made right, two or three restaurants in it. There's enough land there. They had the Hawkeye Lodge, too; so they could have torn the whole area down. This is my goal eventually, and it was theirs, too.

Steckling saved up fifty thousand dollars and wanted to put up a hotel there. So, he goes to Ermal and says, "You can own ten percent of the hotel. We'll give you a monthly land rent, and you can own the land." And Steckling goes to Earl Yoder, who has a construction company, and offers him thirty-six percent if he builds the thing. So all Steckling had to do was put in fifty thousand dollars, buy the furniture, and manage it, and he owned fifty-one percent—which is very sharp. So he got the Carousel going.

Well, he was young then. He didn't know anything about using lawyers. Back then you didn't much anyway, I guess. But they should have. They didn't get all these things agreed, signed, and on paper. Well, the percentage on the land rent went up from where it started, and this and that was screwy.

So they got into a little cat and mouse game. Like, when the restaurant catered a banquet at the Conference Center in the inn: "Well, if you rip our carpet, we're going to bill you!" "If your gravy's on this too much, we're going to bill you for that!" "If you use our tables. . . ." You know. They were doing that to us, and we were doing

it right back. It just got ridiculous.

Well, Neil Trott was vice-president of the company, and he just started up as a broom-sweeper the same way I had. The hotel had a shitty manager in there, and Steckling's living in California. They're all working on the Cantebury-Iowa City and Cantebury-Muscatine, while the Alamo held its own and they let the Carousel slide. He has these young kids—like he had me, like Frank—that don't have any training, and they're running a multi-million-dollar operation. But they're cheap. They do what he asks, and it was working. It was a pretty good theory. He was living in California free, and these places were going.

But there always were arguments between the inn and the restaurant, and between Dave and Ermal. It got so they could hardly talk. They'd be going through lawyers.

Anyway, there's always been this thing between the employees at the restaurant and the employees at the motel: "Fucking restaurant this!" "Fucking restaurant that!" "Fucking motel!" You know. It got to be unbelievable! I had one of them calling me every name in the book, giving me the finger, you name it, in the dining room. I've had Ermal—"Get him out of here! Get him out of here!" You know, I was just over there visiting, trying to talk things over. It was wild!

They had this lady called Lil. She was this real nice lady, I think, but she loved to scratch. She was a little fireball type of woman, puffy blonde hair, makeup here and there. And here's these two punk hippie kids running the place . . . and doing a pretty damn good job! . . . well, sort of. We were doing dumb things, too. We were just

as shitty as she was. But she knew a lot more about the books and this and that than we did. We didn't know that much about business. She'd heard people talk about it in the bar, maybe. But she was stumping us a lot and making us look like idiots. And it really wasn't our fault.

So, with that type of thing, there's always been problems. We'll just have to keep trying. Ermal tries not to worry about it, but the people under him do fucked-up things. They still try to jab you now and then. But we're just as shitty as they are. We're all using three-ten-an-hour help, minimum-wage help and kids. If they tear something up of mine, he doesn't know about it; then we get upset. We do something screwed up to his, and I don't know about it; they get upset. It builds up all the time.

It's just not the right situation for two businesses to be getting along, anyway. We're not going together right. No communication. It's not the same management, and we don't communicate that well. We can't really visit and decide plans. If they don't follow through, I can't go over and say, "Hey! Come on!" Or if I don't follow through, he can't say, "Hey. Come on." You feel like you're going to hurt somebody's feelings. Someone is going to blow up, 'cause that's the way it's been.

I've tried. I've tried! But they think this young kid is trying to tell them they're doing something fucked up. Maybe with the right person in there it will work out. We'll all keep trying. Now we just have to put up with it. We're just going to run the motel and make it a fantastic place, add on rooms, redo the pool area, and figure out ways we could just better ourselves. We'll make the place look good, whatever the restaurant does. The Cantebury is doing it without a real successful restaurant, anyway. So we can, too.

But it's hard. Most people in the area think Ermal owns and runs the whole place. It's hard to keep a manager. You know, you do a good job, and no one thinks of you; they think it's Ermal. Ermal brings people in to show them rooms—"Yeah, and over here is one of my rooms"—while you're standing there doing this and that. We want him to do that. I want him to do that. I want him to play that image if he wants. A customer doesn't want to know that we're separate. But it's sort of hard to take. You work your butt off, and everybody thinks it's theirs. Or they might do a shitty job serving meals, and they think it's you.

So, it's hard, but we try. We're a young group trying to be progressive—having the turn-down service (where the maid comes and turns the bed down), having coffee service. When someone gets a wake-up call, we send a housekeeper up with a cup of coffee, a morning newspaper, and a doughnut or a French pastry. Things like that. We've tried heart-shaped pools. We've tried to keep the whirlpool area up to par.

Since we started off, Frank and I got it real nice, at least at one time. But things are just. . . . Sticking a young guy in there to manage it, and having to go through all these head trips with the restaurant, all the problems with the downstairs, and most people thinking Ermal owns and runs the whole place—it's a tough situation for anybody to be in.

Since then a lot more has happened to Dean and those around him. Heritage operations have come to include everything from restaurants to landscaping services, computerized accounting to limousines. New properties have been bought and sold. Most of the help has turned over several times.

Within a year of this interview, Frank left his post at the Carousel Inn, as did two managers after him. Word was that he was "deprogramming," camping, harmonica in hand, in the Florida Keys. After a short return engagement, between managers number six and number seven, Frank left again, but this time under more hostile circumstances. He and Dean, once great, close friends, were now barely speaking.

Also within a year, Dean got married and began his own deprogramming. He and his bride decided to cut loose for the West. They gave notice at their jobs, sold nearly everything they owned, and moved into a second-hand RV:

"We won't have enough money to get very far when we leave. I guess we'll just head to Colorado and get some jobs."

"Yeah. I just picture cruising out of town, looking out the window—just head west and see what happens."

On Taste

Before, we talked about what's right and wrong in a place. I want to talk about that a little more. You said, for example, that some places, some people, have it right and others don't. How is that? Is it that managers disagree on what the customer wants?

No. I think they are coming to the same conclusions. We want quality. Money is tight, but customers don't mind spending it if they're going to get a lot of quality, if they get the extra little services that don't cost that much, just something else to get control of. If what they get is right—clean and what they expected and more—they'll be happy.

I'd rather stay in a fancy place and spend a little more. Say, it's my night out, or I'm on the road; I won't stay at a little place or a Holiday Inn somewhere. They don't have the little extras. We do. So we go for the quality.

I've got an article here that says the same thing.

People are getting smarter. I'd rather pay good money for a good meal, a healthy meal, than a McDonald's meal and just eat out less. And I think people are getting that way. People are becoming wine drinkers. They're going to the light stuff. People want to pay for something quality. I'm driving a '68 Mercedes. It cost me the same as a brand new Nova, but it's going to save me money, because I can sell it for more. And it's quality. That's what most people are wanting, too, I think. So, that's how we feel about things.

Yeah. But if you all agree, why should there be this difference between places? Why is it that some places don't have the "quality"? What's the problem?

Well, what's the difference between the Carousel Restaurant and the Power Company? That's the problem.

Now, I don't think the Power Company is that great either, but most people do. They are consistent. It's nothing fantastic, but everything is good every time you go. Everybody thinks the salad bar is great.

It looks brand new every time you go in there. Look at the bathrooms, for instance. The whole place looks brand new all the time. You've got good food; you've got good-looking people to look at; you've got good-looking waitresses, and you've got them in uniform. Good-looking people tend to go there, and other people want to be where the good-looking people are. That's the image these days. The Power Company is "the place to go." That's class; that's quality. People don't mind spending more money to go in there than they would at the Carousel, because they're getting the quality. Quality is clean, quality is brand new; quality is something solid. Quality is what's in style, but it's sort of conservative, too, not gaudy.

And that's what we all need to do terribly badly. So we're all in the same boat.

Yeah. But why, then, should there still be this differ-

ence between the two places? Can you imagine a situation where you see a place and say, "That's great!" but somebody from the Carousel Restaurant, like Ermal, says, "Eh?"

That's our personalities. Ermal's a great PR man, but . . . I don't know. He's more from the era where he isn't willing to change. He's an older person, and he's pretty set in his ways now. And he doesn't have much leadership with him. He doesn't have anyone sharp enough to know what's going on at the Coasts and what people want. I'm fortunate enough that I do. That's the difference, I think. I've got a very intelligent man that I work for.

But we're all striving for the same thing, and Ermal is, too. Ermal knows what's right. He reads his Restaurant News.

It's interesting, though. You've described what the customer wants and where it comes from. I gather that you and a lot of other managers hear what people want from the Coasts via sort of couriers. I wonder about that, because I know I'm not like one of those people. But I might be real different than you in that regard.

No! No, you're not. I'm not into that scene. I'm bad enough. Don't forget that!

I play two roles. There's "businessman"—you do what the people want. But a place like the Wagon Wheel is my favorite kind of place. I like the Wagon Wheel, but you can't run a business that way. The Wagon Wheel is not going to make any money or become big, are they?

Actually, I don't go to the Wagon Wheel much. I usually stay home, because I don't like to go out. If I go to the Wagon Wheel, I'm going to see a maintenance man or some bozo from town. And I can't go in there loaded, because I've got to deal with them. So that's why I don't have the opportunity to go.

I have to go to the weird places. If I go anywhere in

town, I probably go to the Sheep's Head for dinner. But I go to the small towns. I go to Wellman to the bar. We ought to go out for dinner or something, take you down to Kalona and see the Chicken House. I'll show you! That's my favorite place. Yeah, the Chicken House. I like the food there. You don't get the best of service, but I understand. I know they are like that. I like the whole scene—Mary Ellen comes to your table. . . . It's great!

I like going over to the Carousel Restaurant, because I can go joke with Martha and that whole situation, see Herb Cochran. You know, I enjoy it.

That's what I mean. A place may be a little cruddy, but that's part of what makes it great in its own way. It's got the Marthas and Mary Ellens. That's why I wonder why, when you're in business and want to make it better, you go for one thing, but, when you're yourself, you go for another.

Well, I know those people. Martha's not that great with someone when she has no idea who they are, if she doesn't feel like it: "Yeah! Sit over here! Wilma! Wilma, two here!" You know, the person off the highway, who's been traveling and has a hangover, doesn't want to hear that, doesn't want to put up with her. I enjoy it, but the person coming off the street doesn't. You have to know them, and they're easily not here enough to know them. But the nice, classy, good-looking girl can come and joke around and say, "Hi. How are you doing, Dean?" And that's fine. It doesn't make any difference. But she could be a lady in front of the customer that she doesn't know.

See, I'm not the majority of the public. I have to look and see who is successful. They're getting the majority of the public. And I see who are the leaders in the business. I've got a guy that reads all the stuff on what is successful, and I know what the people are like around here, you know, probably more than most people do.

I was raised on the farm. I like going to small-town places. I'm used to going and having coffee every day with my dad, every Saturday and all summer, down at the Wayside Inn—the "coffee club," you know, where the farmers get together and shoot the shit. I'm used to that kind of thing, but I do know what the majority of the people on Interstate 80 want.

And you're sure?

The public says what they want: class. Look at all the restaurants, all the motels, all the advertising, everything in the magazines. I can prove it to you. I can show you in any magazine. I can tell you how we're all bullshitted, how we don't know exactly what we want, but we want it anyway. You know what I mean? Everything is perfect on TV. Right?

Yeah. But, maybe when the pressure is off, they really want something else.

Yeah, most people aren't able to admit to the public that they're that way. Most people would much rather wear blue jeans, shitty clothes and be comfortable, and not have to comb their hair when they go out to dinner. But not that many people do it or have the nerve to do it. I do it on weekends, and I'm sure you do it. A lot of people do it.

If I had my way, I'd be running a shitty little hole that's friendly, where everybody liked each other and this and that. But that's not going to get you it. It depends on the situation.

We're on the interstate. We're catching everybody that wants to have a safe place to stay. They want to know that, when they've spent their money, they're not going to get screwed, they're not going to stay in a place that has dirty beds. Chances are, when you go and try and find a homey spot on the highway, it's going to have them. It's going to be shitty. You're not going to get your money's worth. They think that if they go to a chain, like a Best Western, they will at least get their money's worth, and, if not, they have someone to bitch to.

I guess I'm going by what all the big companies do. They're all going for the quality; they're all going for the class; they're all going for consistency.

Yeah. It does seem that businesses are getting better at imagining what the customer wants and then doing it. But I still wonder if the customer they imagine really exists. Maybe all the people staying at the Carousel tonight are saying, "This is OK, but I wish we were in some little cabin that costs six bucks outside of town. . . ."

Exactly! That's what we're trying to do in the rooms. Like, we're making them warm; we're putting in fireplaces, and Jacuzzi bubble pools, unique things. And then we try and make them think they are in a country-French place at the Carousel. I know, it may sound like a joke now, but someday it will be that way. Look at the Cantebury. We still haven't followed through enough with the Old English, but if you can get the whole thing. . . .

People are into fantasies now. I think everybody is, whether they admit it or not. They are into the fantasy. There's so many things that we don't even know about ourselves that we're into, I think. Anyway, that's where we come from with our theories.

On Managing for Quality

Everybody would like to go to a place where you could sit around and shoot the shit, have a good time with the waitress, yet have the food or whatever fantastic every time. You'd take a friend there, and they'd like the food or the room as well. That's what you go there for. But you'd like to be able to be friendly with the help. The first time, a waitress ought to open up and tell you her name, "Hi, how are you guys today?," talk about the weather for a second, and then take your order.

How do you control that? How do you see that they're friendly?

You have to be there all the time and tell them. Get good quality people. You'd rather look at a beautiful lady that's friendly, good-looking, clean. You know: "How you doing today, Rich?"

That's the reason they're there. Work them on tips, a percentage of what you bring in, figure out a way she could get some sort of a bonus for what she does. That's the key for everything, I think. You've got to get some sort of bonus system for them and make them want to be that way. I don't know what your key for writing a book is, but maybe deep inside you want to be successful, or you want to be liked.

Yeah, but does that ever work for you? I gather that you just want to do a good job. What's right is right. At some point you've just had enough, frig it, even if it's good for the place or you're making good money.

Yeah, that's where Frank Deleon is now.

But have bonuses ever worked, ever changed that situation for you?

No, because I knew exactly what I wanted. I wanted to be successful in the business. But for a maid? Someone that's forty years old, someone that's got a family to raise and a husband to come home to? She's got too many other things to worry about than worry about this place. The dollars are the reasons she's there. So, she can do a good job and make more money and get into what's going on in the place and in on some of the decisions. She will be into it. But if she never gets paid for it, she's going to lose her interest. If she works real hard today and doesn't get a reward of any kind, like a pat on the back, why should she do it? Why not come in to work and get in a rut? "I'll just go in to work, put in my time, and come home."

Have you ever been able to do that?

If I ever got in something like that, I'd leave. My goals are to be out on a ship someday, or to be traveling and never have to work. I hate getting up, and I hate working. But now I like what I do a lot. If I wasn't traveling, I'd have to be doing what I'm doing or something like it. I just like being busy, and this I enjoy. I enjoy people.

But I wonder if it's possible that other people, like the people who work for you, want the same things out of life. Do they want something all that different in the end?

Yeah, they do. They all do. No one has the same goals I do. I don't have the same goals you do.

I've put on a different hat for everyone I meet, anyway. And you do, too, you know. You have to treat every employee like a human being, like a separate person. What makes one guy tick by letting him off and paying him for the afternoon—tell him to go hunting—isn't going to work for the wife that's there working. You know? There's other ways to make other people tick. With some people you can get by without giving bonuses. You can just make them tick other ways, and they're into it.

See, most people don't think about these things as much as I do. They've got other things to think about. So, I'm busy trying to figure out every employee we've got and every manager, trying to figure out what's going to make him take what I ask him to do to heart, have him want to do it. My job is making everybody into what they're doing or getting them out. So, I think more about that than most people.

What about the older guys, older managers like Ermal

at the Carousel Restaurant? Is it the same for him?

Ermal managed. He was in the heart of managing and into it, having to work like this when he was a young man. But the way of getting people into it then was different than it is now. He became used to those kind of people, like my dad. Twenty years ago, you would probably get into something if it was good, sound employment and a nice guy to work for. Back then, the thing was to do an honest day's work for an honest day's pay. In this day and age, I think, for the majority of people: "If you've got to work in a motel at minimum wage, get the easiest job you can, make the money, and put in your time." They've got other things to think about.

Our problem is we can't pay our employees enough. You know? So we get these lower-class people and try and make them upper class. You know, it's absurd to try and get them to be professional. How can you expect someone to act like a doctor or lawyer, when they're paid shit, minimum wage. We've got good people. I just wish we could pay them more.

On February 1, 1980, I strolled into the Carousel Inn and suddenly learned that Craig Poock, the manager, had been "let go."

Bernie at the desk:

Yeah, no warning. Isn't that something? They sure keep them hopping.

Jan in the laundry:

Well, I heard yesterday, but I wasn't supposed to say anything. Hush, hush! This place is full of surprises.

I guess it will be different with Dean around.

I'm afraid so.

Dean:

We just had to let him go. We try to keep things professional, but he was just spending too much money. We talked it over, and Craig agreed that it just wasn't right for him either.

It's just too hard to try and motivate people, especially someone who doesn't even know what he wants. Hell, I started when I was nineteen. What did I know? I was stupid. You can't expect someone to run a business when their own life isn't in order.

I'm afraid that I've started to look for more settled people.

Dean, six months and two managers later:

We hired a new manager for the Carousel. You ought to meet this guy! He's one of those guys who looks like he was born in a suit and tie.

The other day, while I'm working with him to break him in, he says, "Say, Dean, how about some coffee and a roll?" And I thought, "Hey, great!" I figured that he'd run across the street or something to get coffee and a doughnut.

But he just walks over to the phone, dials the front desk, and says, "Hey, Bernie. Want to bring us down a couple of cups of coffee and some rolls? Thanks," and hangs up.

Can you imagine?! That's how he's treating our people! Geez! I've got to get out of this business!

Jan Stephenson – The Laundry

n moving from management to housekeeping or the laundry, it is tempting to look for old scripts, for struggles between bedraggled workers and their overweight bosses. But the Strip is far from "On the Waterfront." Conflicts are more subtle and slow to develop. Granted, the strains of the American occupational system are well in evidence. Women with lower wages and more manual jobs are concentrated at the bottom and men with more formal education, better pay, and whiter shirts at the top. Relaxed atmosphere or not, it is obvious who is running things. When, for example, Craig resigned as manager of the Carousel in 1980, ensuing promotions followed an unwritten organizational chart. The opening in the office was filled by a desk clerk who was replaced by her assistant and she by another maid. Such hierarchies are part of the background of daily work that is hardly questioned. Abrupt changes in procedure or personnel can be blamed on the irrationalities of the economy or fickle consumer tastes. Owners and managers with a steady eye to their reports define a roadside mission that is executed in common.

Insiders are simply trying their best to please the public, make a buck, and make it through the day. Those on the top usually join the mission because they are after something, "to show people where my head is at," "to make that million dollars," or just "to fit in." But the people on the bottom are not so much anticipating a future as fleeing a past.

Janice Stephenson, who runs the laundry in the Carousel, can speak with some authority about the Strip as an occupational refuge. She has been around more than most of the other employees. In thirty-some years of marriage she has helped raise and support a handsome family including a crowd of grandchildren. She and her husband took their very first vacation together last year. She spent fourteen years working as a nurse's aide and then four years running a screw gun on the line for Bader Manufacturing Company. In 1979, she did not so much come to the Carousel as leave Bader.

How did you start out working here?

I got mad at the man and walked out! I had surgery on my wrist and was told by the doctor and the insurance company not to go back on the job. They tried to put me back on it, and I got mad and walked out.

It was hard work. Of course, it was better pay, six dollars an hour, but it wasn't when our income tax came due. I'm not going to work all year long and then have to dig up seven hundred dollars, besides what they've already taken out of me. It doesn't pay to make that much.

I like this job. I really do, when things run right. I used to walk in the door at Bader, stand there all day, and pray for 3:30 to come, so I could get out the door. I hated it, somebody always looking over my shoulder. They have these guys walking around with stopwatches. You have to learn, you know, if things are going real fast and you see them coming, slow down or they'll find a way to make you go like that every second. The foremen will just kind of look around and say, "This should be done in two hours!" If they would do the job, even for one day, they would have a different outlook on things. It was a knock-down-drag-out constantly.

It's been a lot easier on my nerves here. I know that. I don't have somebody over me screaming all the time. "Go faster! Faster!" and all that. This is what really surprised me here. They are so easy to work for. As long as you do your job and do it right, they don't bother you. They sit down and talk things out in a reasonable way, and that's it. That's one reason I like it here. And we all do our work. We try to go out of our way to be extra nice to the guests, do little things for them.

"We"? Who do you mean "we"?

I guess around here I call everybody "we." I wouldn't talk about Bader like that. Never! But here, you know, everybody works together and gets along fine. It makes a really big difference. I just couldn't believe it when I first started here.

Compared to a knock-down-drag-out life on the line, the Carousel is nothing short of amazing. In exchange for decent treatment and a fraction of her former wages, Jan spends five days a week handling a torrent of dirty laundry. The housekeepers need their uniforms and rags cleaned by 8:00 a.m., and soon after, enough linen for eighty-four rooms and twice as many beds. Jan is not one to complain: "Basically, it's no different than doing your laundry at home. Of course, there's a lot more of it!"

Before the housekeepers finish stripping rooms, the laundry is packed with mountains of dirty linen—bath towels, hand towels, face cloths, pillowcases, fitted sheets, top sheets—of all sizes and colors, to be sorted, washed, dried, and folded before the next round. To get all this done, Jan is allotted a pair of commercial dryers and washers, a part-time assistant, and eight hours, supposedly 7:00 to 3:00.

The equipment provides as much of a challenge as the linen itself. Rather than an automated washer, Jan works two tubs, one with an agitator and the other an extractor, on hand-set timers. Here is how it goes: place five sheets or an equivalent amount of towels and pillowcases in the agitator with a half-scoop of detergent and a dash of fabric softener; set the timer for four minutes; when the four minutes are up, pack the load in the extractor, setting it on rinse for one minute and extraction for two (you have one minute to spare—start another load in the agitator!); then it goes into hampers awaiting dryers. Everything, including Jan, must be in continuous motion for several hours. Through months of experimentation, Jan worked out this system on her own, and I daresay, few others could keep up. For example, in the one minute between wash cycles, Jan cannot only handle all the loading and sorting but also fold as many as seven sheets. When I tried it, I could barely fold three, none of them as neatly as Jan insists. None of her assistants has ever been able to do more than five.

On mornings after a full house, Jan is probably as busy as she ever was at Bader, but now she is more in control. For example, soon after she started at the Carousel, she discovered that her designated hours were not practical. Dirty linen came down to the laundry too late in the day to be done by 3:00, and clean linen was needed too soon after 7:00 to catch up the next morning. So Jan started to come in at 6:00 and leave when she knew she had done enough, usually around 2:00. She has to get up earlier, but she is glad to have a little time in the afternoon and "keep the girls happy": "Housekeepers are getting paid by the room, and if they have to wait for linen, they're getting ripped off. It's only fair." She is proud of the way the motel looks ("our rooms are beautiful") and welcomes the chance to talk with housekeepers and maintenance men as they pass through. She is even consulted on color schemes as rooms are redecorated.

For workers like Jan, then, a place like the Carousel is a refuge not from hard work but from alienating, dehumanizing discipline in other occupational settings. Out of pride in workmanship and respect for co-workers, Jan disciplines herself through a private game:

I'm always setting quotas for myself. I think of it as a challenge. When I come in here in the morning this place is a mess, heaps of dirty sheets and towels all over the place. I take a look at the clock and imagine how long it will take to get it all done, sorted, washed, dried, and folded. Then I go like mad, and I always get it done on time. I usually have a few minutes left to sit at the table and have a smoke, look at all that linen, folded, sorted by colors, neat on the shelves, waiting for the girls to come down.

Tammy Freeman–Housekeeper

If there is a typical worker at the Carousel, she is about twenty years old, earning minimum wage in a job she will leave within a few months. She is a housekeeper. There are anywhere from five to ten of them on the regular, weekday staff and at least a half-dozen more on nights and weekends. Since they are paid by the room, their checks fluctuate with the trade and the size of the staff. It is not what you could call a dependable livelihood, much less a career. And it is strenuous, exacting work. No one complains of having too few rooms to clean.

On weekdays the "regular girls" punch in about 8:00 a.m. and ready for the day. While they chat, don uniforms, and check the carts, the head of housekeeping translates motel talk from the desk into routines for the day. Until she picks up her section assignment and keys, a housekeeper can only guess how hard she will work and how much she will earn that day.

Sections are assigned equally with some allowance for varying talents. Tougher assignments go to women with the experience to handle them, while novices work up to speed. Cleaning a room is supposed to take half an hour, and that is the way housekeepers are paid, regardless of the clock. The actual time it takes depends on your pace and a number of other concerns. For example, down-and-outs are frequented by businessmen who barely crease the sheets. Waterbeds are a challenge to make no matter who slept on them. Weekday trash fills one bag; weekends, two or three: "You never know what you'll find on the other side of the door." You may have to wait for supplies or, even worse, a guest who lingers until noon. A new maid may take an hour per room and still have to return before earning the head housekeeper's okay.

There is a camaraderie that pulls them together. They compliment each other on work well done: "Your rooms just sparkle!" They share supplies and tips on how to "make it out" (leave before going on your own time). They trade stories about home life and the guests. Whatever the detriments of the traditional entrance—knock, announce youself, and go in—it contributes to a rich lore on the job. Almost everyone tells the story of a maid who half-stripped a bed before discovering there was someone in it. They share complaints about the vacuums, the uniforms ("Why can't we wear pants?"), the mess, and, most of all, the way they are paid.

We don't like it. On days like today it's bad, because the rooms are all real pits. There was all kinds of garbage and everything to pick up, because there was this wedding party last night. You can do it. I made it out. I did thirteen rooms, and therefore I got paid for seven hours with an extra half-hour for cleaning up the cart and setting it up. So that's seven hours, and I made it out in exactly seven hours. But other girls who haven't been here as long are going to be here longer than that, because they don't know exactly what they're doing. So they're going to get paid for seven hours, and they're going to be doing eight hours of work. But it's kind of an advantage sometimes to me or to anybody who can work fast, who's been here for a while. Sometimes you get paid for seven hours, and you're out in five. So, in effect, you're getting paid more per hour. And it gives me a feeling of achievement. In that way it's an advantage.

It also makes it pretty impossible to get overtime, like the maintenance men do. For forty hours, we have to do at least fifteen rooms a day, five days a week, no matter how many hours you're really here. Even if you could do it, there usually aren't that many rooms to go around. The only way I've been able to put in for overtime is because I'm the assistant head housekeeper on Saturdays. So I get ten hours on Saturday. When we have two or three housekeepers quit, all the load just gets thrown onto the other five housekeepers on the floor. So in cases like that I've gotten overtime. In a year I've put in overtime, but I haven't been paid for it, except maybe on two paychecks. That's because of how the days fall on the calendar, they say.

"They" could be just about anyone. Piece rates are standard in nonunion motels. Besides, most of the housekeepers would not recognize the owners by name or on sight.

Most of the time they spend alone in the rooms or hurrying between sections, supply closets, and the laundry. A head housekeeper confided: "They don't want to be watched, and people don't want to see them." It is hardly because they are loafing.

A "good" housekeeper is dependable, neat, and, above all, fast. After filling her cart with the appropriate linen (assuming it is ready), she heads for her section with an arsenal of rags and sprays: "green stuff" for tubs, sinks, and floors, alcohol for mirrors and chrome, and custom concoctions of every variety. One of the first things maids do on entering a room is assault what they smell with "pink stuff," lemon-air, and smoke-eater. Then they remove the linen, trays, and trash. The only treasures they can keep are deposit cans or bottles left in vacant rooms.

If a half-hour sounds like plenty of time, you have to imagine the mess that people leave and the cleanliness they demand. Beds must be made symmetrically and without a wrinkle. *Everything* must be washed and polished. If you are lucky, that is, if guests have not stolen too much linen of late, you can wait till afternoon to lug thirty or forty pounds of wet towels and dirty sheets to the laundry. Before the head housekeeper will okay a room, there must not be a single hair or waterspot in sight. Every item of furniture, every hanger, towel, piece of stationary, lamp, ashtray, and bar of soap must be in its place. She will check everything, down to the angle of the brochure on the dresser. A room that may have borne a nonstop drunk the night before has to look as if the decorator just left.

Again, the idea is to encourage the illusion that the place, like the people who maintain it, is free of history or purpose except for those the guests provide. For me, the most memorable image of a housekeeper is in a final ritual. On her way out she rakes the carpet, covering the tracks of the vacuum and her feet, removing the last vestiges of her presence. The room no longer looks as if she cleaned it; it is simply clean.

Yet, as invisible and disciplined as they are, each woman works in a style that is her own. They find ways to shape the routine around favorite TV programs or to leave parts of it, like dusting light bulbs, for a slower day. One maid will develop an efficient, lock-step procedure while another will pride herself on improvisation. That is their prerogative, as long as a few rooms are ready for walk-ins early in the day and the rest are immaculate by 5:00. With a sniff and a quick look around, the head housekeeper can usually tell who serviced the room, not because one is cleaner than another, but because every service bears the signature of the servant. With a little care, visitors might also see that the Carousel and the strip do not just house commodities or "experience" for sale but also people to meet.

Tammy Freeman has been a housekeeper at the Carousel for nearly a year, an unusually long time. She offers some insights into her position and herself.

The way I ended up here is complicated. I'm not sure even I can remember all the places I've been. I'm only twenty-one, and I have a hard time remembering them all, at least in the right order. Until tenth grade, I was in a different school every year.

My family moved around a lot. I was born in Iowa, in Oskaloosa, but I only lived here for like three years. My dad was manager of a TG&Y store, and he got transferred around. First he went from here to California. They asked him if he wanted to go, and he said, "Sure! I'll go to California." We lived in Downey and then El Segundo. I don't remember much of it, just the beach and stuff. I probably remember that because my parents made home movies. I only lived there until I was like in third grade. Then we moved to Wisconsin, another TG&Y, and finally back to Iowa. He managed a TG&Y in Mason City. Then, when we got to Dewitt, Iowa, it was a restaurant. It was just a small restaurant, still there, the Tower Cafe.

They ran that for a while, and then my parents got divorced. I turned rebellious, really rebellious, then. I hated every minute of it. I was always "Daddy's little girl," and then I got separated from him. Everytime I got mad at my mom, I'd say, "I'm going to run away! I'm going to live with Dad." And I did run away about four times in junior high and high school. Practically everyone in my family has been divorced and remarried. Anyway, they sold the restaurant and split up the money. My dad went back to Oskaloosa, and I went with my mom to Iowa City.

We moved around three places just in Iowa City. I went to three different schools—Longfellow, Central Junior High, and Ernest Horn—before we moved to West Branch. It was hard. We were on welfare when we came here. Mom was on ADC. First she was a waitress; then she got a job bookkeeping at Wagner Pontiac, where my uncle worked.

My ninth-grade year, I went to live with my dad in Texas. He had gone to Texas from Oskaloosa because he got offered an assistant manager's job in a Ramada Inn down there. I lived there, in a room in a Ramada Inn, for three months. That's where I had my first job. I washed dishes in the restaurant. I was only fourteen or fifteen years old, so I couldn't do much.

I have had so many jobs, you wouldn't believe it. It's kind of bad. Like, after we moved back to Iowa and I was in high school, I couldn't hold a job. I was with the wrong crowd and everything, you know, kind of a bum.

When I was in high school in Oskaloosa, I worked in Hardee's part-time. But I only worked there for like three months. I didn't like it because, for one thing, my aunt owned it. And, you know, I just didn't like the food. I don't like selling something that I wouldn't eat. There's no nutrition in it. When I eat, I like to eat something that I'm going to get something out of, instead of just making my stomach full.

I was a waitress at Country Kitchen, too. That was my first job when I moved back to Iowa City, right after I got out of high school in '77. My dad got remarried, and I like Iowa City better. I hadn't had a very good relationship with my mom during my high school years. So I decided to come back and see if I could get to know her a little bit better, try to resolve our differences. I moved back in with her, but we just couldn't get along. So I ended up staying until I could get everything together and get my own place. Then I moved out again.

Anyway, I just didn't like that type of job. I don't like being a waitress at all. The public can be very rude, especially when you're trying to do your best, you know, and sometimes it just doesn't work out that way. They're in a hurry, or maybe they think that you're not good enough; you're not doing the best job you could do. Maybe they think your mind is on different things. I don't know what they're thinking, but maybe they're thinking they're better than you are. A lot of times that's the case, I think. You're "just a waitress," you know, "a low-life." They give you minimum at Hardee's, and at Country Kitchen they take a dollar away for tips. You usually end

moving. I guess, though, it's no harder than being a waitress. As a housekeeper you can slow down whenever you want to, but you pay for it, too. At least you don't have to put up with as much public. Here, too, you're always supposed to have a smile on your face. They tell us that over and over. Dean tells us all the time, and it makes sense, but it's hard to smile all the time, especially if you're having a super bad day. But if you see someone walking down the hall, most of them don't even look at you. If they say "Hi," you smile and say hello back. That's not that hard, not as hard as it is in a restaurant.

If I was going to work as a waitress, I'd have to work someplace like the Power Company before I'd work anywhere else. For one thing, you make more money than you would at a place like Country Kitchen. Besides, the people that go there are usually people that have money, and they have more manners—I think! They respect you a little bit more, especially if you work three to eleven or the graveyard shift, when you get a lot of drunks in there.

Most of the people who stay here are pretty nice, but every once in a while. . . . It only takes one person to ruin your day. Unless you can change it around and look at it from a different perspective, it kind of bums you out.

I haven't had any real bad situations lately. Once (it didn't happen to me, but it happened to one of the other housekeepers) we had a bunch of Navy guys in here. In a roundabout way, one of them asked her to come up to his room and mess around with him after work. And she was really insulted by it.

Or like, we call from downstairs in the morning to find out if they're in or not so we can get in to clean. It's better than when we just used to knock on the door, but people still get mad, because we wake them up, call too early or something. But we can't do our job unless we get in. This morning it started out real bad. I could only get into one room when I started out! That makes for a long day. But the people were all pretty nice. Before, you'd knock on the door, and a man might come to the door with his underwear on or just a T-shirt, as if you're not really there. Sometimes they'd come to the door and look at you like you just insulted them or something, just by being there, standing in front of them.

I look at housekeeping as one of the most important things in the motel that has to be done. If we didn't do a good job, the motel wouldn't be doing as good as it is. That's one of the things that keeps me going, like when I think about how other people put down people like housekeepers. Maybe they had an experience with a housekeeper before who didn't do a very good job. Like, they came into a room that was really dirty. Then I can understand why they have misconceptions. But people are people. There are some housekeepers, like I say, who just come in here for the money, and they don't really care. But I pride myself on being a good housekeeper. I want to do a good job. If I'm going to be housekeeper, I'm going to be a good housekeeper.

If I could, I'd tell those people that there are good

housekeepers, and there are bad housekeepers, just like there are good waitresses and bad, just like everything else, as far as that goes. We're here to clean their room, and, if it wasn't for us cleaning their room, they wouldn't be here.

But it's hard to get through to them. You have to understand yourself mainly, why you're doing what you're doing. But most of the people that come in here, you can't really say all that much to them to make them understand. Like, I was going to say, "Think of one of your daughters or their children working here. . . ." But I guess that's not really true. People with more money, if they had money all their lives, of course they're not going to be working in a place like this. They're just lucky.

Four Months Later

Now, I'm on my second job since the Carousel. I tried housekeeping in a nursing home, but the disinfectant cleaners they used made my hands break out in hives. Besides that, it was too depressing.

Now I'm working at an answering service, answering a hundred different telephone lines. It's a sitting-down job, but I figure, after running my ass off for over a year, I deserve a break. Besides, it's a night job, and that is when Rudy (my boyfriend) works.

I miss the Carousel every once in a while—mostly just the people I worked with. I miss the job a little bit. It's hard to keep my weight off since I'm sitting all the time.

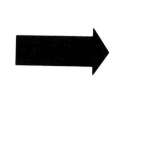

Chapter 4. The Carousel and the Strip

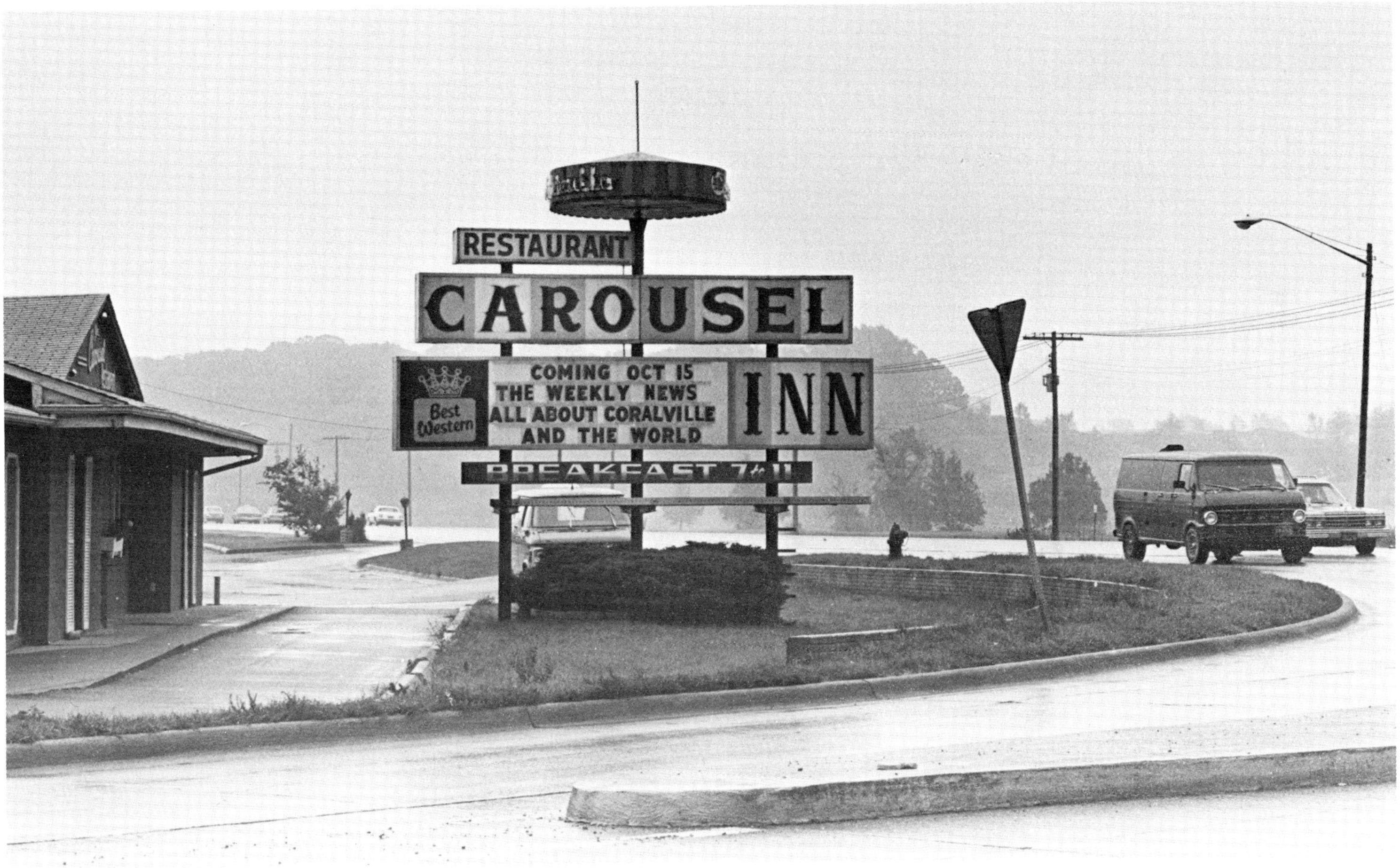
RESTAURANT
CAROUSEL
Best Western
COMING OCT 15
THE WEEKLY NEWS
ALL ABOUT CORALVILLE
AND THE WORLD
INN

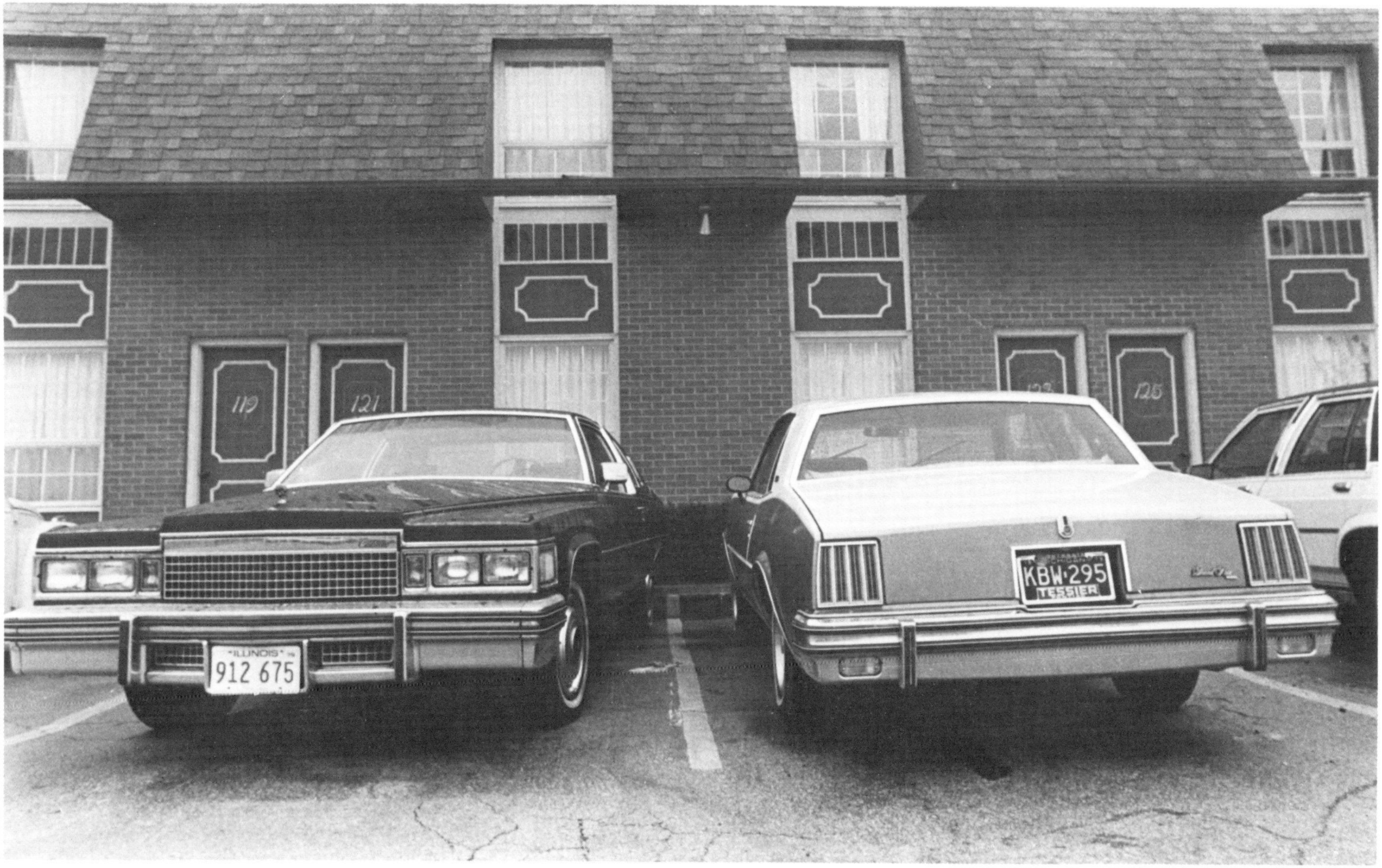
119
121
125
ILLINOIS
912 675
KBW·295
TESSIER

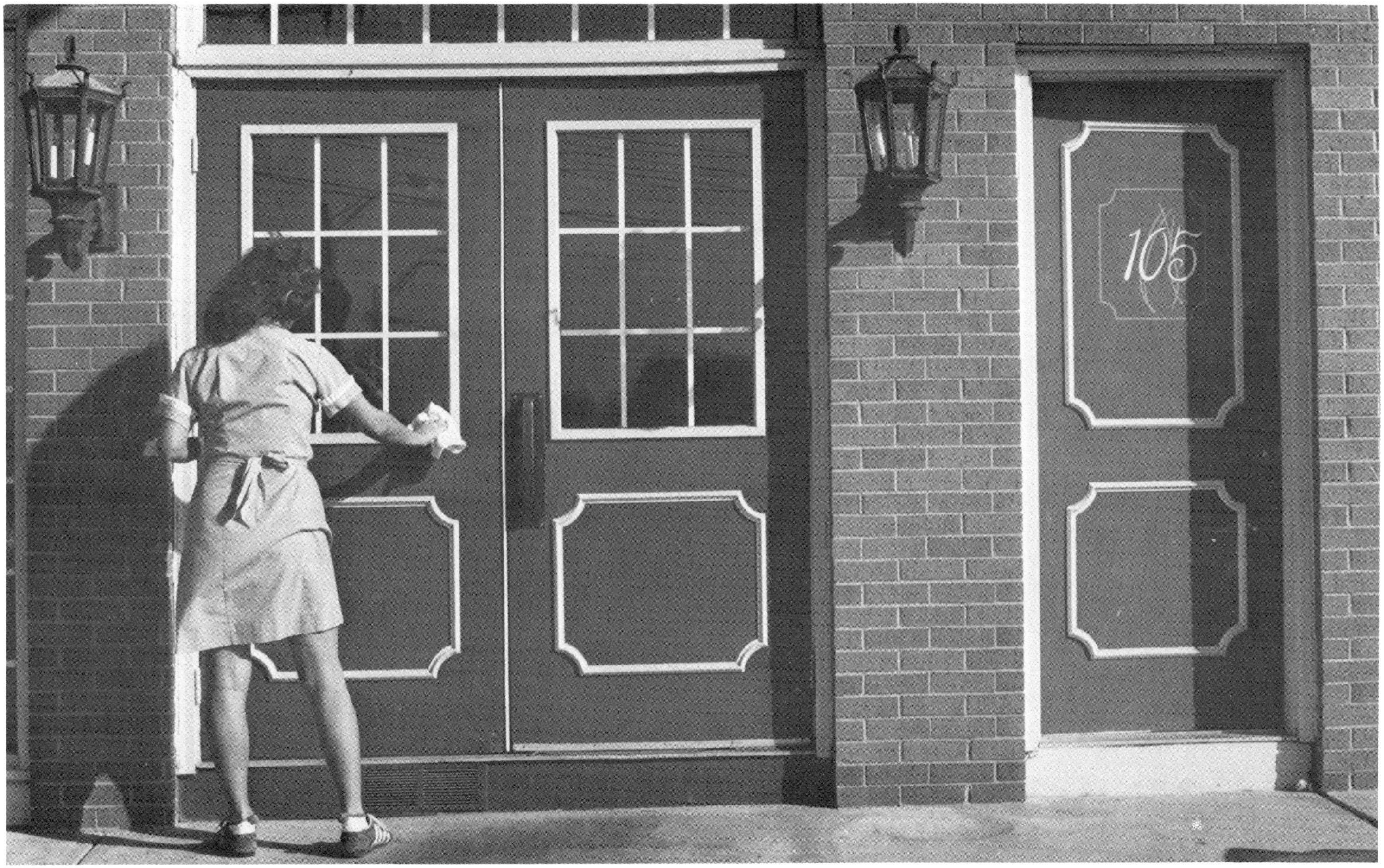
105

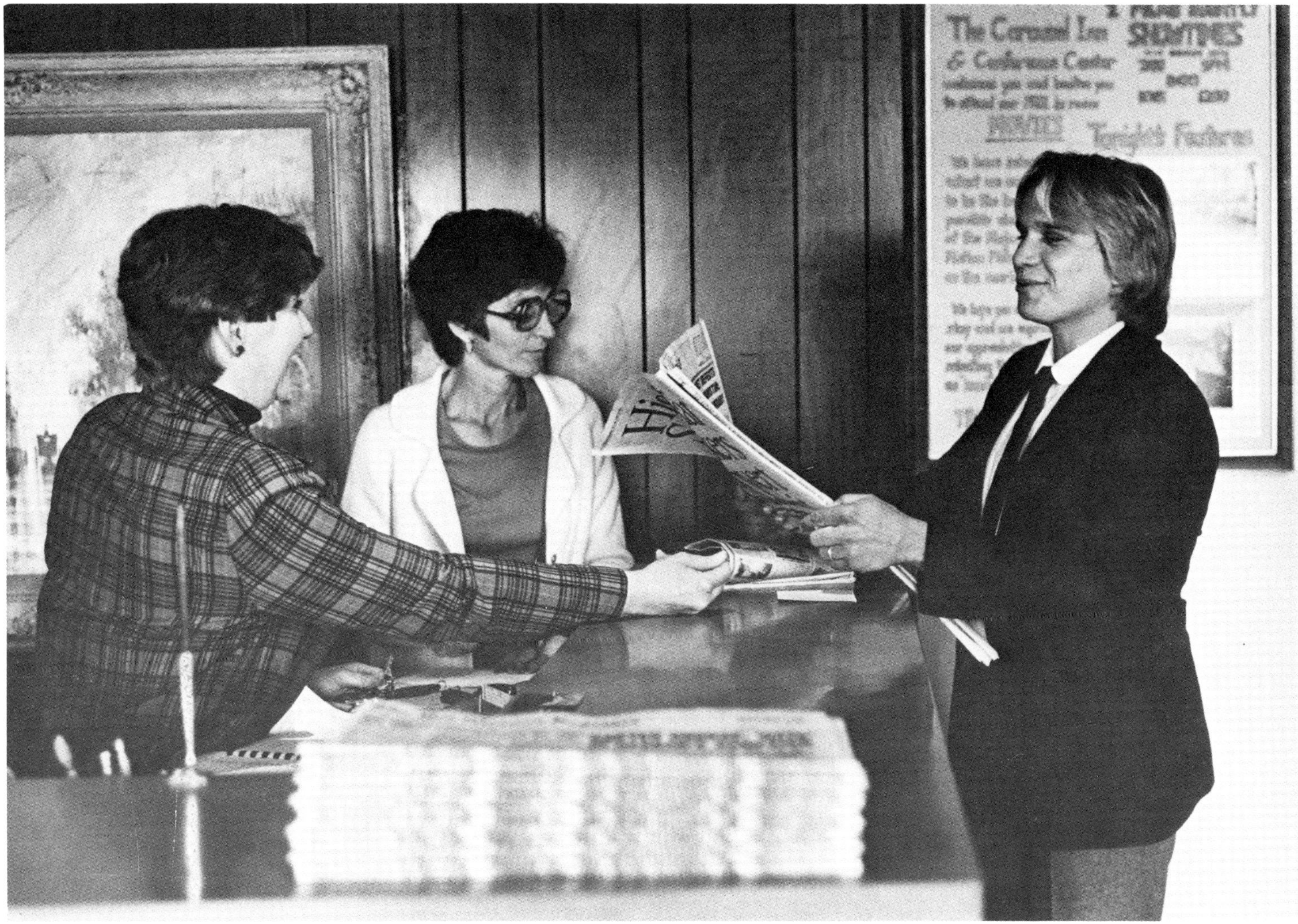
The Carousel Inn
& Conference Center
SHOWTIMES
Tonight's Features

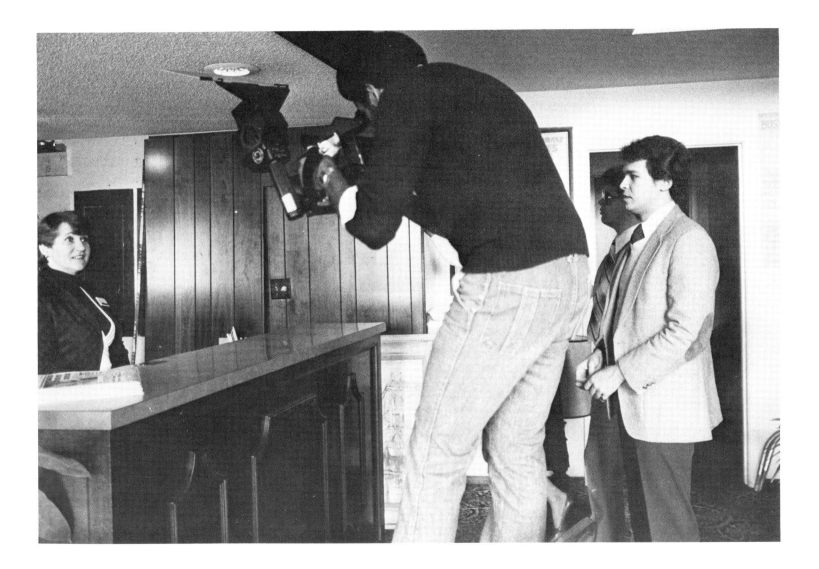

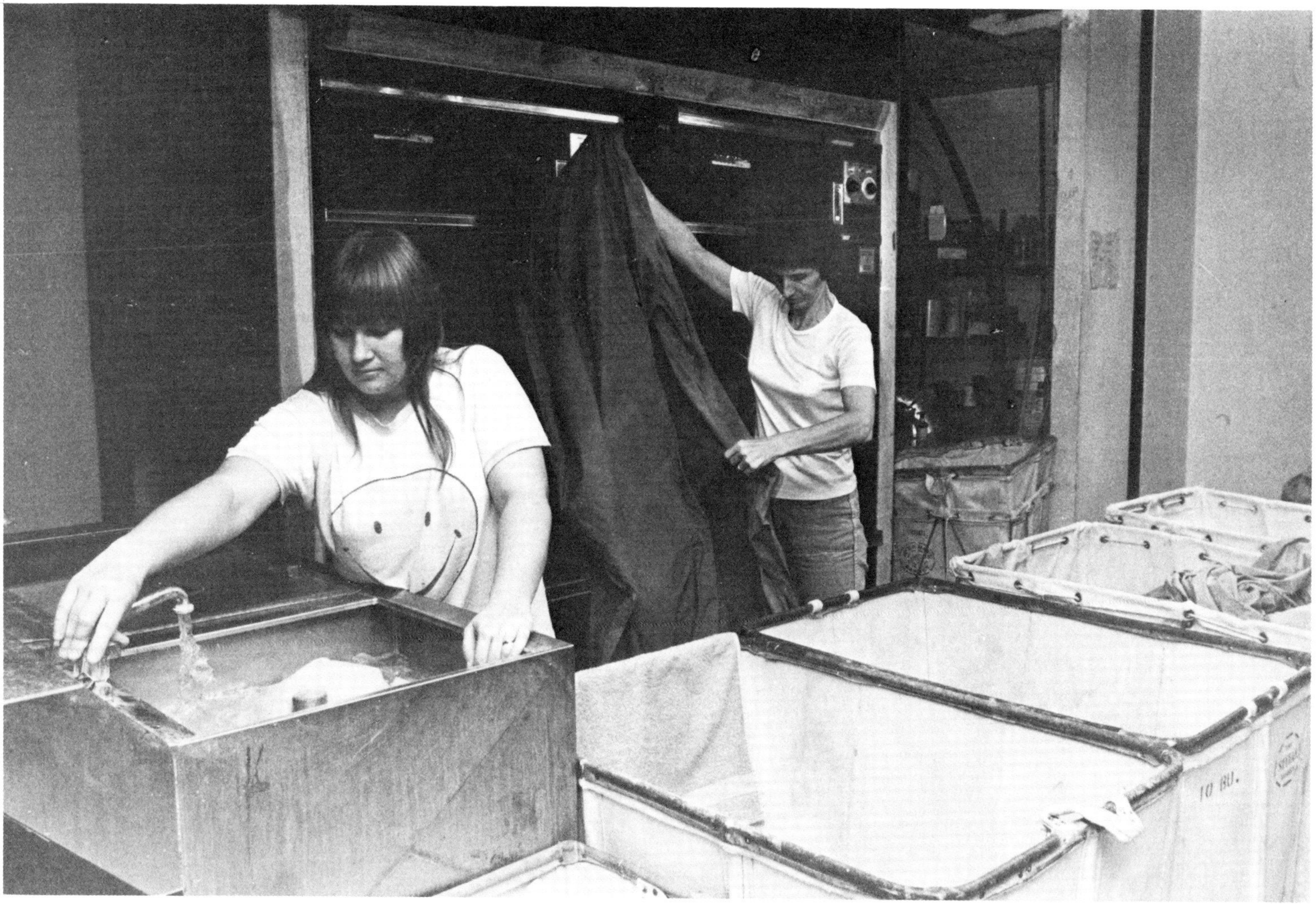
10 BU.

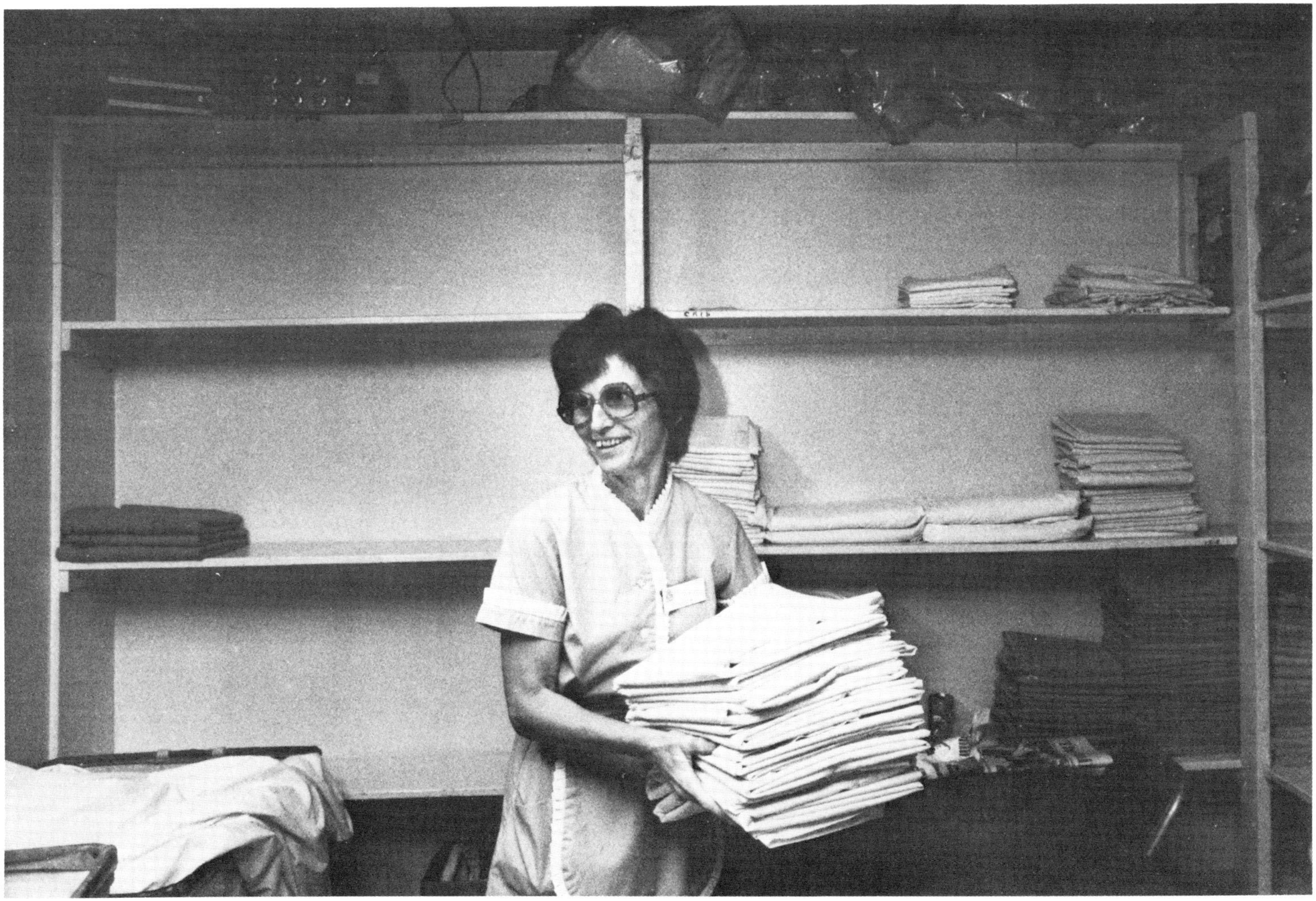

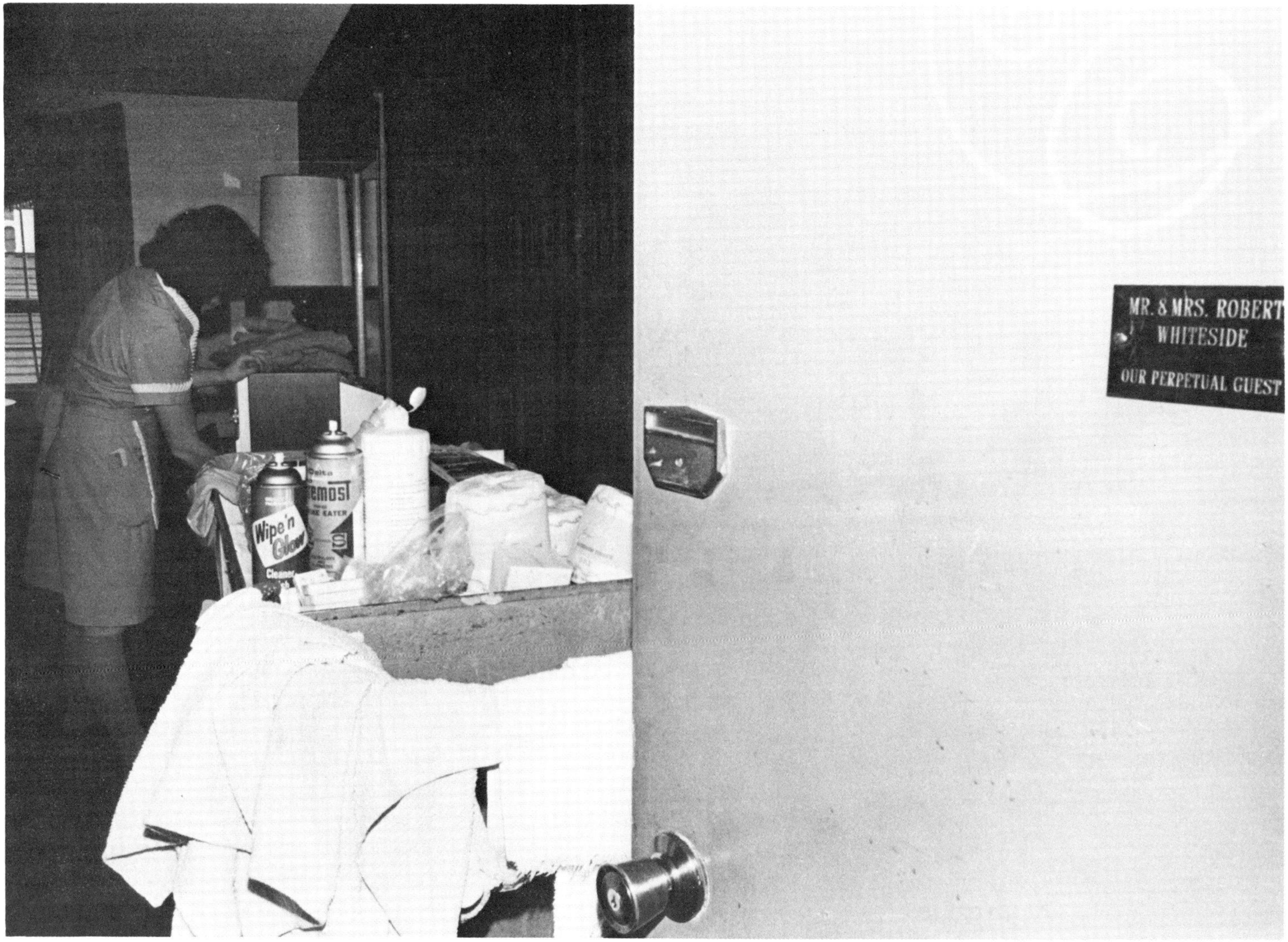
MR. & MRS. ROBERT
WHITESIDE
OUR PERPETUAL GUEST
Wipe 'n Glow

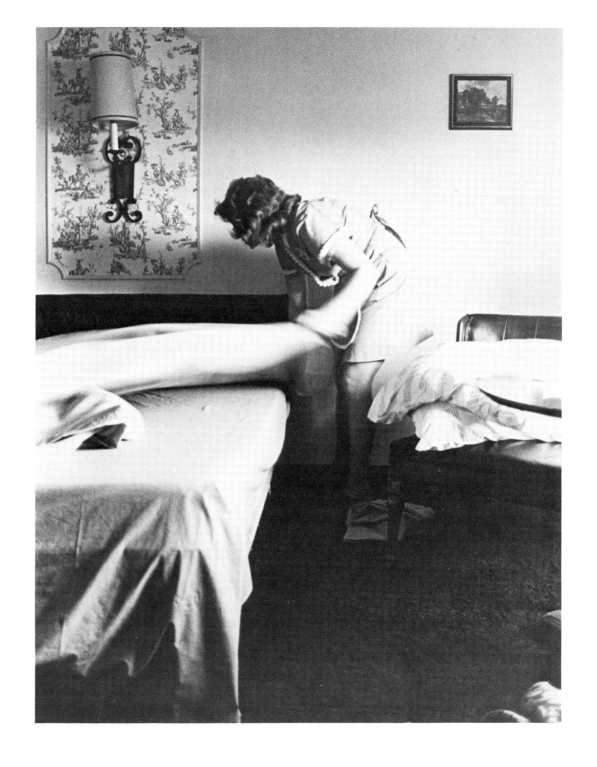

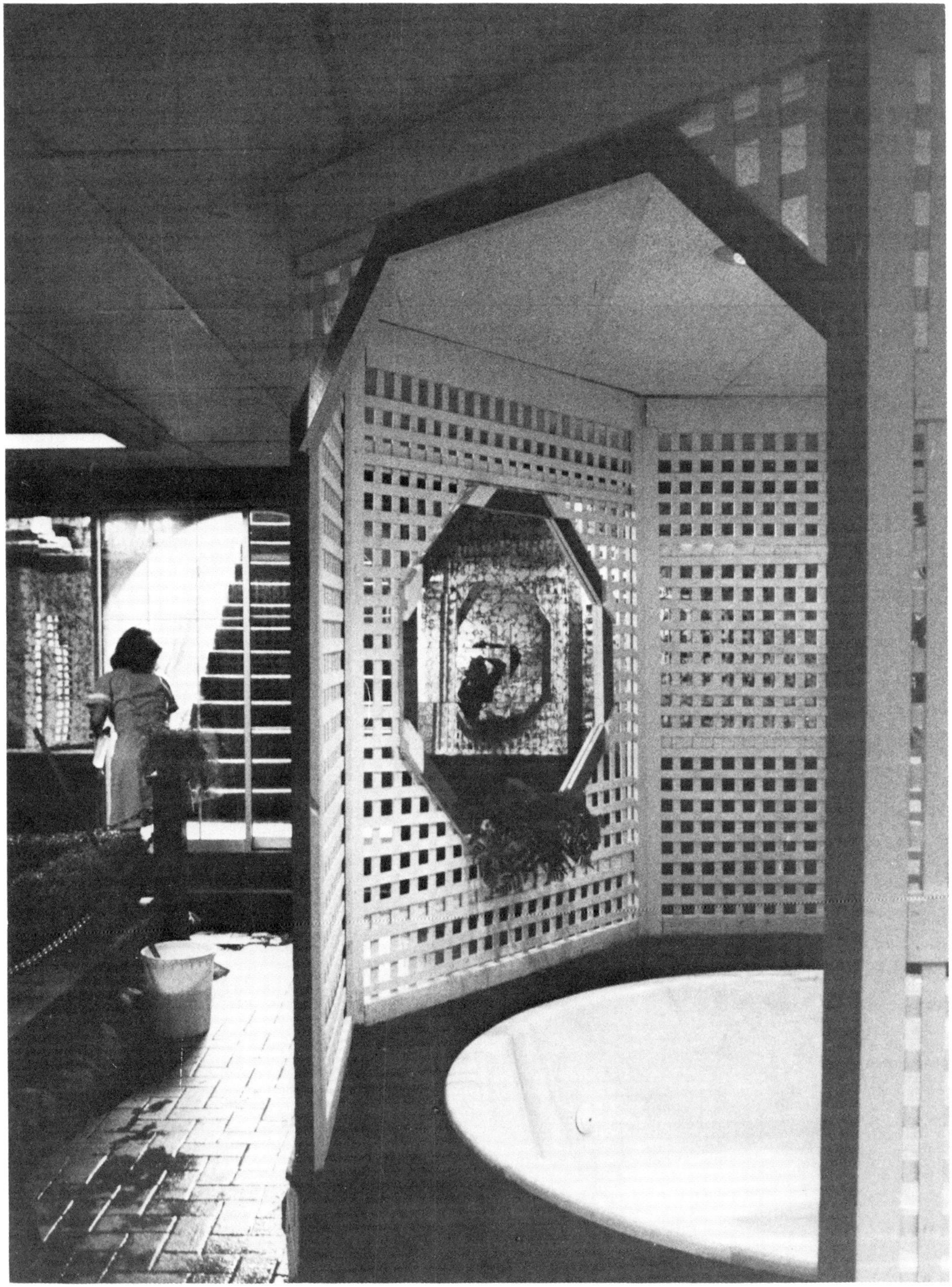

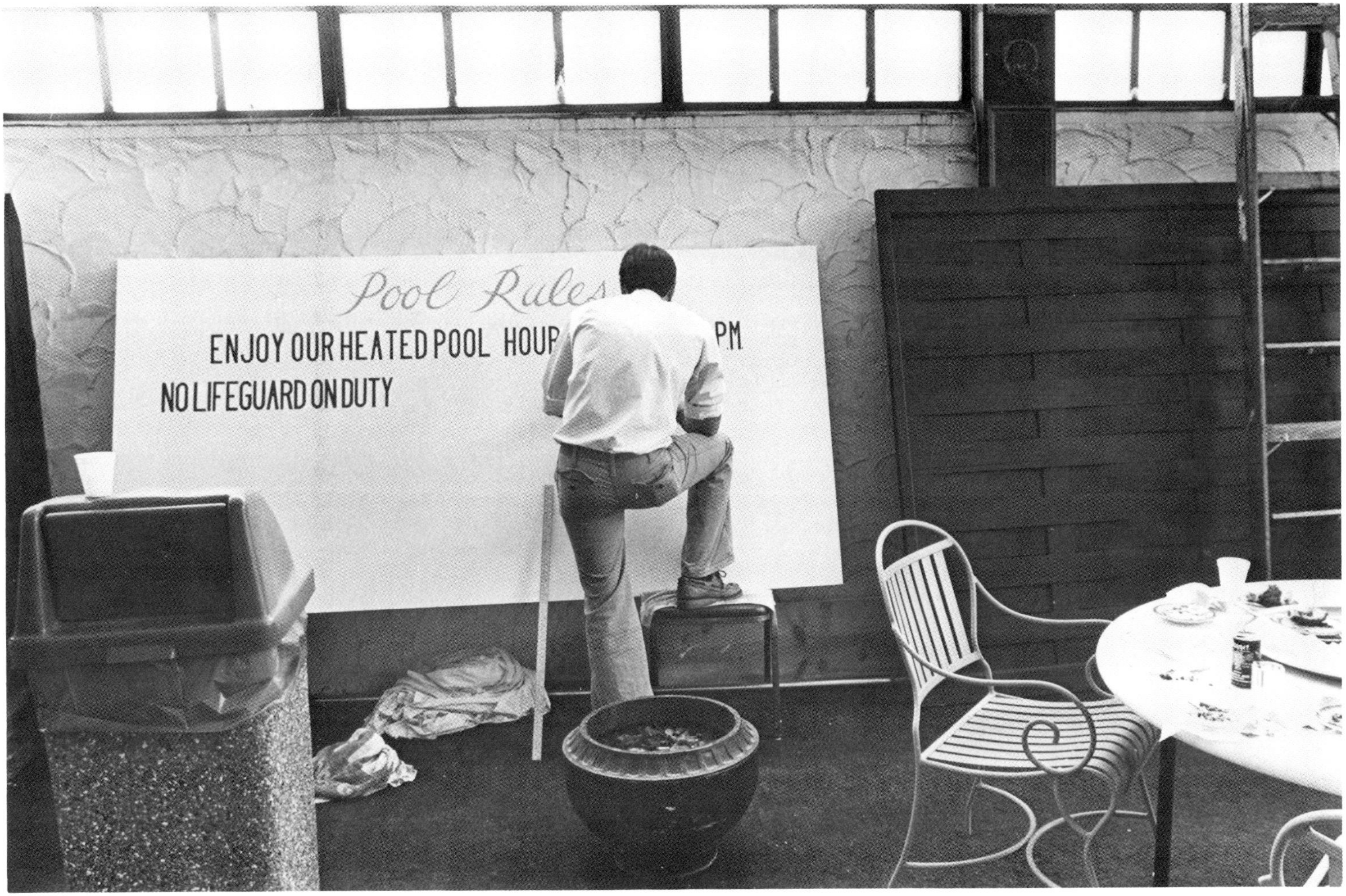
Pool Rules
ENJOY OUR HEATED POOL HOUR
PM
NO LIFEGUARD ON DUTY

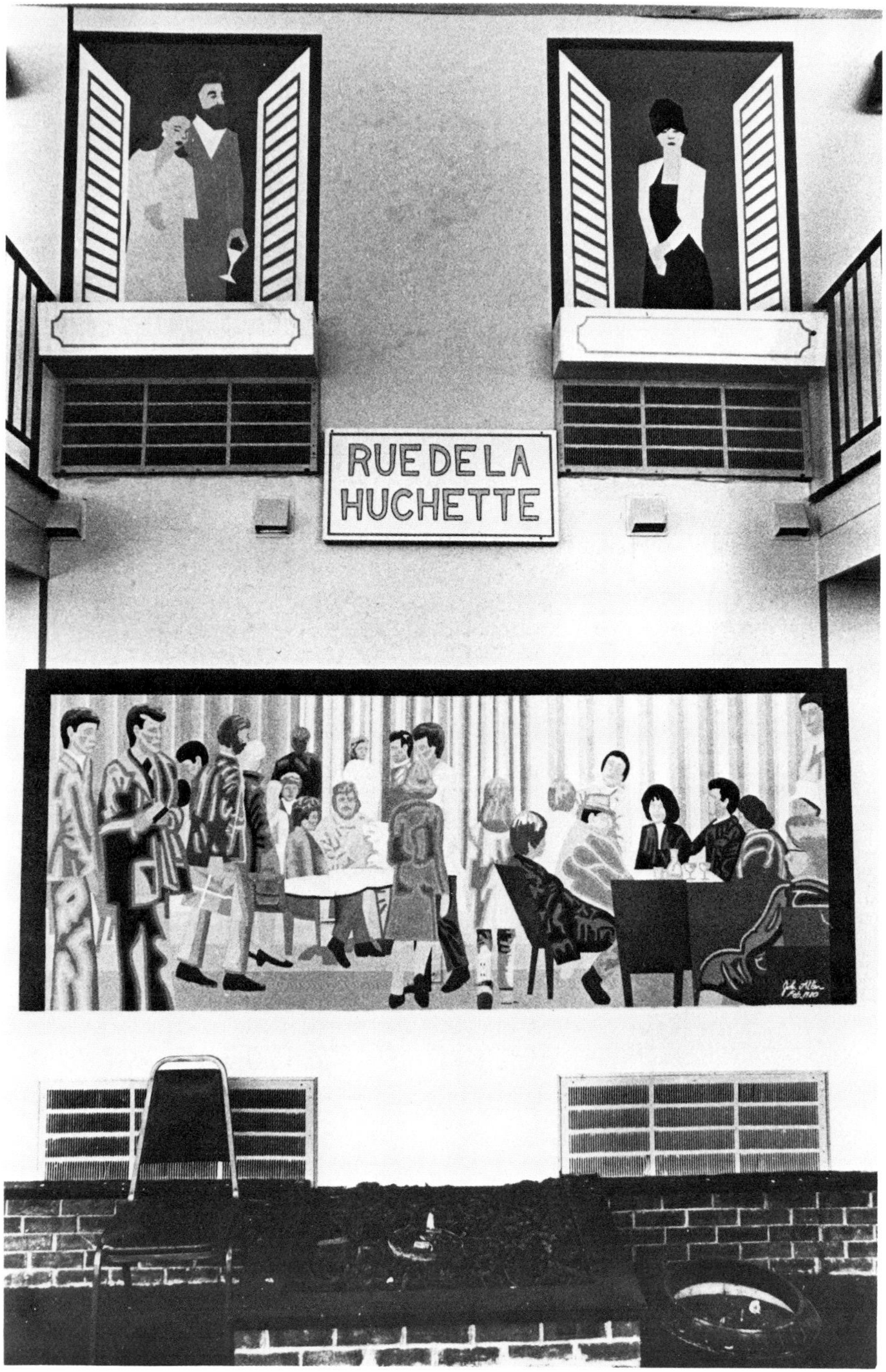
RUE DE LA
HUCHETTE

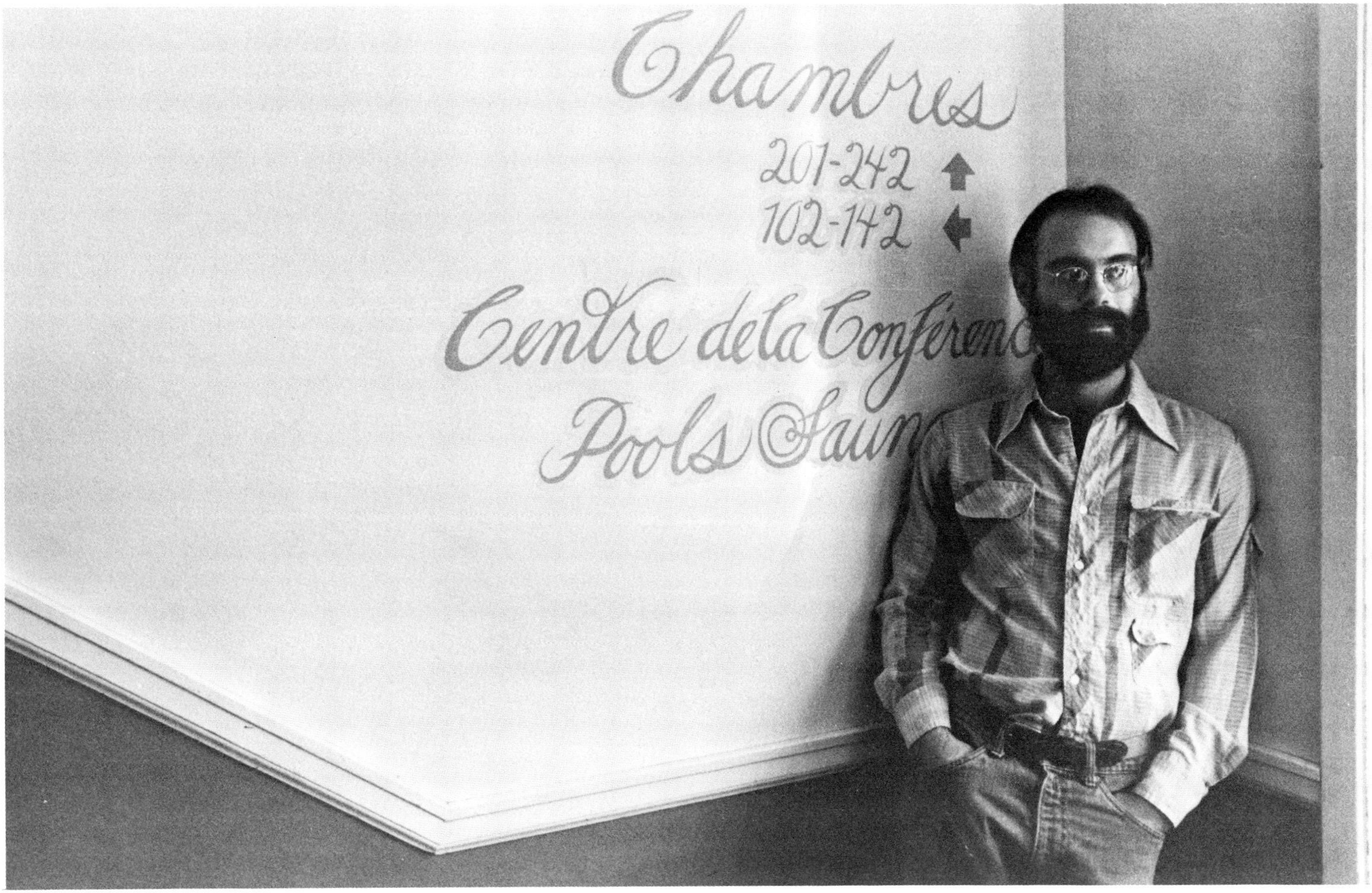
Chambres
201-242
102-142
Centre dela Conférenc
Pools Saun

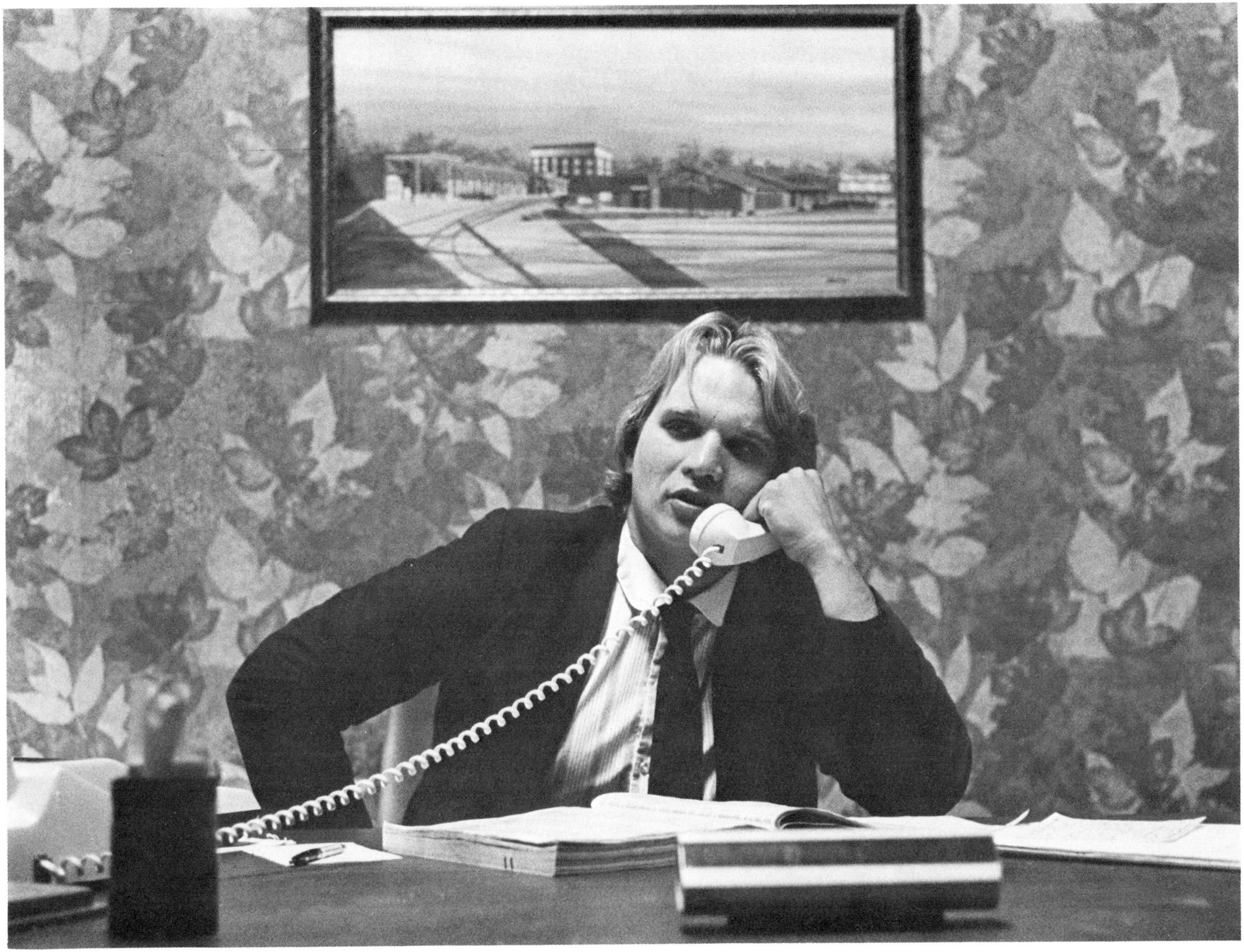

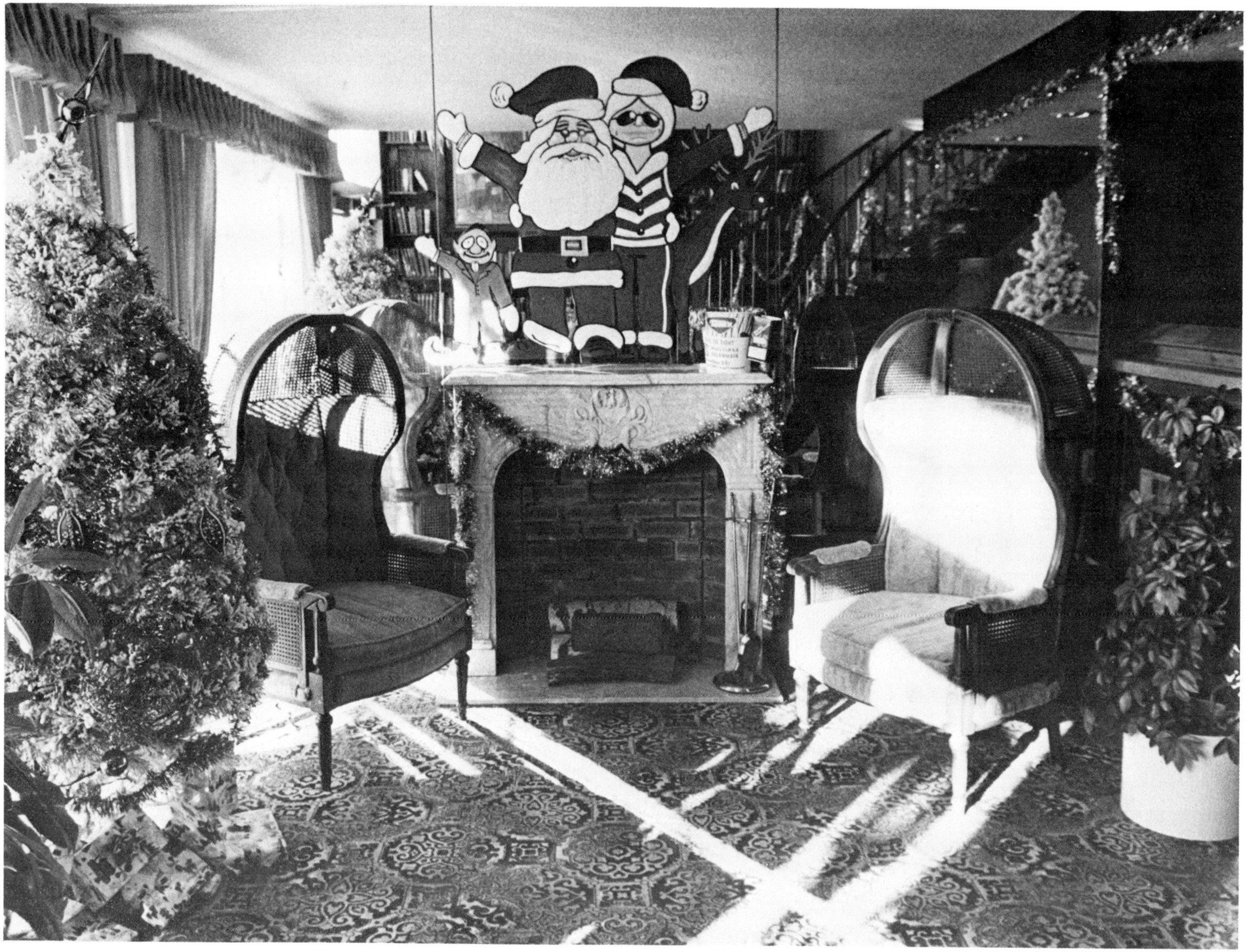

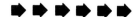

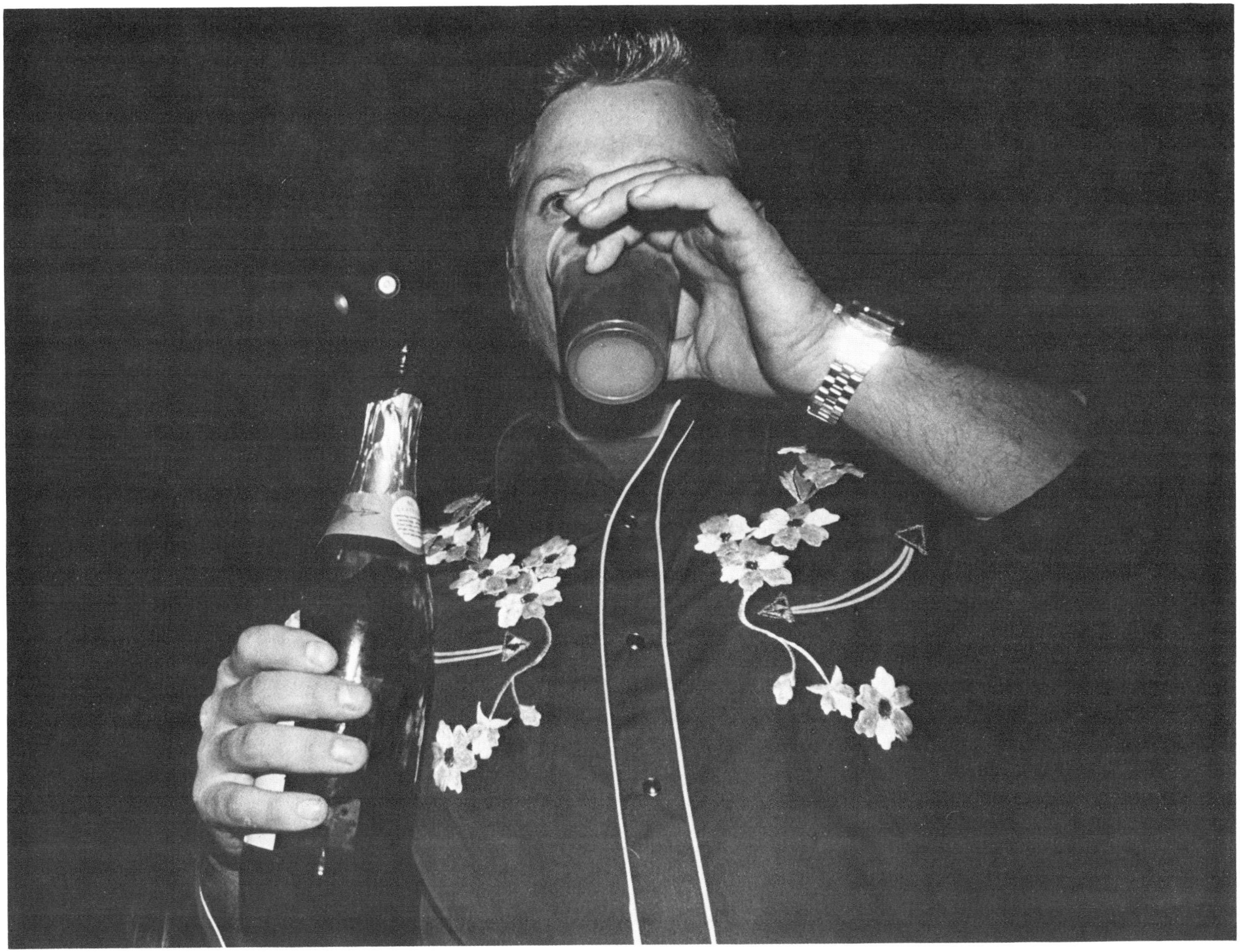

ormal reactions to the strip range from quiet resignation to celebration and disdain. They are as diverse as American tastes. In the hustle of everyday life, a strip may, indeed, seem hardly worth attention: if you have seen one, you have seen them all. But if you have an empty tank or a bulging bladder, a taste for Warhol and Whoppers, any strip is a welcome sight. If your tastes run more along the lines of yogurt and Yosemite, every strip is just a blight. Judgments are rendered in off-hand quips and full-blown theories of art and society. Yet, as diverse as these reactions are, they are uniformly consumer-oriented. In question is the quality of the patron's experience, not the quality of the *exchange* between patrons and service providers. Few workers can afford such self-indulgence.

At the very least, I hope the Carousel staff has helped argue against a one-sided view. The strip should not be considered solely a vehicle for satiating the public, because there is more than architecture or cuisine at stake. In particular, I fear that improvements on the traditional strip, serving up more of the good life for consumers, will mean less of the good life for service providers.

Such fears might well be fostered in any commercial setting. Even before meeting John or Tammy, we might guess that they would describe their place as a process rather than a commodity. We all know that bosses and consumers judge our labor by its market value, but we know, too, that we are more than what we produce, more than "just" a housekeeper, sign painter, homemaker, or professor. Donning an insider's point of view may once have resembled scaling the canyons of social class. But now, I believe, the barrier is less between groups than

between roles or frames of mind. In fact, when insiders describe their reaction to the strip *as consumers*, their tastes are much like our own. Their perspective as workers, then, is not presented to replace the consumer's but to complement it. A place like the Carousel does not have to be diagnosed as an alien or pop phenomenon. Instead, it can be a meeting place for the insider and outsider, the producer and consumer, in us all.

With such a view, sites along the strip like the Carousel are as difficult to judge as any American place. Each encounter begins with a complex and quite individual story of car payments and softball games, visions of success or experience with failure. We see the ups and downs of people in motion—Frank touring the halls, Brad rehearsing inspection, or Jan admiring linen over a smoke. It is hard to see how anyone could know and care about these people and say their place fits some tidy message. Such complex and likable people deserve more than the usual "eh?," "ah," or "bah!" muttered by passing motorists.

As unique as their stories are, they share themes that are common on as well as off the strip. Probably most familiar are tales of reckoning with "outside" pressure. For example, the organization of the Carousel, informal as it may be, is experienced like an alien force. On the strip, as in office complexes, industrial parks, and Main Street, U.S.A., men with drive or vision are concentrated at the top and women with fewer choices at the bottom, and both are ultimately responsible to the marketplace. Whether they welcome or resent their positions, it is a fact of life that seems inherited rather than created. Greetings between managers, staff, and the public are ritually staged to ease the tension. Even owners distinguish their ideals from a reality they must maintain for employees and consumers. Americans may no longer be separated by caste, but lines of power and wealth still separate bosses, workers, and consumers. When Frank speaks of "keeping the ladies happy" and Dean of "what makes a guy tick," when Jan describes her amazement with decent treatment and Tammy her embarrassment in front of a guest, they articulate some of the alienation that is prevalent in American commerce, an alienation between people. We are tied together less by feelings of mutual obligation than by roles in a social script.

Yet in the relaxed atmosphere of the Carousel this sort of alienation receives less attention than another, more psychological sort. It is the dislocation many people feel between the "two me's." First, there is the continuous or "real me," the person with a childhood, hobbies, moods, family, and friends, a life that defies description. And then there is the "hired me," the person whose life begins and ends with a punch of the clock, who is defined by routines or operations manuals. On the job and in their evaluation of it, people reveal a tension, sometimes profound, between these two senses of self.

Again, such alienation is hardly peculiar to the Carousel or the Strip. For example, in contrasting John and Jan or in hearing Dave or Dean compare themselves with Ermal or their fathers, we can see a difference of whole generations. Older workers tend to stress the hired me or belittle its dissociation. Compared to the hardship surrounding World War II, decent pay for decent work is enough. Reconciling your on- and off-the-job presence is a luxury barely worth pursuing. Younger workers, concentrated on the Strip, tend to be less easily satisfied. Raised, like the strip itself, amidst postwar affluence, they look for personal fulfillment as well as material gain. How, they ask, can I handle a job that is not really me?

A full stock of solutions is evident at the Carousel. Kathy and Dean are the dualists. They neatly compartmentalize their two selves. If the hired me is uncomfortable,

there is always the real me sequestered at home. Brad and Mike are the rebels. Rather than checking their personalities at the door, they scrawl them over everything they can. Frank and Craig are the reformers. They negotiate a fit between their personal and vocational lives. Dave, Tammy, and Jan are the optimists. With patience and hard work, they trust, any sense of dislocation between the real and hired me should fade away. John is the pragmatist. He assumes that alienation comes with the territory. Invest as little of yourself as possible and get out.

In a sense, they are all pragmatists. They have sought a way to earn a living, do a job, and be themselves in a fashion. Their search is remarkable, not because it is peculiar to the strip, but because outsiders seldom recognize its importance. Workers, like consumers, have needs that commerce should meet. The strip should be evaluated for how well it meets both the taste of consumers and the need of workers to reconcile personal liberty and occupational opportunity.

What is unique to the strip, at least in workers' estimation, is how much success they can enjoy. They take pride in their work and care for each other. They may have to tolerate low pay and unpredictable conditions, but they have the freedom to craft their response. Freedom is the key. In this sense, the strip has more in common with historic frontiers than with modern industry. The mixture of challenge and opportunity makes the strip a refuge like the boom towns of yesteryear.

The opportunity was first developed by backwoods speculators like Virgil Bowers only thirty or forty years ago. Small-time entrepreneurs followed, pioneers like the Loghrys, Prochnows, and Stecklings. They risked fortunes skimmed from hometown enterprise for a fling on the burgeoning American roadside. With hard work and luck, a few survived. Some of them earned enough to invite family and friends to join them. As the highway system was more fully developed in the 1960s, their fortunes were less dependent on tourist adventurers. More affluent and auto-mobile citizens secured their fate as settlers did for sooners more than a century ago. The sons and daughters of newcomers or less successful pioneers began to find employment on the strip as well. The material rewards were slim, but the promise was great. Young people and women with few credentials or contacts labored beside their bosses. With perseverance, it seemed, they might rise as rapidly as their employers and, if not, at least be spared the drudgery of more "civilized" work. The legacy of those frontier days persists on the strip today.

But there are signs that the frontier is closing. As consumers demand a more perfect escape from their own oppressively perfected jobs, more and more capital must be invested in amenities, uniforms, and quality control. Simple eateries or cabin courts like those in which the pioneers staked their claim are, indeed, a thing of the past. The "authentic," fantastic experience of pedestrian malls, theme restaurants, or architected strips are beyond the means of small-time entrepreneurs. Instead of mom and pop sharing the profit, loss, and labor of roadside service, the strip is increasingly occupied by managers and workers following the directives of absentee owners, franchisers, and investment groups. The story of Dave Steckling's rise from jack-of-all-trades to jet-setter is a story, too, of the widening gap between capital and labor.

From this point of view, strip critics, workers turned demanding consumers, are their own worst enemies. In sponsoring the perfect escape, they are helping to create a work environment that is more confining. This is the underside of progress.

The strip has been a place of personal trial, a place where an individual might win or lose a fortune, make a statement, clown through the day, or just make a buck and get out. Whatever their fate, people have been free to express themselves in their work. They could add or

subtract some of the real me at will. But as their performance, the hired me, is honed to more exacting specifications, there is less room for adjustment. If you are lucky, you happen to have the "right" attitude; more likely, you just feel alienated. The frontier, the refuge itself, increasingly demands escape.

This change is evident in microcosm at the Carousel. Dave Steckling grew up on the Strip and built parts of it with his own hands, but now he more often handles reports from his management corporation. The young people who rose with him, like Dean and Frank, began with simple ambition and a sense for what is right. Hardcore detail men are their replacement. Management, maintenance, and housekeeping, once shared by the Steckling clan, are now delegated to strangers related through payrolls, time clocks, inspections, and monthly reports. Their meetings in the hall, though friendly, are awkward enough to attract comment. Workers know as well as managers that greetings are staged reminders to get with it, to get "happy and humming." The Carousel is still far from a factory, but in a short time it has moved well along a similar path.

Nowhere was this more evident than in a rash of improvements in the Carousel during February 1980. These were not capricious but deliberate efforts to better the motel, to make it a more profitable and attractive place. The business had long been successful, but it was time to grow. There was mounting pressure to contain costs and deliver the "class and quality" that would attract increasing trade. The Cantebury had an established market with businessmen and the Alamo with the budget-minded, but the Carousel had not really "found its niche" for the future. Moreover, as new properties occupied Heritage management, operations in the Carousel seemed out of control. Since the mid-1970s, when Dean and Frank built up the business, nearly every employee had been replaced several times. Each time novices were trained by their predecessors, adding quirk upon quirk to the routine. The breakdowns showed that labor costs had risen above accepted standards. Changes in key personnel meant this was an opportune time to consolidate the Carousel's success and direct it toward the future.

Many of the initial changes were quite spontaneous. Craig was finally convinced that he was not right for the job, and Dean sought a more settled replacement, a detail man. In the meantime, Dean readied for his own exit to new frontiers. Tammy held on for her week of vacation and then quit.

But many of the other changes in personnel were less amicable. The head of housekeeping was directed to trim her payroll by firing four housekeepers. Kathy was given the "choice" of quitting (rumor had it that "she didn't smile enough" at the desk) or moving to the office as a secretary for the manager. The position of assistant manager was eliminated. In a matter of weeks, Heritage decided to assign secretarial duties to the desk and give Kathy another "choice": resign or move to the new, computerized accounting service at Heritage Systems. Kathy reluctantly made the move while she lined up another job and quit soon after. So ended the career of one of the most senior members of the Carousel's staff.

At the same time, management's problem with the characters in maintenance came to a head. One day, while showing some people around, Dean discovered the latest addition to the shop. Some pet mice scurried about an elaborate maze constructed of plastic tubing. It was a secure home, but it looked as if a band of rodents had the run of the shop. What made matters worse was a slight drop in the Carousel's score on a recent inspection, this one a genuine surprise. The mice were just the last straw.

In charting the relaxed atmosphere of the Carousel, Brad and Mike had finally encountered its outer limits. Management's response was to separate them like a pair of mischievous school boys. Dean sent Mike over to the Alamo. A couple of months later, Brad had returned to

odd jobs in Wellman and Mike to the night shift in a feed store. They felt utterly betrayed. Brad complained: "Dean is just two-faced. That's what pissed me off. He said, 'Oh, yeah, we're still friends.' But I said, 'Not like I thought we were.' I learned in that big a place there's no place for friendship. Dean's a good company man, 'cause he don't care who he shits on. No matter, like if Mike and I are friends or if I've been friends with Dean for ten years, as long as it looks good on his record when he sends it in to Steckling every month. That's all he cares about. I couldn't do it. *No way* I could do that! But Dean can." Mike adds: "That's the big difference between Dean and me or Brad. Neither one of us could do what he does and be able to sleep at night."

Although Brad and Mike find it hard to believe, Dean did care, and he was not sleeping very well those days. In fact, he could barely wait to escape himself. He explained: "Sure, they're friends of mine. We grew up together. But, hey, this is business. Imagine you're a little old lady from southwest Iowa, staying at the Carousel while you visit some sick relative at the hospital. And here come these two guys marching down the hall in motorcycle jackets. You just can't handle that kind of thing."

Other members of the staff exchanged opinions in the hallways, some standing up for management and some for maintenance, but no one was terribly surprised by the outcome. For everyone the lesson was clear. No matter how far removed from public view, your attitude had better be right. There is no longer a place in the Carousel for characters or rebels, the cowboys of the roadside frontier.

Along with these changes in personnel came equally significant changes in procedure. Everyone was vigorously reminded to avoid overtime and to be sure to smile at the guests. The shop was stripped of girlie magazines and games, cleaned and repainted. Housekeepers were advised to pay more attention to their uniforms and show more deference to the guests. For example, they were to phone each guest from downstairs before going up to clean.

Changes were particularly visible in the laundry. Since housekeepers were held up making calls, the dirty linen came down later in the day. The laundry assistant was reassigned to cleaning public areas, and in the interest of avoiding any potential overtime, Jan was told to stick to a 7:00 to 3:00 schedule. She complained that her work might never get done—no more visions of tidy linen "waiting for the girls to come down." In place of the challenge that Jan daily set for herself, managers advised her to relax. They would "help" her take the peaks and valleys from her routine. Just work steadily, put in your eight hours, and go home. With such small, well-intentioned adjustments, the Carousel took a step closer to the factory that Jan had fled.

Given the heads that rolled about them, few employees voiced objections above a whisper. Everyone seemed to be waiting for things to settle, but then there was "the union thing." It was the first assembly of Carousel staff and Heritage officers since the Christmas party, but this was a very different affair. It was organized by employees, and managers were uninvited guests. Naturally, everyone tells a slightly different version of what transpired, but Tammy offered a fairly typical account from a housekeeper's point of view.

The whole union thing started when one of the employees here, Brad, just got really upset. I think maybe it was a personal thing more than anything else. But I'm not sure.

He started going around to all the housekeepers and the maintenance men, telling them that he wanted to call the union and giving reasons why he wanted to do this, things like how we get screwed for our overtime. (The housekeepers don't put in much overtime, though. But the maintenance men do.) He said he knew who to call [an AFL-CIO number in the phone book], and we didn't

figure it would hurt. We figured, if anything, we could just find out about it. So we all agreed.

Brad called this guy, and he was supposed to have been here at noon the next day. So, at noon we were all sitting in the employees' lounge, all the maids and all the maintenance men. And we were really excited, you know, to find out what the guy would say, because at that time we didn't have enough supplies, we were always having to share vacuums, the elevator to the laundry was always breaking down. There were just all kinds of things. Anyway, we were all excited. We really wanted to talk to this guy. And he never showed up.

But, about fifteen minutes after we got in there, here comes Dean and Neil from Heritage and Bruce, who was the manager at that time. They came storming in the door, and, man, they were furious. You could see it in their eyes. They were mad!

They said, "Where is he?!"—'cause, supposedly (we didn't know it at the time, and that's why the guy never showed up), if you're trying to get the union in somewhere, you don't meet in the same building. It's against the law or something. Then he said, "Who's responsible for this?!" And Brad spoke right up and said, "I am."

Dean and Brad had been friends for a long time. They went to high school together and everything. So there was a big argument between them, and then they went outside and started arguing.

We were all left sitting there not knowing what was going to happen. Neil stayed and started to talk to us about it. He asked us first why we wanted a union. And we mainly just said, "Well, we just wanted to find out about it—just curious as to what the benefits could be of being in the union." Finally he calmed down and told us what he knew about the union, trying to talk us out of it.

He told us mainly bad points. Like, you only get a fifteen-minute break in the morning and a fifteen-minute break in the afternoon, half an hour or an hour for lunch. You have to account for every minute in the day. You can't go to lunch or take breaks whenever you want to. (We don't get paid by the hour, you know; so as long as we're done by five o'clock, we can take our time—which is a good point.) Anyway, it would be more a just-come-to-work-do-your-work-and-go-home thing than a friendly atmosphere.

I've never been in a union, so I really don't know, but that's what he was telling us. Jan, who was working in the laundry at that time, had been in a union before, and she said that he was right. She sat there and told us he was right.

We couldn't figure out who told them that the union was coming here. In fact, we just found out who called a little while ago. Now it doesn't surprise me one bit.

Anyway, Neil talked us out of it. That was pretty much the end of it. Brad ended up quitting. Mike, his buddy, is still around. He was transferred over to the Alamo, and now I don't know what he's doing—odd jobs, I guess. Otherwise, things are pretty much the same.

It is tempting to treat this scene as a climax in an epic tragedy—a foreclosure on the frontier. But that would be to parody the truth. Several months later, employees still debated the identity of their informer and similar details, but otherwise, in fact, that meeting was the end of it.

In a couple of weeks people settled into routines. Few of the original cast remained, anyway, and they counted themselves lucky. For a while, Jan enjoyed her promotion to head of housekeeping, and others actually welcomed management's newfound control: "At least now we know what is expected of us." Many felt flattered that the Carousel at last drew attention once reserved for newer properties like the Cantebury. There was less talk of *their* "relaxed atmosphere" and "freedom," but they could be proud to provide a better atmosphere for the guests. The February Massacre and the union thing were not giant calamities but small steps down a familiar trail earlier blazed by manufacturers.[1]

In "getting their act together" for the market place, people are driven apart. Decision making and manual labor are more rigidly divided between management and staff. Consumers and workers spend less time in genuine exchange and more time making and taking orders. Workers find less place for the real me in their lives on the job. As much as the traditional strip has estranged consumers, improvements on the strip promise more profound alienation. The legacy of the strip as an economic frontier is, indeed, fading, not through histrionics but small "improvements" accumulating across the nation.

The human side of this development is, I believe, most visible close up, in the movements and expressions of people in a particular site. Its pervasiveness is visible through a longer lens. The Carousel and the Cantebury are affiliated with thousands of inns around the world through Best Western International, Incorporated.[2] Like Heritage properties, the typical affiliate is an independently owned motel of eighty to one hundred rooms on a highway or off an interstate. Fewer than 20 percent are in central business districts. Every year about twenty-eight million people stay at a Best Western. More than 80 percent of them arrive by automobile, and about six of every ten make their lodging decision behind the wheel. Though barely visible in workaday life, Best Western has become a major interest on the strip.

In 1948, a year before the Loghrys opened their drive-in on what was to become the Coralville Strip, an independent motel owner named M. K. Guertin organized a few neighboring inns in California. It was not much, just a friendly agreement to recommend each other to guests.

Over the next decade the circle of friends slowly grew to about fifty with a half-dozen staff members overhead, but many other motels in the West waited to join. In the mid-1960s, the organization incorporated under the name of Western Motels and established a headquarters in Phoenix. As the roadside boomed in the following decade, even more affiliations were requested, now from as far away as the East Coast. With little effort, a California clique was becoming a national organization.

The pains of growth were well in evidence those first years. It was a casual group dedicated, not to profits or growth for the collective, but to individuals who would fiercely guard their independence. Members elected officers from their ranks and directed them to follow rather than make policy. They assembled for regular meetings where consensus was supposed to emerge, but conflict was the rule. There were more strangers among them. They fought bitterly on the one hand to organize more effectively and on the other to do as they pleased. If you recommended a place down the road, you wanted someone to assure its quality, but you also did not want anyone telling you what to do. At the same time travelers were showing a preference for standardized chains. Holiday Inns, Incorporated, with its rigid controls, was becoming the biggest lodging entity in the world. Faced with this competition and their own unwieldy numbers, Western pioneers were forced to make the same sort of choice that bosses routinely make for their employees: preserve small freedoms or recognize economic reality by engineering for profit. In its own way and on a much grander scale, Western was in the same position as the Carousel on the eve of the February Massacre.

In 1974, the realists prevailed. In recognition of its national scale, the organization was renamed Best Western and restructured to empower a seven-man board of directors chosen by the members. The members hired a professional management team to direct a staff that now numbered in the hundreds. Their leader was not some roadside yeoman but Robert C. Hazard, a *cum laude* Ivy Leaguer with experience in American Express and IBM. Affiliates would still be independently owned and operated, but the organization was to give them the look of a chain. In fact, Best Western aimed to dispel its image as "merely" a regional referral service for mom-and-pop motels. Since four of five frequent travelers (travelers on the road seventeen or more nights per year) prefer chains over independents, this was, indeed, a realistic choice.

Under Hazard's aggressive leadership, the Best Western crown was displayed more prominently in each affiliate. A single, toll-free number linked travelers and agents to a new International Marketing and Reservations Center. Quality controls were more rigorously enforced. Between 1975 and 1978, 390 properties were dropped for failure to meet well-defined standards. In most American cities where there is a Best Western, it is top-rated by the *Mobil Travel Guide*. Members were offered central purchasing, insurance, and millions of dollars worth of advertising. In 1976, magazine layouts alone reached 85 percent of the adults who stayed in hotels, motels, and resorts that year. Between travel guides, television, outdoor advertising, periodicals, and promotions, motorists see the Best Western logo billions of times per year. Foreign affiliations expanded by the hundreds, and fly-drive tours were organized in-house and through TWA, United,

Pan-Am, American, and Eastern Airlines. Construction was begun on a new, 60,000-square-foot, ten-million-dollar headquarters in Phoenix to house, among other things, a fifteen-million-dollar reservations computer system with the potential for satellite links to tens of thousands of agents around the world.

After twenty-five years of fracas, all this was accomplished in barely five. By every economic measure it was a success. Between 1975 and 1979, Best Western increased its share of the market, as they define it, from 5 to 11 percent, and Hazard is now shooting for a third. There are more than 2,500 affiliates—double the number in 1974—with a total of 150,000 rooms in 1,500 cities in eighteen countries. That is more than anyone in the business, including Holiday Inns. Like Holiday Inns, Best Western grosses about a billion dollars per year. By some estimates, the two take in more than 20 percent of all the receipts of hotels, motels, and tourist courts in the United States. Recently, large prestige hotels have joined the organization. The Barbizon Plaza in New York City reports having gained 100 to 150 room-nights per week from the Best Western system. Some 80 percent of Best Western guests are repeat customers. The movement from frontier circle to well-oiled corporation has been thoroughly supported in the marketplace.

In 1978 Hazard lorded over a convention of the membership like Marshall Dillon in Dodge City. They called it a "Round Up," an apt allusion to their legacy but ironic given what transpired. Some three thousand people whooped it up at a "Camelot" night, Oktoberfest, square dance, and barbecue. They heard from Andy Williams, John Davidson, Edwin Newman, and former President Ford. The tab for three days ran close to half a million dollars, which is a tidy sum, even compared to the $15.4 million paid in dues and fees that year. Quite the "Round-Up"!

Hazard chose the occasion to announce ambitious goals for the future. He urged members to pay higher fees for their space-age computer and to expand in met-

ropolitan areas. He asked for tighter quality controls, even if some properties would be eliminated. He recommended that affiliates drop their personal names and use only "Best Western." Such advice was unspeakable just a few years before, but rapid success turned heresy to prophecy.

After the Round-Up, Best Western sped closer to Hazard's goals and further from its frontier past. The computer came on line, and more rigid quality controls were instituted, forcing out some members and ranking the others "Deluxe," "Superior," or merely "Comfortable." Landon Associates, an image and identity firm in San Francisco, was hired to help dissociate Best Western even further from its mom-and-pop origins. The chain is now considering a more "international" name and logo.

Potentially the greatest break with the past came with the formation of B-W Financial Services in 1979. It is a wholly owned subsidiary of Best Western International begun in cooperation with Helmsley-Spear Hospitality Services, a giant real estate and lodging firm in New York City. The key to their joint venture is Helmsley-Spear's ties with an awesome array of financial organizations: banks; insurance, credit, and mortgage companies; government-backed investments, time-sharers, pension funds, and syndicators. Capital is their game, and they aim for Best Western to get it at competitive rates—competitive, that is, in the major leagues. B-W now helps owners negotiate loans and package portfolios; analyze market, operation, and finance conditions; coordinate closings; and challenge tax assessments. It offers staff planning studies "to maintain payrolls at maximum productivity and minimum cost." It even offers a complete management package for investors who want to avoid all day-to-day responsibility. They are, in effect, invited to pick motels off the shelf like stocks, drilling rights, or the family jewels. B-W calls it "a long-term passive investment."

Best Western properties are still independently owned

and operated, but the word "independent" has a hollow ring. In a short time the association has moved well away from its mom-and-pop roots, in reality if not in image. It shares its interest on the strip with international monopoly capital. Along with success, class, and quality have come tighter management controls and wider chasms between workers, owners, and their agents. The sorts of changes that were evident in the Carousel are truly pervasive. In fact, when viewed against this background, the Carousel has shown remarkable humanity, sheltering personal liberty in the race to modernity.

But the race is on, and there can be little doubt about its outcome. Pop preservationists and chic urbanites have already begun to celebrate old tourist courts and drive-ins like snail darters or powder horns. Whether viewed as an era of intimate freedom or crude profiteering, the frontier days of the strip are nearly over. Many insiders as well as outsiders came to the strip in flight from modern industrial organization, from the alienating world of shop discipline and capitalist aggression. ("You deserve a break today. . . .") But the strip is rapidly repeating the history of industry itself. Judging from productivity alone, this represents admirable progress. Successful businesses are delivering better goods and services and more "authentic" escapes to a larger public. But here insider and outsider part company. For workers, the refuge increasingly resembles the trap.

This tragedy is too large and systematic to be blamed on isolated defects of character or taste. Razzle-dazzle offerings on the strip are not essentials so much as symptoms of its purpose and remnants of its past. With the latest market reports, developers bury their legacy in malls, barnboard, and salad bars with well-appointed staff. These are not the acts of sinister protagonists but of reasonable men and women seeking to profit from the fantasies of consumers.[3]

If the human significance of this development is suggested in the Carousel and its pervasiveness in Best

Western, its dynamics are boldly evident in the fast-food factories that line the strip. In the roadside race to modernity, they have set the pace.[4]

Over the past twenty years, restaurateurs have joined the ranks of big business. They have capitalized on Americans who eat out more often and spend more money doing it than ever before. Between 1963 and 1980, annual receipts for the dining experience rocketed from thirteen to sixty billion dollars. This expansion was broadly manifest, but it was concentrated among the chains that grew up on the strip. Since 1963, average annual sales of chains have grown twice as fast as the restaurant industry as a whole. For example, between 1967 and 1972, annual sales of public eating and drinking places in America rose by 48 percent, but chains gained 113 percent. By far the greatest gain was registered by fast-food chains. They tripled their sales and increased their share of the market from 2 to 31 percent. Much of their growth came at the expense of traditional restaurants, independents with full menus and sit-down service. In those five years independents' share of the receipts shrank from 72 percent to 55 percent. Franchising itself has become highly concentrated. In 1978, fewer than a dozen firms gained control of more than half the sites and sales. Now subfranchises, chains within chains like Gino's Incorporated with hundreds of Kentucky Fried Chicken stores in the East, rank among the giants of food service. About 40 percent of all the restaurant employees in the country work in franchises, and most of them in fast-food outlets where franchises control three-quarters of the trade. Golden arches and decorated sheds, then, signal more than architectural trends or "hamburger row." They mark the leaders of roadside commerce.

As clearly as utilities, banks, and manufacturers, they constitute an industry. In a 1978 text on the subject, Harvard business professors Wyckoff and Sasser meticulously document the industrialization of the dining experience. Rather than arcane theory, they present real-world cases, "situational analyses," set within the service economy as a whole. What they find in *The Chain-Restaurant Industry* are models for growth and success.

Some of that success they attribute to broad demographic changes such as the increase in two-income households and the declining birthrate since the mid-1960s. More Americans now have more disposable income and are at an age when they are more likely to spend it away from home. But that still does not explain the phenomenal growth of chains and of fast-food franchises in particular.

Restaurants are notoriously tough business, highly competitive and subject to fluctuating consumer tastes. And their expenses are relatively fixed or, as they say, "uncontrollable." The direct cost of food and labor consumes about two-thirds of each sales dollar. These costs have risen dramatically as consumers have shown greater cost-consciousness. The key, then, has been to increase productivity when there seems so little room to do so.

Here, according to Wyckoff and Sasser as well as government and trade publications, is where the chains made their gain. In exchange for "a head start on the learning curve of business" (and miscellaneous arrangements), franchisers are able to harness the initial capital and borrowing power of franchisees as well as continued royalty income. Variable costs, such as advertising, finance, inventory, and training, are spread over a larger base. Collectively franchisees have more to invest in business improvements and their implementation on site. For example, centralized accounting with point-of-sale computers provides quicker and more accurate information for decision making and control. Harder technology has helped contain otherwise fixed and escalating costs of food preparation: liquid nitrogen freezing, microwave thawing, forced convection ovens, and the like with computer sensors throughout. Modern food service has accommodated celloid chemistry, dairy and meat substi-

tutes, and new oils for frying. Most of these innovations were developed by food and equipment suppliers, but chains sponsored their introduction and proliferation to deliver more consistent and affordable products.

Fast-food chains made their greatest strides by assaulting one particular problem of traditional restaurants—labor. Food service is woefully labor intensive. Restaurants take in about half as much in sales per employee as modern manufacturers, and with higher wages traditional restaurants have, in fact, lost ground over the past twenty years. But their loss has been matched by fast-food gains. Through industrial engineering, they have turned labor from a fixed to semi-fixed or variable cost. The key to fast-food success is increased productivity through tighter labor control.

By limiting menus, they not only reduce waste, simplify inventory, and increase purchasing power, but also rid themselves of expensive, trained chefs. Portion control further reduces the need for skilled employees. Much of food preparation is left to the production lines of suppliers so that orders need only be "assembled" on site. Drive-in windows, walk-up counters, salad bars, and the like appeal to consumers' new taste for informality, but their key advantage to owners is reduced labor costs. Self-service along with disposal utensils eliminates waitresses, busboys, and dishwashers. The layout behind the counter is carefully designed for maximum productivity. Fast foods are assembled like widgets on the line, while competitors founder in the job-shop tradition.

These and similar "improvements" point to labor control as the key to a latter-day industrial revolution on the roadside. Independent, full-service restaurants are an endangered species, not just because of their architecture or cuisine, but because of the uncontrollable expense, talent, and temperament of their staff. Fast-food chains are taking their place by designing for readily replaceable help, people who will work on call for low wages in radically simplified, programmed tasks. The

leaders of roadside commerce demonstrate that alienation in the workplace is hardly the result of coincidence or
sadism. It is pervasive because it is part of the formula for
success. Whether their game is widgets, lodging, or the
dining experience, operations that best discipline their
workers for efficient production will surpass their rivals.

For this reason, big chains face their fiercest competition, not from middle-sized operations, but from the
smallest. Independent family enterprise is easily romanti-
cized, but in the real world it is highly disciplined.
Whether through ruthless patriarchy or intimacy in a
common cause, mom, pop, and the kids labor fiercely for
meager rewards. At the other end of the spectrum, corporate giants apply capital and industrial engineering to
the same end. Middle-sized operations are caught in between, where morale, productivity, and profits are most
endangered. Trouble is only to be expected when memories of freedom or common interest remain fresh in mind.
Managers, subfranchisers, and minority franchisees
rebel. Workers begin to organize in self-defense. It is the
Bermuda Triangle of management. Wyckoff and Sasser
explain: "Minimizing the depressed profits of the 'Bermuda Triangle' requires a careful shift from a highly per-
sonalized, informal management style and structure (typical of entrepreneurs) to a . . . style [that] stresses the
ability to work through other people by means of organizational structure and delegation, formalized reporting
and procedures, highly specific and frequent measure-
ments of performance, and a greater separation of 'own-
ership' and 'management.'"[5]

In leaving the frontier, sites along the strip like the
Carousel are making their way through the Bermuda Triangle. Survivors are not only winning profits and consumer support but also correcting some of the injustices
of the past, as in the areas of equal opportunity and occupational safety. Mom and pop offer freedom *if* you are
willing to work as long and hard as you are told and if you
are one of their kind. Highly disciplined corporations are
able to offer more consistent class and quality to more
consumers.

Yet before applauding such development, we ought to
recall some of its less tangible but profound human effects. Along with success has come greater alienation
between and within the people who occupy the strip. It is
written in their faces, exchanges, and stories. It is probably most obvious in places like the Carousel, passing
through the Bermuda Triangle, but it is also evident on
either side. With this vantage we can return to the Coralville Strip to compare the signs of the future with the remnants of the past.

The Coralville McDonald's is on First Avenue, "the new strip." The store is brand new with lush landscaping and Tudor ornamentation. It is close enough to a state-of-the-art store to be mistaken for those featured in national advertisements. Whatever your opinion of McDonald's or franchises, this site can represent some of the most modern and sophisticated attempts to satisfy consumer tastes.

Diamond Mil's is an owner-operated bar serving irregular meals and regular country-and-western music to a much more limited clientele. Millie Ollinger has rented the building as it stands for more than ten years on Highway 6, the original Strip. Mil's, then, can represent the mom-and-pop operations that once dominated the strip.

Obviously, neither business literally represents anything beyond itself. They have distinct histories of providing different services to different people on different sites. Each is modern and successful in its own way. But we still can view McDonald's as a sign of the present and compare it to the past that Diamond Mil's suggests. In the difference are some lessons on the strip.

Chapter 5. Model Offerings

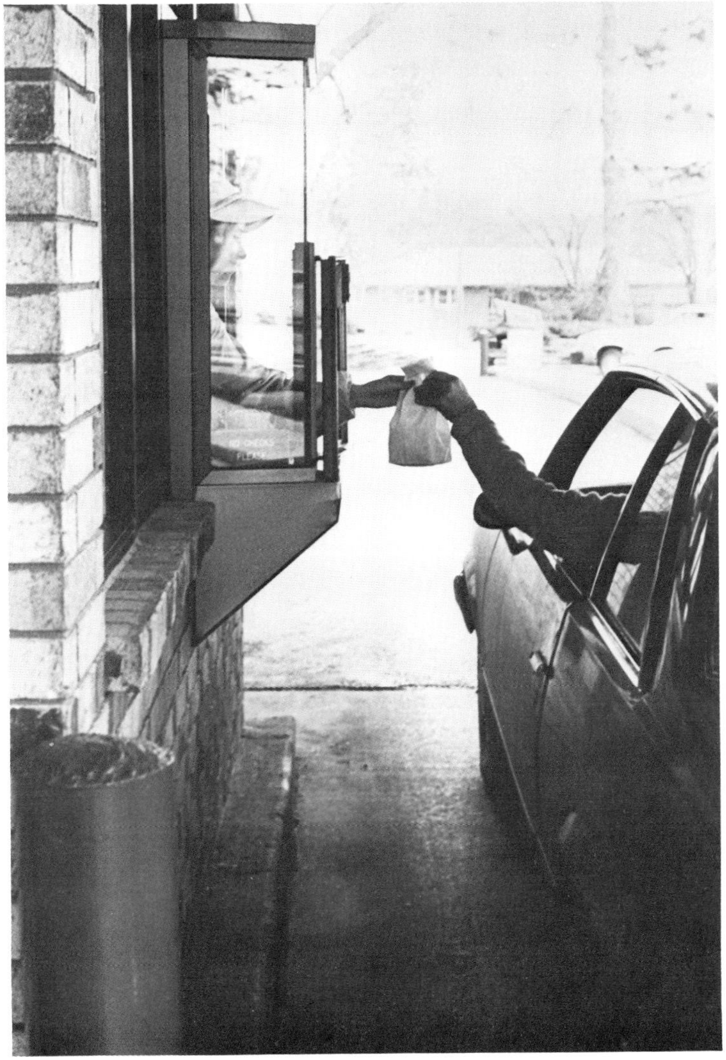

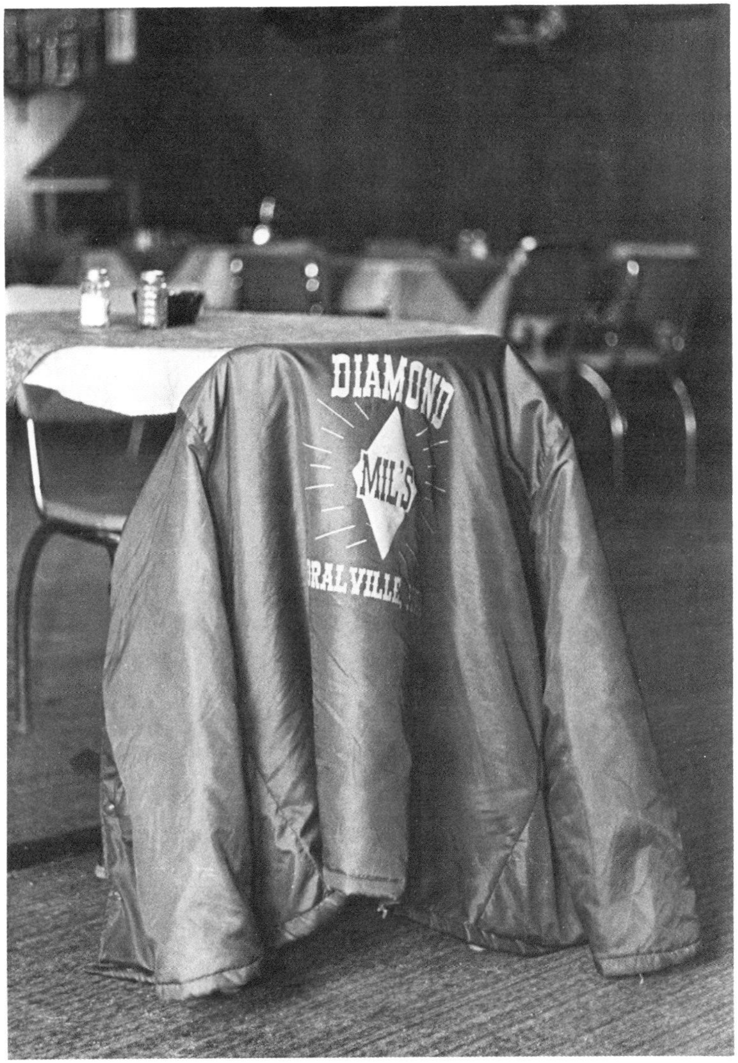
DIAMOND
MIL'S

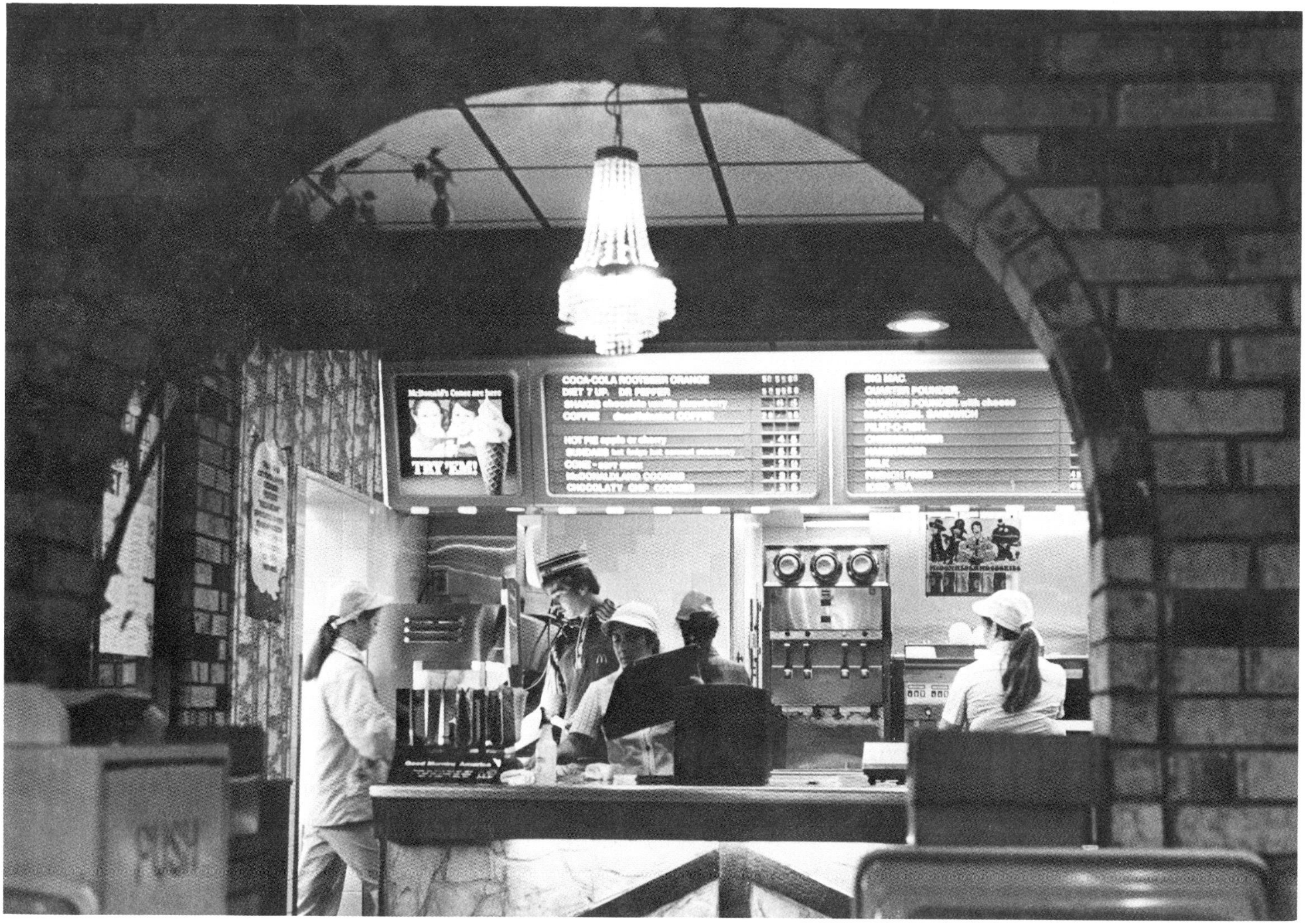
COCA-COLA ROOTBEER ORANGE
DIET 7 UP. DR PEPPER
HOT PIE apple or cherry
McDONALDLAND COOKIES
CHOCOLATY CHIP COOKIES
TRY 'EM!
BIG MAC.
QUARTER POUNDER.
MILK
FRENCH FRIES
PUSH

Mac's–Making It Your Way

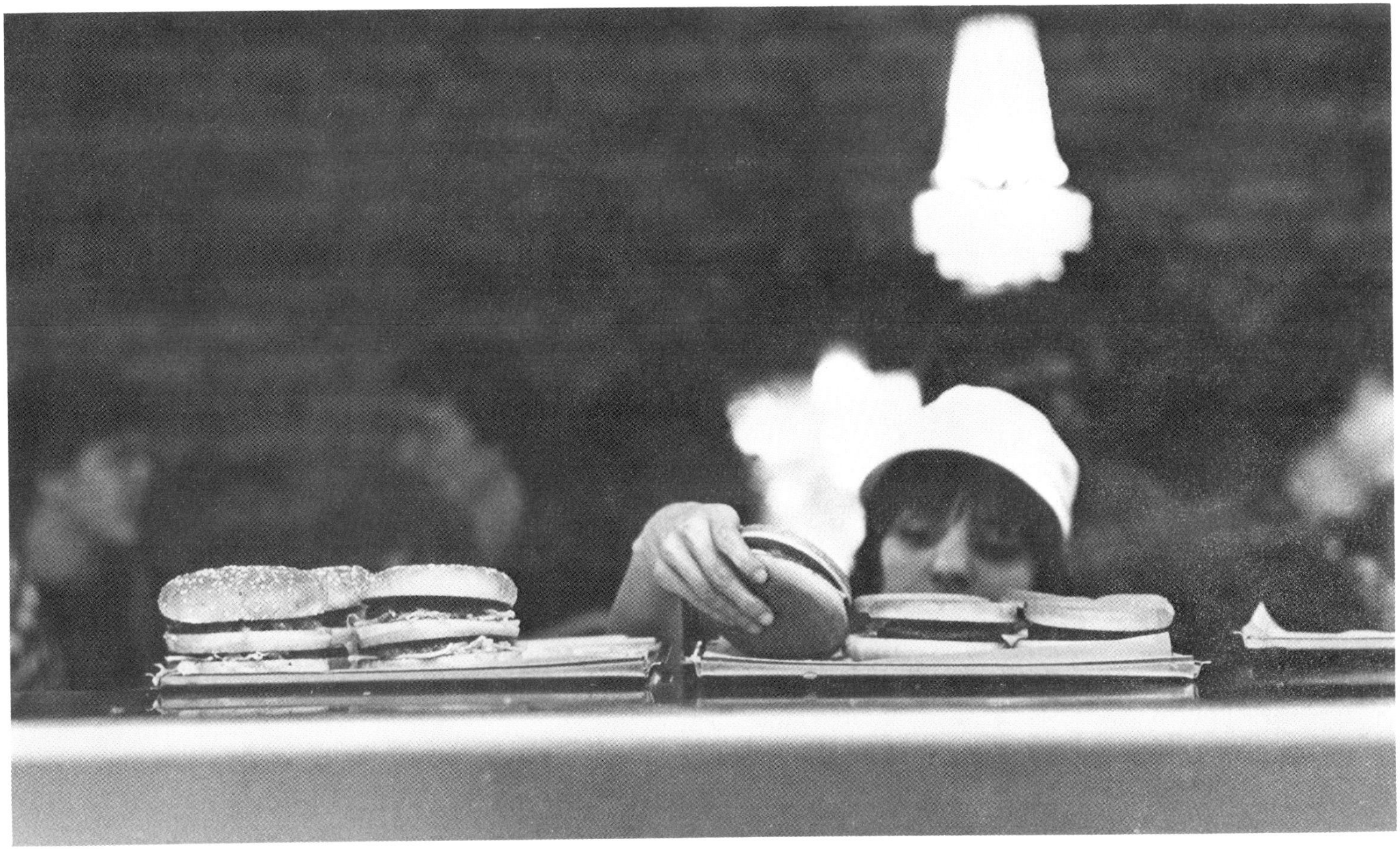

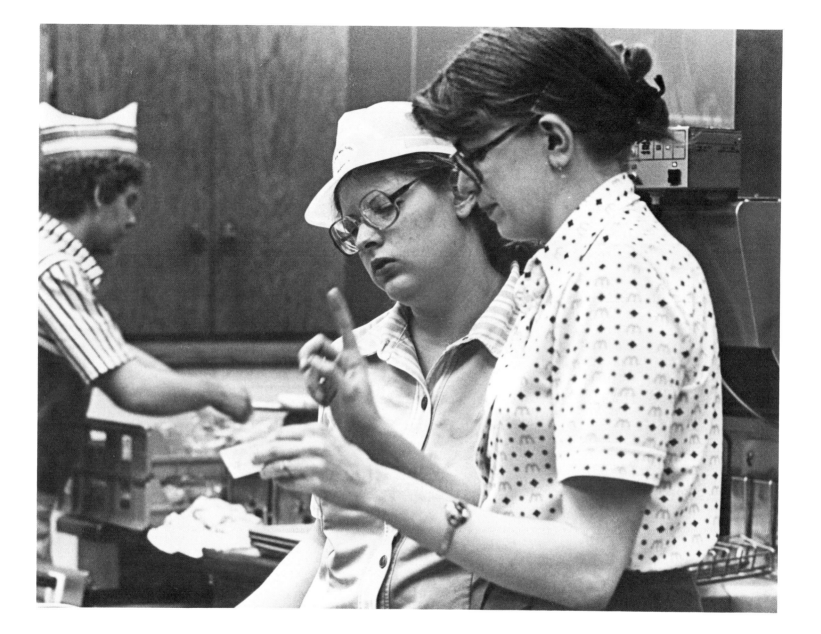

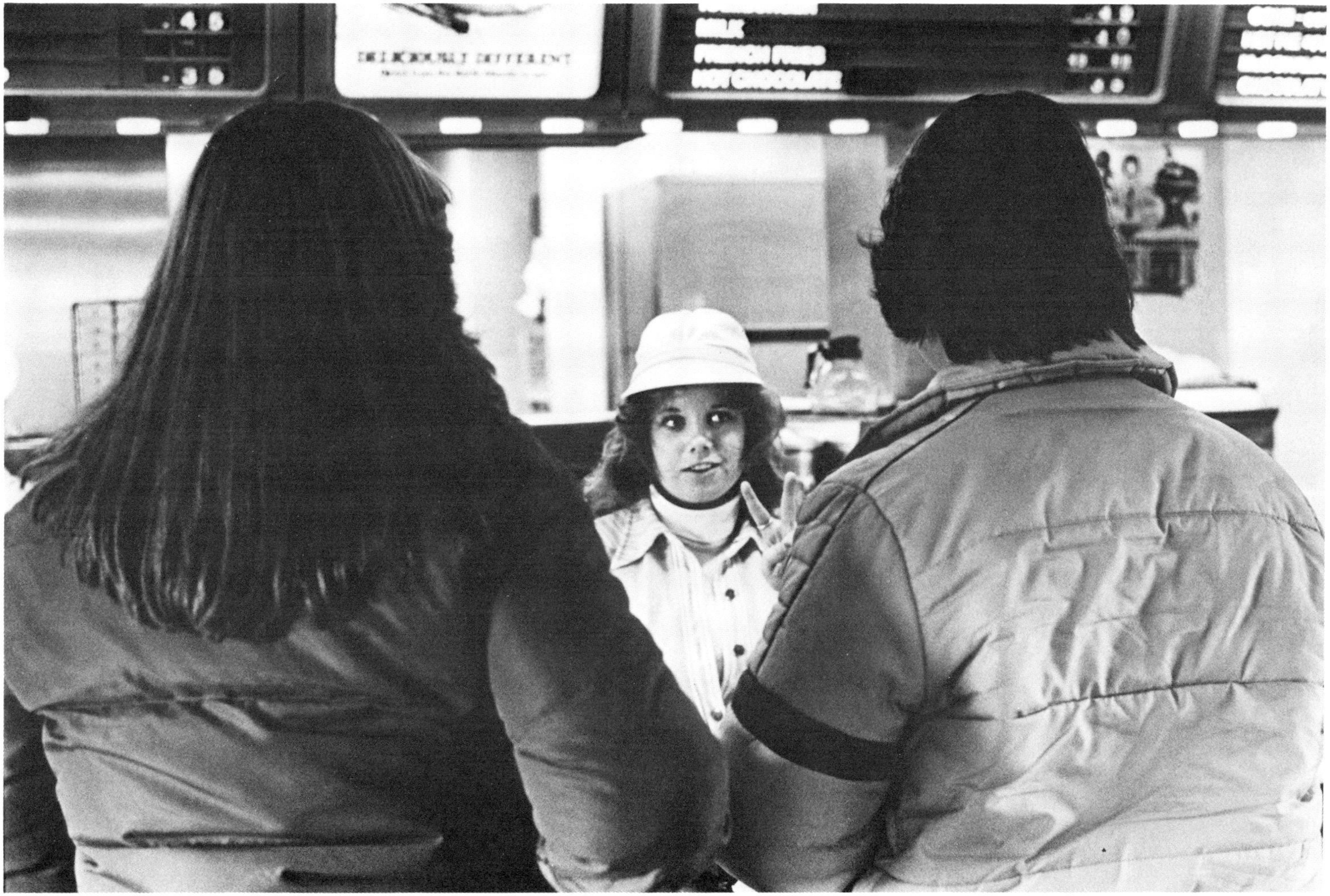
MILK
FRENCH FRIES
HOT CHOCOLATE

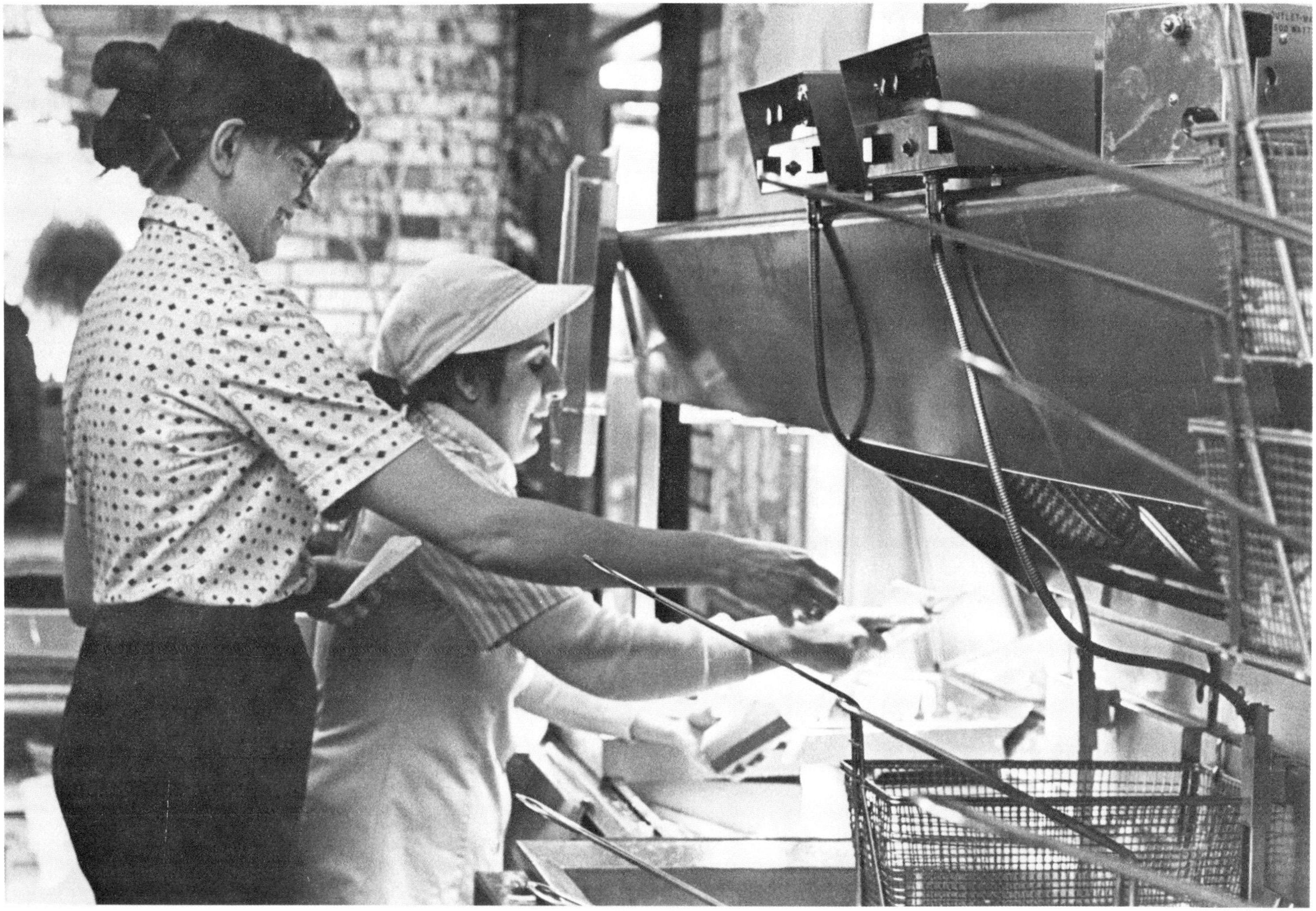

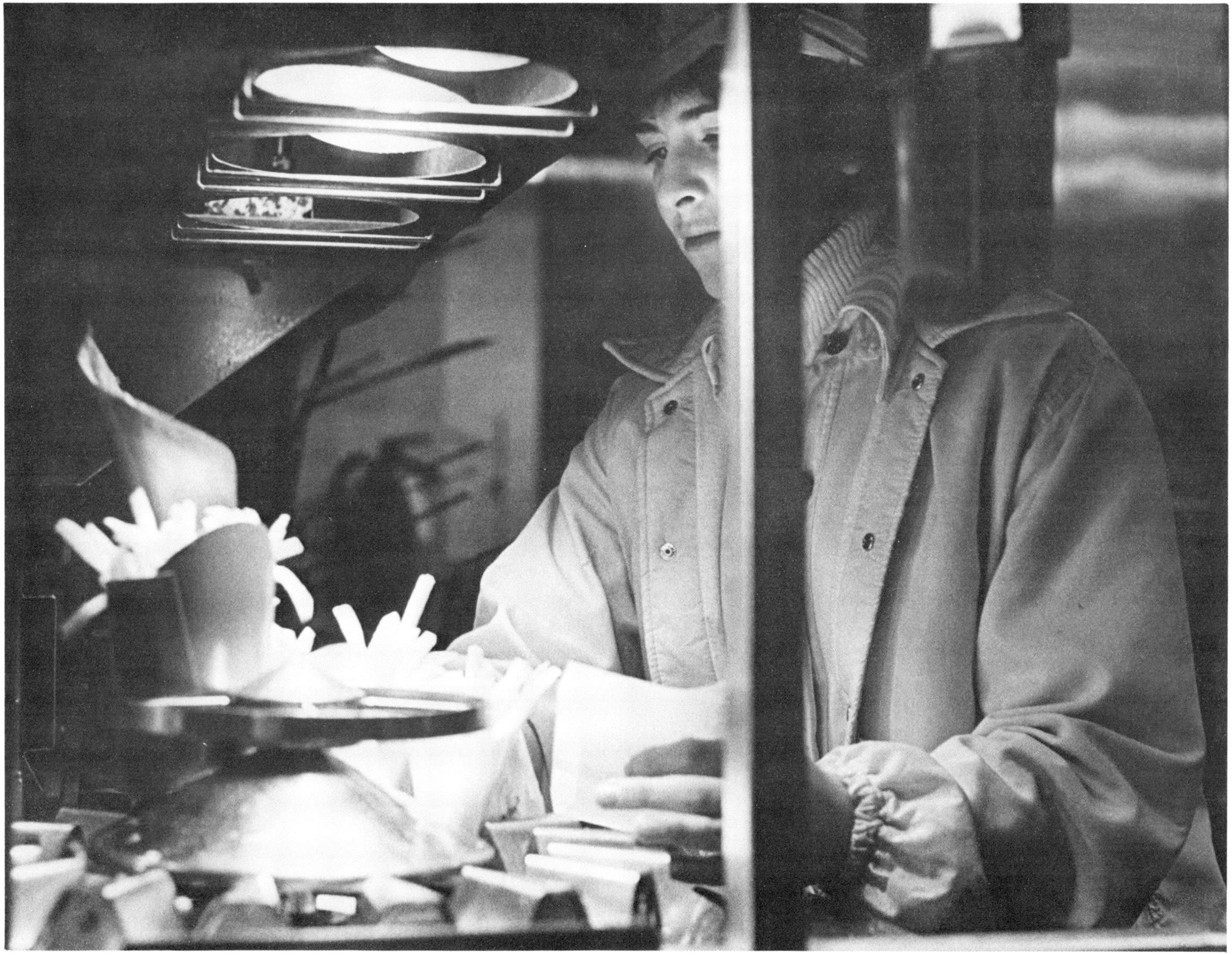

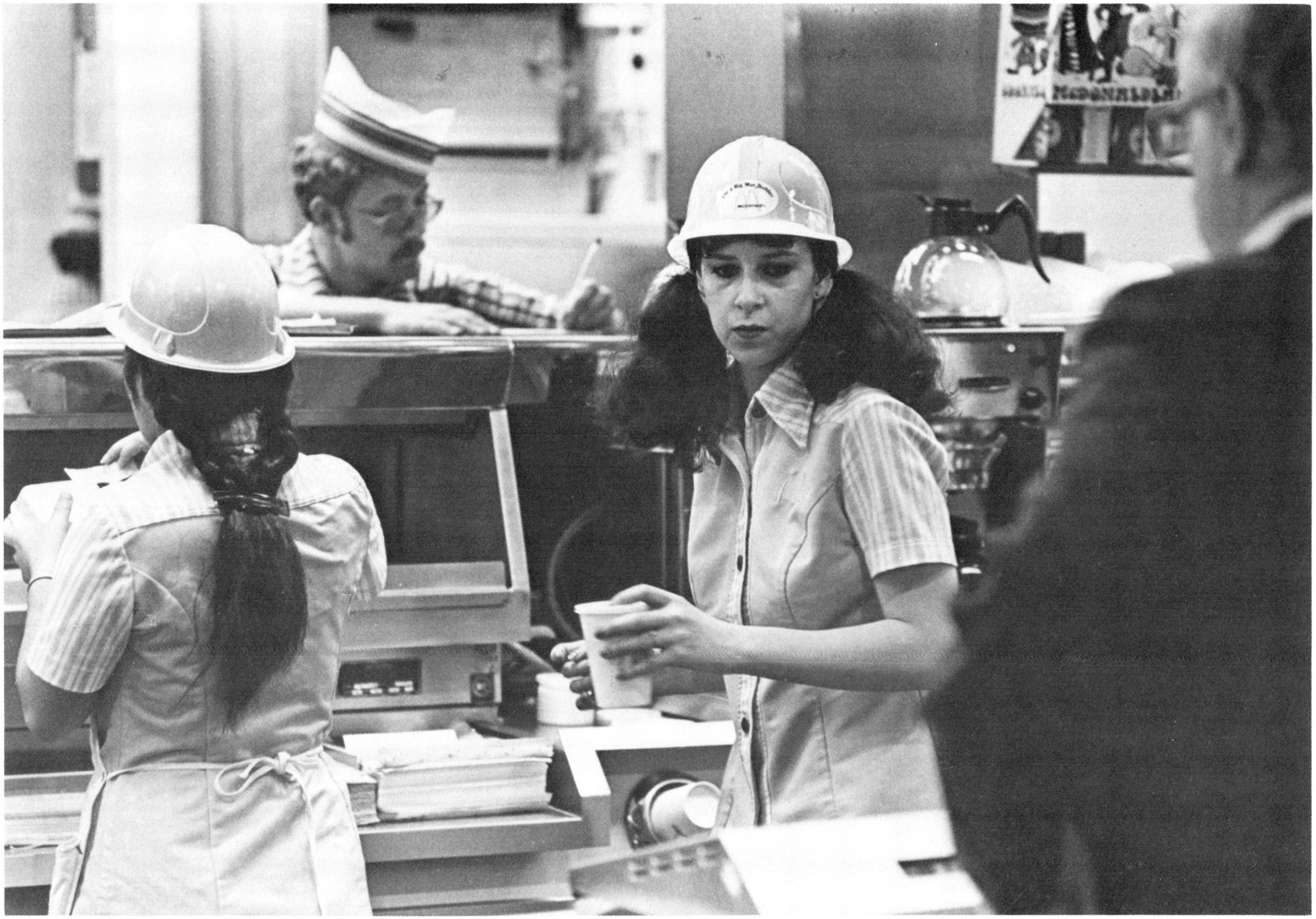

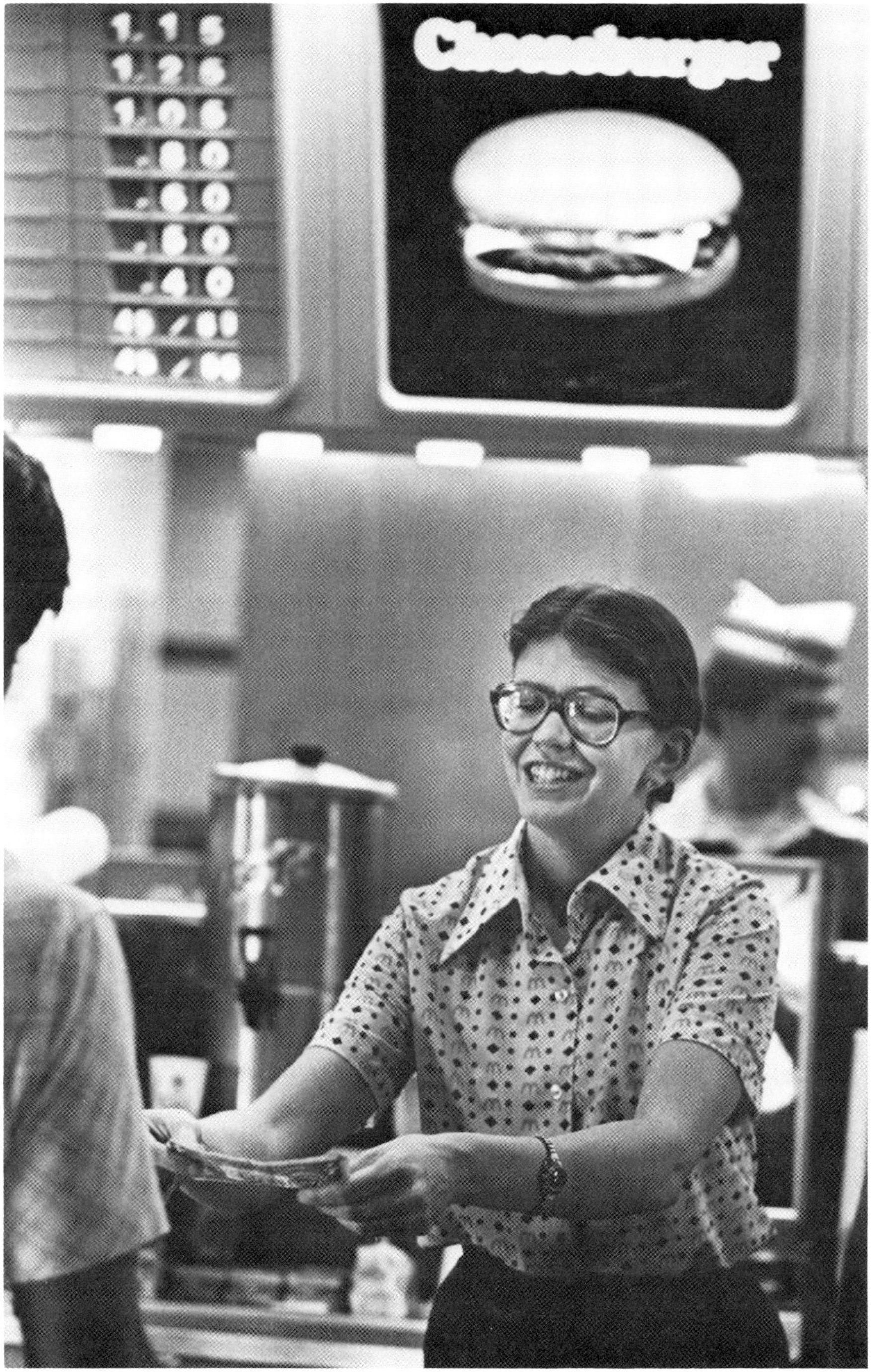
Cheeseburger

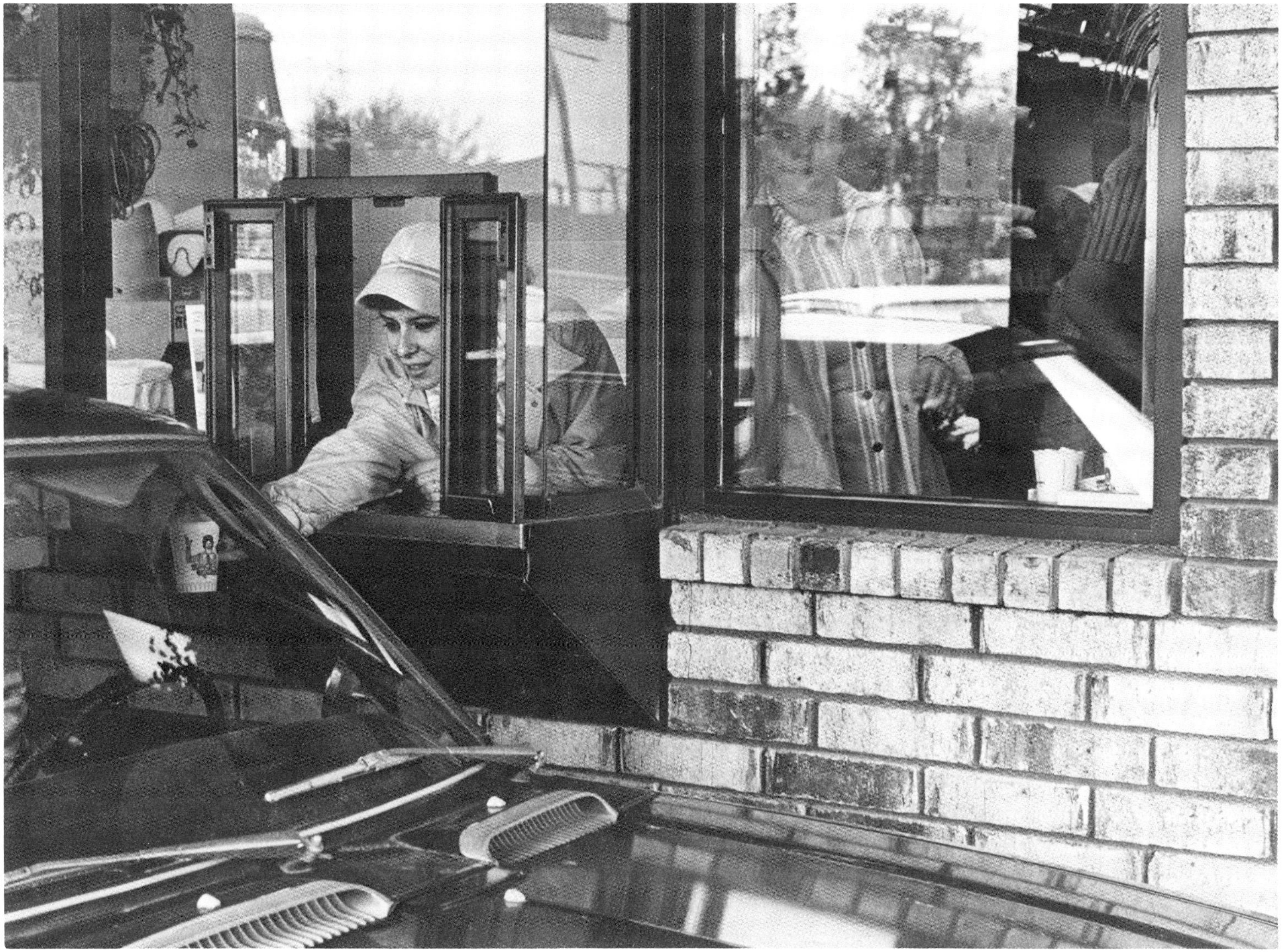

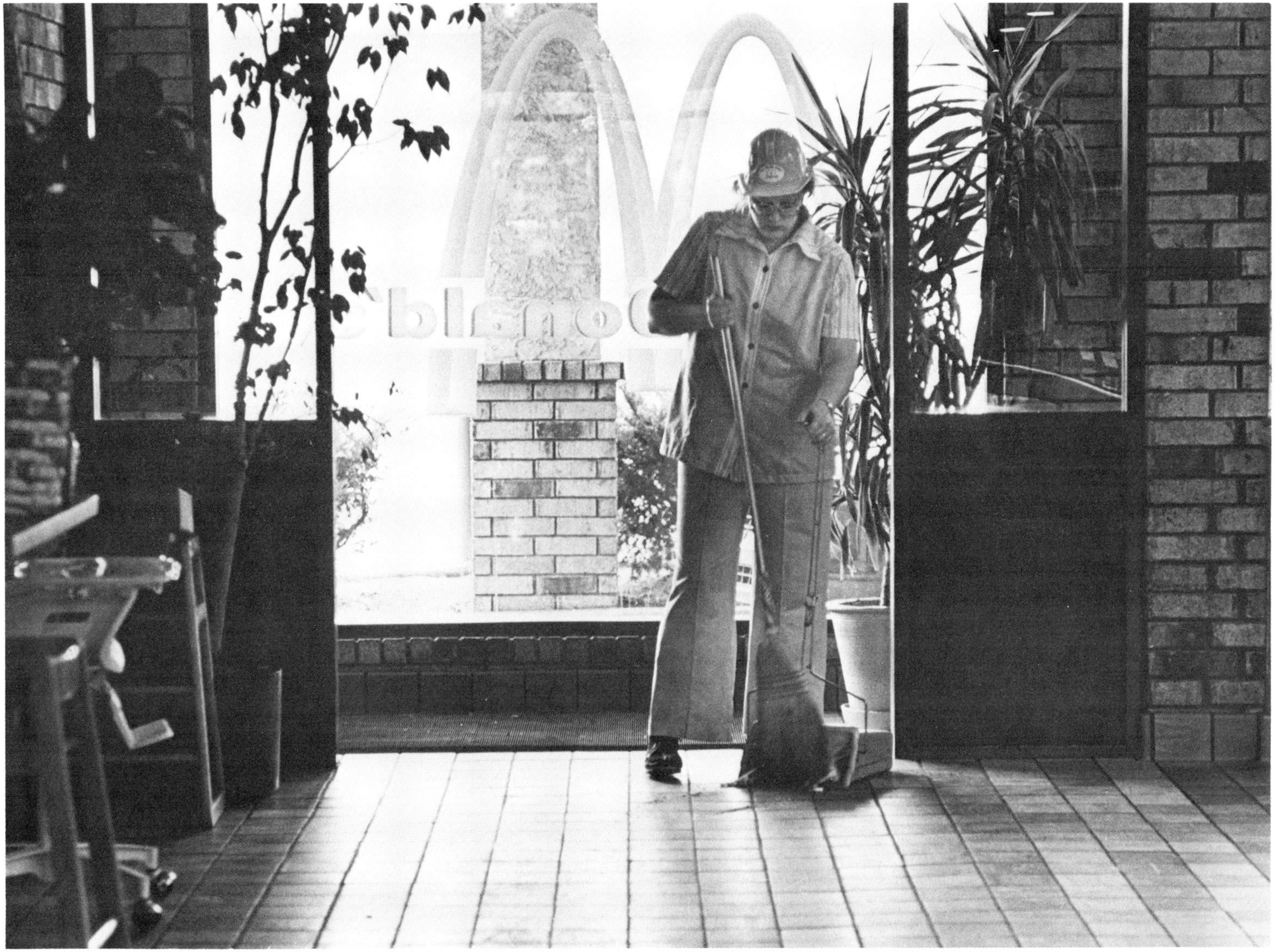

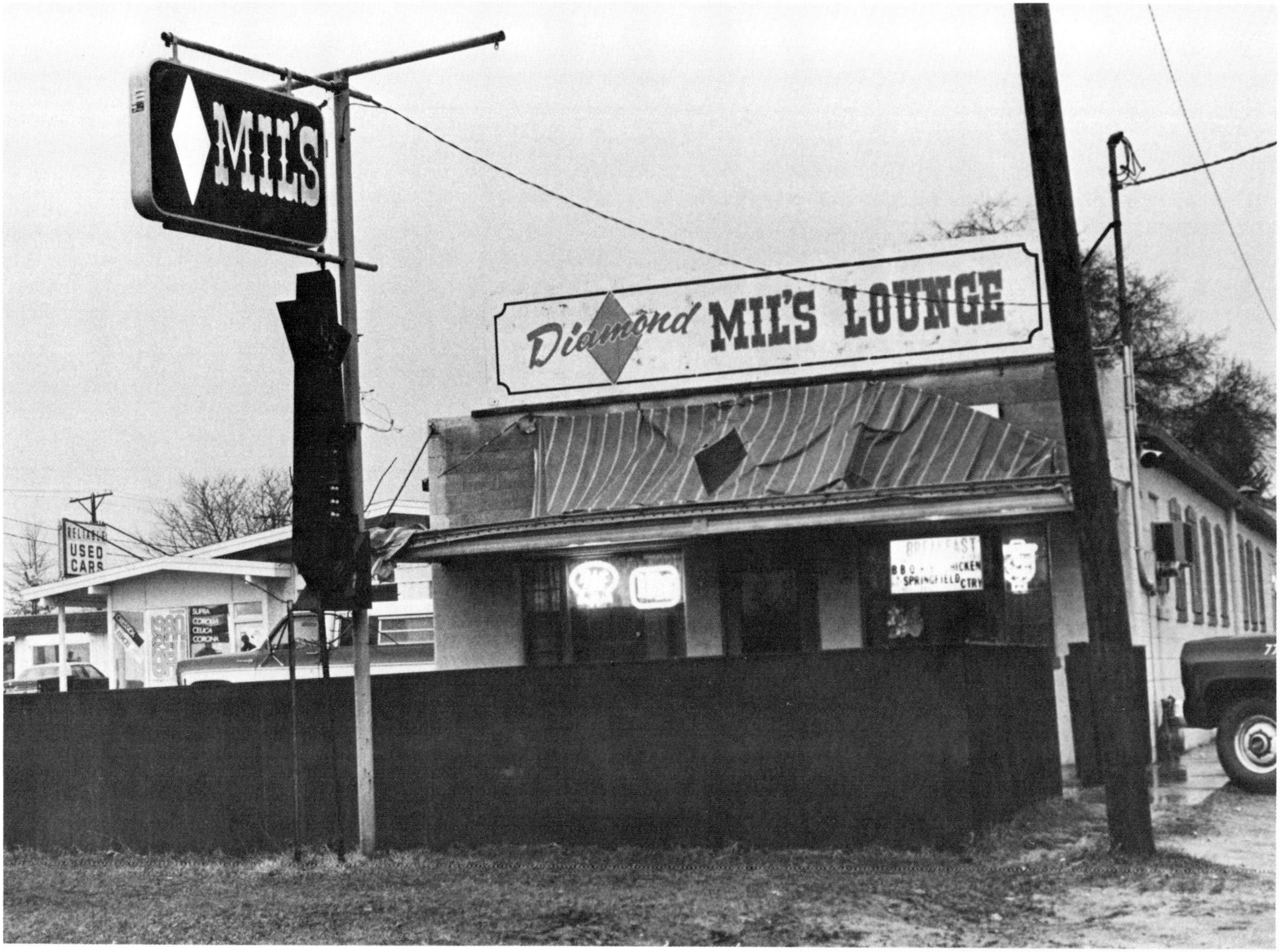
MIL'S
Diamond MIL'S LOUNGE
USED CARS
SPRINGFIELD CTRY

Mil's

Diamond Mil's is a model mom-and-pop operation or, more properly, a ma operation, Ma Mil's. In the afternoon, a slow, quiet time, you might stop and strike a conversation with Ma that would touch upon the history of her bar, the routines, the decor, the regulars, the music, local politics, or sports. I have put together a monologue that addresses such things in her own words.

Of course, it is not a typical discourse in itself. She usually does not have time for much gab. Most of her patrons know her only as "Ma," "Diamond," or "Millie," that plump woman who dishes out hugs, "Darlin's," and "Honeys" as amply as the potatoes and gravy at her lunch line. When things get busy, at noon or after 8:00 p.m., she struts here and there to direct the help and make sure everyone is having a good time. She may put an arm around your shoulders, give a hearty squeeze, and chant, "Can we get you anything?" or "Had enough to eat?" or "How about a smile, sweet thing?" She asks a regular about a sick nephew or wonders if a construction job will get workers indoors before the cold sets in. With newcomers she may talk politics, the Hawks, or TV. It is her bar, and its atmosphere is inseparable from her personality and the image of the patrons.

Outside the bar, insofar as she is known at all, she is considered, as she puts it, a bit "crabby." She defends her business against the slightest threat with all the grace of General Patton. On summer evenings, rattling a cowbell wildly over her head, she screams support for her softball team and derides their opponents with awesome vigor. All of this attracts the affection of her patron family and the contempt of her enemies. She simply has "no use for"

the town fathers, the Chamber of Commerce, and the ABC crowd, or, for that matter, most of the world surrounding her home for close to sixteen hours per day.

While other strip businesses "beautify" their sites with plantings directed toward passing motorists, Millie confines her landscaping to a small yard behind a plywood barrier. An attached, bounded drinking area is required for licensure, but a cheap rope fence would have sufficed. Instead, her landscaping is reserved for customers, neatly partitioning her homey bar from the hostility and chaos beyond.

This introduction to her place is set in one of those quiet afternoons. She just got out of the University Hospital. In fact, the stitches from her intestinal-bypass surgery will not come out for another week. She figures that her family has too long a history of heart disease and she too many vices to trust another diet. Besides, "Maybe I won't be so crabby, if I don't have all this fat to drag around." A few patrons linger over a draft, their pickups lined outside. Near the dance floor the jukebox plays "Take This Job and Shove It," while the television tunes in a soap over the bar. Millie has time to chat while they ready for the evening rush. As usual, things are not running as smoothly as she would like, a little too messy and behind "schedule." While we talk, Millie barks instructions, takes deliveries and some ribbing from the regulars.

So this is Diamond Mil's, my bar.

You should have seen it before. In 1971, it was just an empty room. Some of the carpeting was here and paneling. We had the dance floor with a black wrought-iron fence around it, but it was an empty building. They had

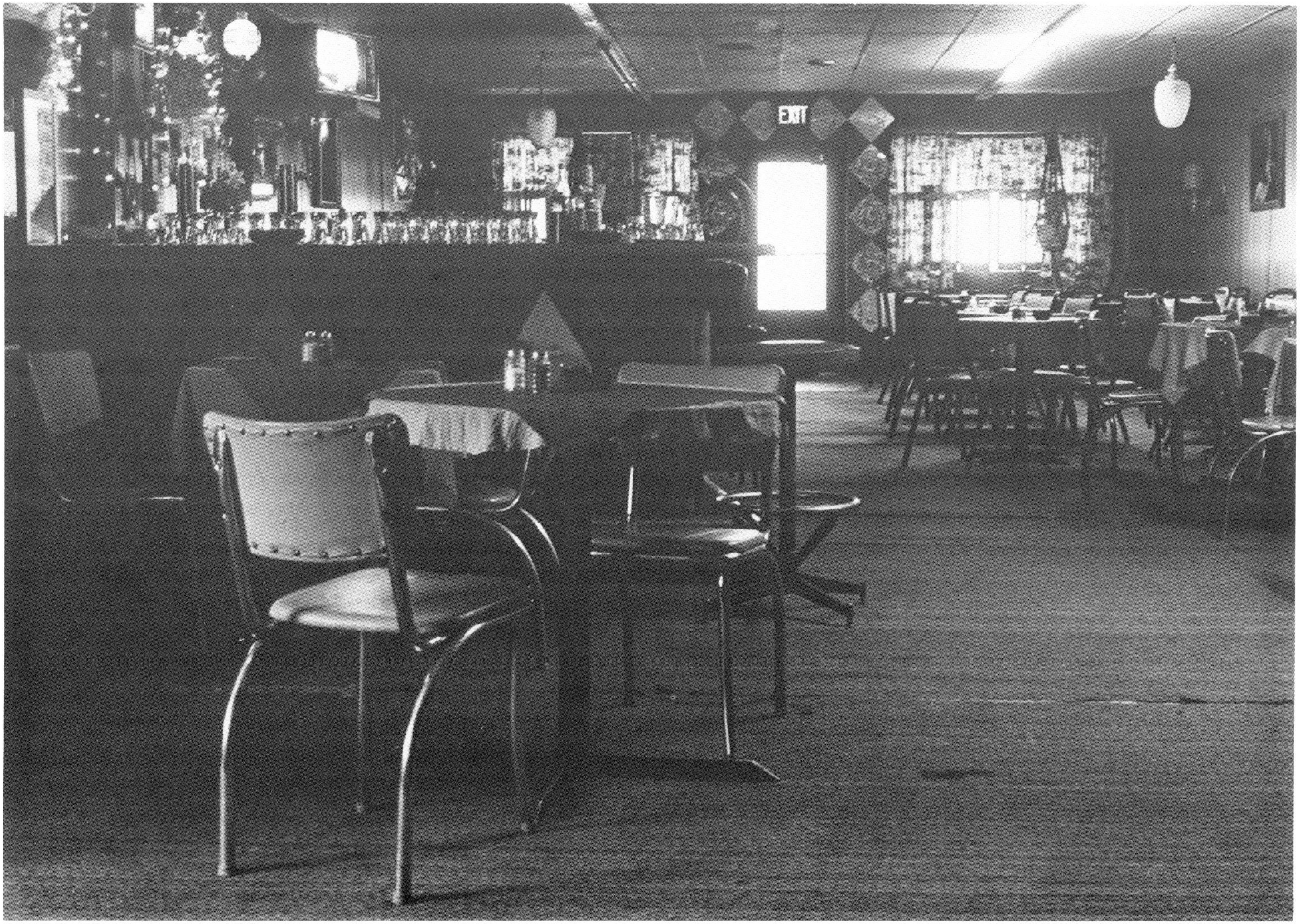
EXIT

used it for pinball machines and stuff, like Funhouse, U.S.A., but they closed up. And before that it was an old mattress factory with two cement floors. There's like nine inches of cement here. So we had to use a jackhammer to get down for a drain. That was the biggest challenge.

Then, once we got that done, a guy (I can't remember his name) built the bar here. I didn't even have a back bar, just card tables in the back when I started out. We had enough carpet to patch in here and there, and we built our bar. Then my husband made all these tables. But we didn't have that right away.

First I only had draft beer. That's all, because I was going to run it myself, just open at four in the afternoon. This went on for, oh, six weeks till I about killed myself, and I decided I better get some help. I used to do all the cleaning and everything. I'd work till two o'clock in the morning and then have to drive thirty-five miles home to Keota. My husband worked nights at the VA, so he already commuted back and forth to Iowa City. I had been working different places around here probably ten years before I decided to have my own business.

It was the challenge I wanted. I first worked at the University Hospital as a supervisor of the cafeteria coffee shop. But I always wanted to be a hostess, so I went and was a hostess at Howard Johnson's for two years. And then I wanted to learn to tend bar, so I went to the Carousel. I used to run the Port-of-Call Bar down there.

It was a fun place. It really was! They had their whirlpool, and regular people would come down. It was kind of like a family-type thing. But once in a while—say, they'd be down there having a good time—one of the personnel would come and say, "Don't be so noisy. Hold it down. We have a meeting down in the room." Or, before I had to close at 10:30, they'd be calling down to say, "Bring the customers up to the upstairs bar." Well, I didn't feel I had the right to tell the customers where to go. I mean, if they wanted to be up there, they'd be up there, you know. Some of them would get a little upset,

too. They'd say, "Well, why don't you open your own bar? You're good in a bar, Millie."

Well, I never had thought about opening my own bar. I'd tell them that I don't have any money. I was driving back and forth from Keota, thirty-five miles, and my check was like $62 a week. Well, there was a lady staying at the Carousel, Mrs. Bidney, Muriel, from over in Illinois. Her husband, Stan, worked for Tugger Tractor there. He had never been sick a day in his life, but then, nine months before he was supposed to retire, his kidneys went bad. So she stayed at the Carousel while he was in the University Hospital. All their lives he worked and she worked, so she'd never been out anywhere. But she'd come down to the bar; she had me to talk to at night. We became good friends, and she said, "If you ever need any money, why, I'll help you." I never thought any more about it, but she kept saying, "You're going to open your own bar!" I'd say, "I don't have any money," and she'd say, "I'll help you." Not long after that, her husband passed away.

But everybody kept on it. Different customers said, "There's a building up the street. Go look at that." So, one noon hour, I come up here and looked through the window. The place was closed, had been for several months, but I decided then I wanted to do it. All you needed to put in was the bar, because the carpeting and the paneling and the dance floor and everything was there. Where the stage is at was a wall to a great big kitchen. So I'd have to move it back and build the stage on my own. And I had to pay for it on my own.

So I decided to borrow $5,000, and I called her up. I said, "Muriel, I'm ready," and she said, "Okay." A day or two later she called back and said, "Millie, I can't let you have the money." She said, "Never thought anything about it, but Stan died and I can't touch it for nine months. But you just go to the bank and get the money. I will back you." So I borrowed $5,000 dollars with her security.

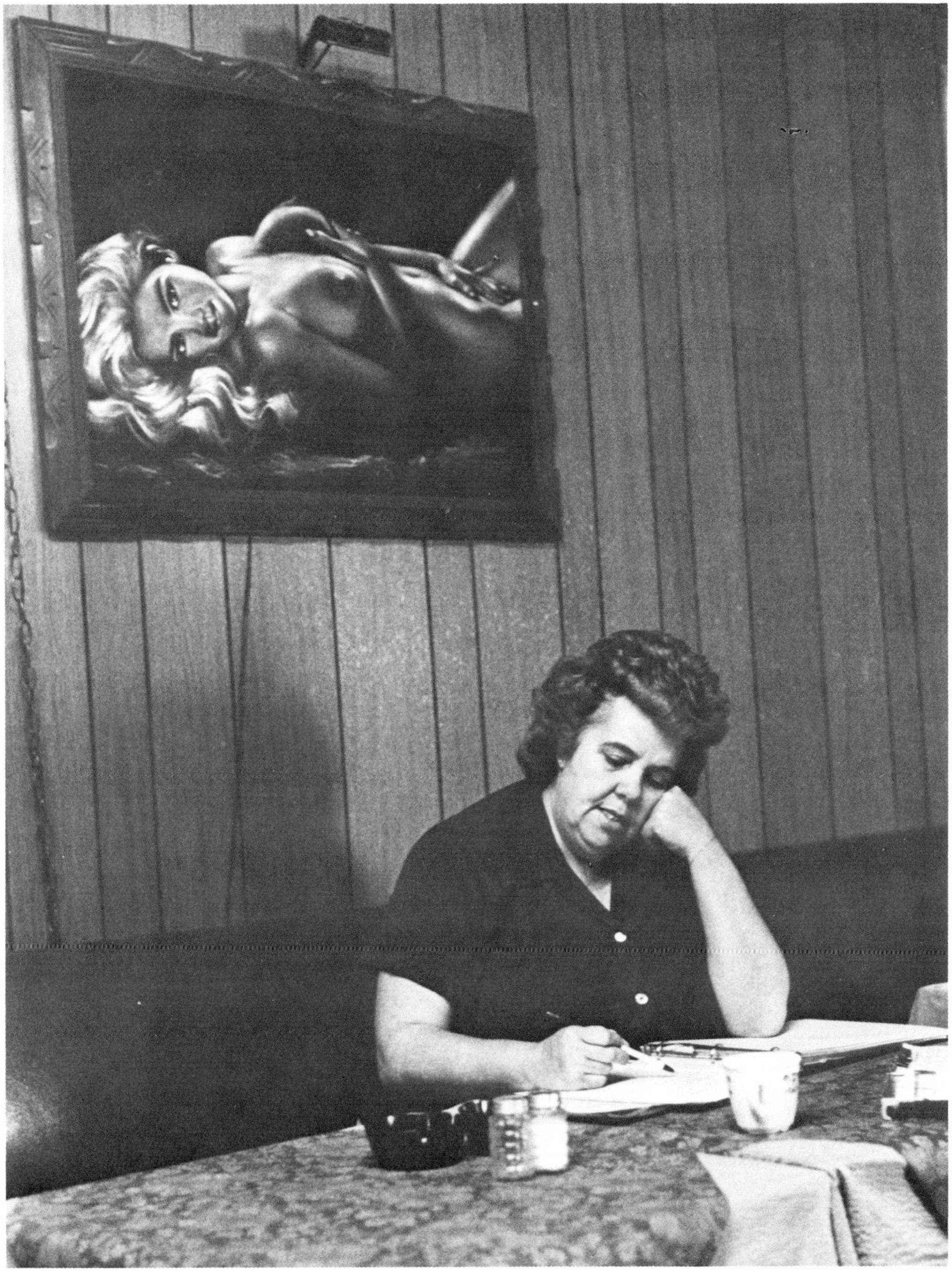

We're still close—like I stood for her when she remarried. She comes here every fall on their anniversary, stays all weekend. She has one grown son, a businessman out in Michigan. He comes and stops to see me, too. We're all good friends.

And so it was a lot of hard work. It was just push and shove. I didn't have much to operate on, just the $5,000. The first thing I bought was this player piano. That was $475. It's an antique, and I've been offered a lot of money for it, offered $1,200, but I won't sell. Once, I was just about ready to, and my daughter, Donna there, said, "Don't you dare sell that piano." It's been in every business I've ever had. This one is electrified—I think it's unplugged right now—but sometimes we sit here and have sing-alongs. I've got a truck driver that comes in here; he's a fabulous piano player. He'll come in on his way home at night and play two or three songs. I've got a couple of them, in fact, that come in right here, sit down and play. They enjoy it. And they don't play it electrically, you know. They play it!

But I've taken it everywhere. It was here, my first place, and I took it with me when I bought Bill Hopp's in Cedar Rapids. And when I sold that place, it went with me down to Cou Falls, right across from the Ranch Supper Club.

I called those places "Diamond's Water Hole." I didn't want to use "Diamond Mil's #2" or anything like that, but I wanted people to know they were connected. I got the original name when I was up at the State Fair. I knew I was going to open up this bar, but I didn't know what I was going to call it. I was just sitting there, you know, waiting for the kids to come back from wherever they went. I was looking up, and there was "Diamond Jack's." Everybody was having a big time, just really whooping it up, and I thought, "Diamond Jack's . . . Diamond Lil's . . . Diamond Mil's!" And that's how I named it. I just called the other places "Diamond's Water Hole" to show, you know, they were connected.

I bet you didn't know that Diamond's Water Hole in Cedar Rapids was the first club Mickey Gilley ever played in. I used to have people from Nashville—Cal Smith, Freddie Hart. I had Stonewall Jackson, Mickey Gilley, Trilly Cole. I brought her up to Cedar Rapids. I've always been country my whole life—Always. I've been to Nashville. I've got a lot of valuable records, like I've got pretty near all of Jim Reeves. I was a fan of his even before he ever got killed. And I've got a lot of 78 records.

Anyway, if you've never worked in a bar, you wouldn't know. It's interesting! Look behind the bar. We have an automatic dishwasher. (You watch this gal here.) It puts the soap and everything right in there. See, there it's on. You just turn this way; your water comes there. And it has the soap, and that's clear. There, that's your rinse water. And it's all hooked up to jugs underneath. And here's the tap box, where we keep our keg beer—holds four kegs of beer. It came from the Big Ten Inn, down on Riverside Drive, when they had their sale. And then this here is a glass chiller. You bring them out, and there you have your frosty mugs. And we have our blender here.

There's my buddy Mickey! I've got pictures of him all around. See, he signed this one: "You're beautiful! Love You Always, Mickey." Here's one of him and all his band. This is the road manager here. This is his club down in Pasadena, which is about fifteen miles out of Houston, Texas. Yeah, Gilley's Club. It's in the World Book of Guinness. It's the largest club in the world. It seats 3,300. It's not fancy (in this one you can see the tops is cardboard), and there's just little tables. Nothing much, you know, but the biggest in the world!

A lot of this stuff on the wall, signs or whatever, the companies give them to us. But look at this, an old Ford horn. (Honk! Honk!) This guy was going through, and it was my birthday. He went out in the car and brought this in to me. (Honk! Honk!) We had more fun with that baby, got it about wore out, squeezing it so.

Catfish $2.
Pork Steak $2
Sausage/Kra
4
Bill Wells
Ed Ketsenburg
Elliot Ohrens

Pabst
Blue Ribbon
BEER

And this is things that different customers gave. This here (is it a Buddha?) was sent to me in the mail with a note saying they thought it looked so much like me. So I don't know who sent it! Ha! I guess they were making fun of my boobs or belly or something. Ha!

My liquor license is there. When I first came here, 1971, it was like $750. It's up to $950 now. It's pretty much a matter of putting up the money. You can't have any felony. You know, if you're an upstanding citizen, as long as you try to run things half-way right, there should be no problem.

This here is my little bartender here, Georgia. This gal is the one who paints. She's an artist. She painted those bags over the air conditioner there for me. They're just garbage bags to keep the cold air from coming in. There's one that says "Mil's Ranch," the one with the cabin by the mountains. We had her put that on there, because I said, "That's where I'm going to retire! That's Diamond Mil's Ranch." Isn't that right, Georgia?

[Georgia:] "Yeah. But I forgot to put the tail on the windmill."

I wondered what was wrong with that windmill!

[Georgia:] "Yeah, I was halfway to Texas on my vacation, and I said, I should go back and put the tail on that windmill."

She made those macrames up front, too. She does that for me. She's always doing something.

These other paintings I got from a guy in town. Pretty wild, huh? He just came in here—he was a little down on his luck at the time—so I bought a couple of them. Customers seemed to like them, so I bought a few more.

Back here's the dance floor. Right now it's set up for lunch line. We just got done so everything's messy still, but this all comes off. This is where that wall was. We cut the wall out and moved it back for a stage room. Then that made my kitchen. It's really very small. I've just been serving food, oh, about two years, anywhere from fifty to seventy people a day. I do all the cooking, just like you're cooking at home. I don't have any deep-fat fryer and all. Everything is made in a big cast-iron skillet or an electric roaster. Like today, I had barbequed beef and I had ham and beans on cornbread. I have country-fried steak or fried chicken, just like you'd cook at home. I have two specials a day, and then we make some salads. In fact, there's some left if you're still hungry. We haven't put everything away. Anyway, the meal is composed of your meat and potatoes—we have mashed potatoes or country-fried, potatoes and gravy—and a vegetable, your bread and butter, and then your drink is extra. $1.90 is what I get for a meal.

(We've just got to get this cleaned up! We all was kind of late for work this morning. Jim overslept, and I had phone calls, and all. This has been a backwards day for us. . . . Jim, want to get this floor right away!)

We just clean this up and leave it during the week. Then on weekends it all folds and goes back, so we have our dancing here when the bands come in, Friday and Saturday. Of course, we have special parties, too, like our Oktoberfest. Or I have private parties, anniversaries, family dinners. We have a lot of hospital parties here. On Fridays I've got several groups that come out. They bring their hors d'oeuvres or I fix them some. And if they want a keg of beer, I'll just set it up on a table and sell it to them for what it cost me, if they're regular customers. My only stipulation is that, if they have it on a Friday night, they have it all gone by 8:30 before the band starts. Otherwise other people come up, getting free drinks, and we've got to pay for that band, since I don't get a cover charge, you know. We have a regular happy hour, too, from 4:30 to 6:00, with cans of beer like 50¢ and draughts 35¢ or liquor, like double shots in a tall glass for a dollar.

The one thing you just have to see is this place on a Saturday after a football game. You wouldn't believe it! We'll have to get you here early and sit you in a corner just so you can watch. We get them in here after the

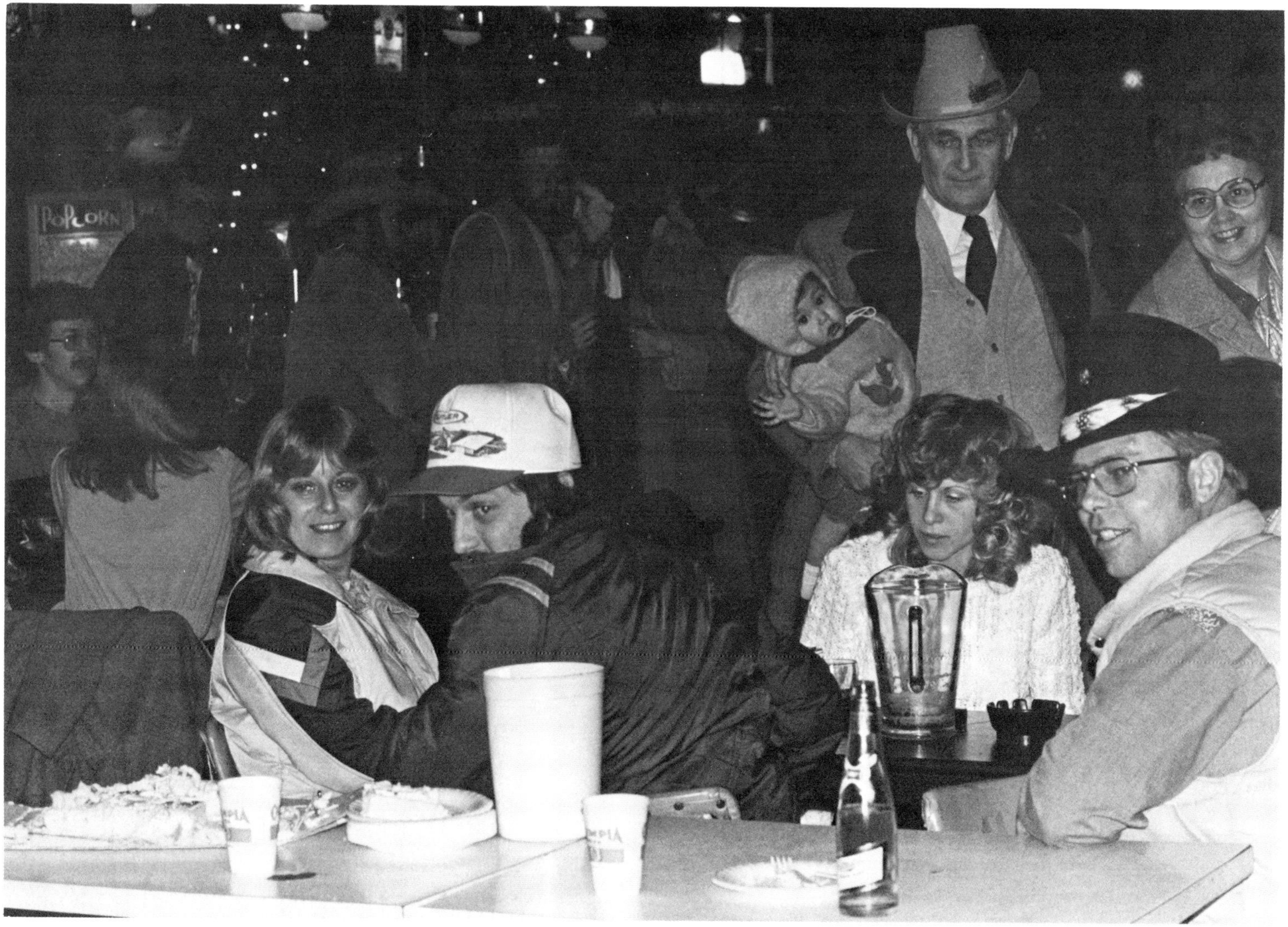
POPCORN

game, fill the place up—every inch of it, including the yard outside, every inch! They sing; they dance on the tables. It's wild! You know, I get a lot of locals in here. Well, they come in around 3:00 just to get a seat at the bar so they can watch!

The music means a lot. Like over here is our jukebox. As you can see, we have country and western music on here! There might be a few seasonal things. For Saint Patrick's they put on Irishmen songs, or there's ones for Easter time, New Year's, or Christmas. But you'll never see any rock on here. You know, I think you can control a place with your music. That kind of determines your clientele. It really does. A lot of people think I'm crabby about my music, but I have been strict because I am country. I maintain I have a country bar, and so why should I put on disco and rock, when everybody else in town has got it? And I've had a lot of people traveling through say, "Boy, you have got a super jukebox!"

Like this row here, the one farthest to the right, never comes off. Of course, there's a lot of Mickey Gilley's on here. And I was to Hawaii, so we have "Tiny Bubbles" with Don Ho. And there's a lot of Jim Reeves'. I'm a real Jim Reeves fan, like "Rock Island Line." (See my railway sign on the stage there? "Rock Island"—I got that when they were building the Maiden Lane bridge. The only thing I ever regret is that there were two of them and I didn't get them both!)

The other records change, the yellow ones. They go by how many times they've been played, unless there's some that I really want to keep on. Hagen's TV takes care of it, and they're very good to me, good to deal with. Of course, I still have to keep an eye on it. Lots of times you run into it with a female vocalist, you know. Or take Ronny Milsap—he's a super, super guy, but some of his songs lately are getting really hairy. He's got a couple of them out where he's just like yelling, you know. I like harmony. I like a song that's got meaning to it, not a song that's got three words, repeating them over and over;

there's no meaning to it, just a bunch of racket. I can go along with country rockers. There are some pretty country rock songs, but still. . . .

Sometimes the jukebox men will come in when I'm not here, or I'll have a new gal behind the bar who will call them up—"We heard this song; we want this song"—and they put it on. This happened a few months ago. I had a whole bunch of songs on here; I didn't even know what they were saying. Well, it turns out somebody had called down and asked for them on the jukebox. I said, "Hey, look. Either I call or I authorize it. My help is not telling me what I'm putting on this jukebox!" So now nothing goes on unless I okay it.

It's the same way with my bands. I do not have loud bands. When you come in here, you will be able to sit at your table and carry a conversation when there's a band playing, or they won't be playing here. When my girl goes up to the bar there, and the bartender can't hear her order, they're too loud. I have local bands that won't play here anymore because of this. They can play other places, but this is my establishment and I'm paying them. If they're too loud, I'll point them to the door, plug in the jukebox and turn her on.

These other places (I won't mention any names), they say it's just so loud the place vibrates. They think they're cutting me, pretending to be country, but they aren't country. They just are not! To get country music you may have young kids in the band, but you have to have some old folks in there, too. You can't have a whole band of beboppers and try and say they know country music—'cause they don't. So many of them, the young ones, are trying to record these old songs, and they're just killing the old tunes. I know, because I grew up with these old songs—"My Happiness" or . . . I could name you country songs that you never even heard of! I grew up with them. I'm pretty near fifty years old, and I've listened to Nashville ever since we had a radio, an old Delco with batteries. With me and my brother it was always country.

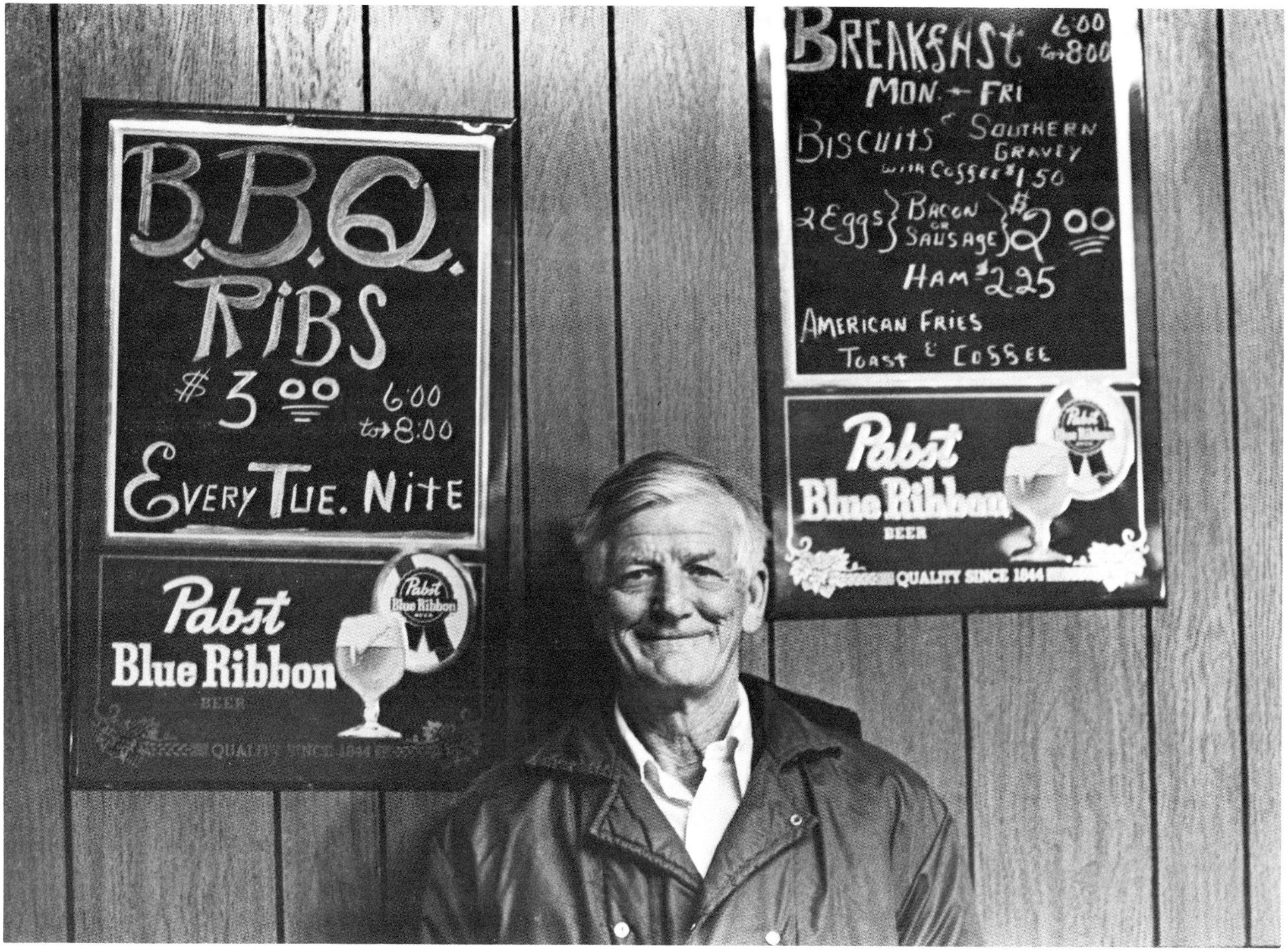
B.B.Q.
RIBS
$3.00
6:00 to 8:00
EVERY TUE. NITE
Pabst
Blue Ribbon
BEER
QUALITY SINCE 1844
BREAKFAST 6:00 to 8:00
MON. – FRI
BISCUITS & SOUTHERN GRAVEY
with COFFEE $1.50
2 Eggs } BACON OR SAUSAGE } $2.00
HAM $2.25
AMERICAN FRIES
TOAST & COFFEE
Pabst
Blue Ribbon
BEER
QUALITY SINCE 1844

So I try to hear every band before I hire them. If they'll tell me where they're playing, I'll go and listen to them. When I get on my feet again, I'm going to have to go and do a little crusading for some different bands. I like to keep them motivated.

We all sure work for our living. I have Georgia helping me on Mondays, Wednesdays, and Fridays. Then I have Millie Graham, who worked down at the Ming Gardens for years. She's got red hair, and she works on Tuesdays and Thursdays in the daytime. And then my daughter Donna helps me at noon till one o'clock, through lunch, then she goes back to Anna's Place where she's a hair stylist. She works Monday nights, too. And I have Pam Wagner that works the bar nights, Tuesday through Saturday. And I have two Pattys on the floor for band nights, just Friday and Saturday. We get by somehow. My sons help out. Nick, my second son, works on Saturday afternoons. My older sons, they both build Wausau Homes, but if we run short, one of them will tend bar, too. He used to tend bar before he took on this full-time job. So, one way or another, we get the work done.

Then, of course, there's "Jackson" over there. His name is really Jim Reid. He comes from Muscatine. He worked down at Ina Mae's for years until he lost his wife. He has a sister, Vinnie Drafahl, here in town, so he moved up here, and he does the dishwashing and cleaning for me. He's almost ready to get retirement now (he said the other day he's got to apply for it). But every bar needs an older gentleman around to do odd jobs, you know. We call him "Jackson." I think my son gave him that name. He didn't like it at first, but now it's kind of part of his life. He's very lonely, you know. Anyway, everybody teases him, and he loves it.

I wish you had a chance to meet Gay. She's moved to Springfield, Missouri, but she worked for me for five years, and she remembers everything. Why, they came up here last Saturday night. Gay mentioned things I'd forgotten about, funny things that happened like when we first opened up. I sat there and thought about them all night.

Oh, we've been through some tough ones, I'll tell you. It's laughable now, but you can imagine: you go and buy a bar three times bigger than you've got, like I did in Cedar Rapids, and you try running two of them. Gay run this one for me, and I went up there and run that one. That was something!

She's like . . . she is a daughter. Well, she calls me "Ma." Her mother died when she was two, but she has a stepmother, from Eagle Grove originally. She married a Detweiler boy, that played with the Nashville Trinity Band, but now he's on the road with a group called the Plumber Boys. They seem to be coming through every couple of weeks with their baby, playing different places in Iowa.

And, boy, that girl's got a brain on her. I don't care who walked in here, where they was from, how long it had been since they'd been here, she could tell you everything about them. You've never seen anything like it. If you came in here and you had a drink and you came back four years from now, you'd walked through that door and she'd say, "You're drinking Blue Ribbon beer, aren't you? Or have you changed since then?" You know? This is her.

I used to be that good, too. When I first opened, I could pick out salesmen, where they were from, what they sold, and what they drank. But I think when I had surgery, five or six years ago, I lost a lot of it. Maybe it was the anesthesia.

But we have a lot of nice people. Like there's Big Don, an NFL scout from Minnesota. He's just a real big, supernice guy, and he always come to see Donna and I when he's out scouting in the fall. They come from every walk of life. You know, most bars are either a college bar, or they're an old farmer's bar, or they're a businessman's bar. But there's everybody here. Like this guy from Sioux City come in one day, and he said, "Millie, how do you

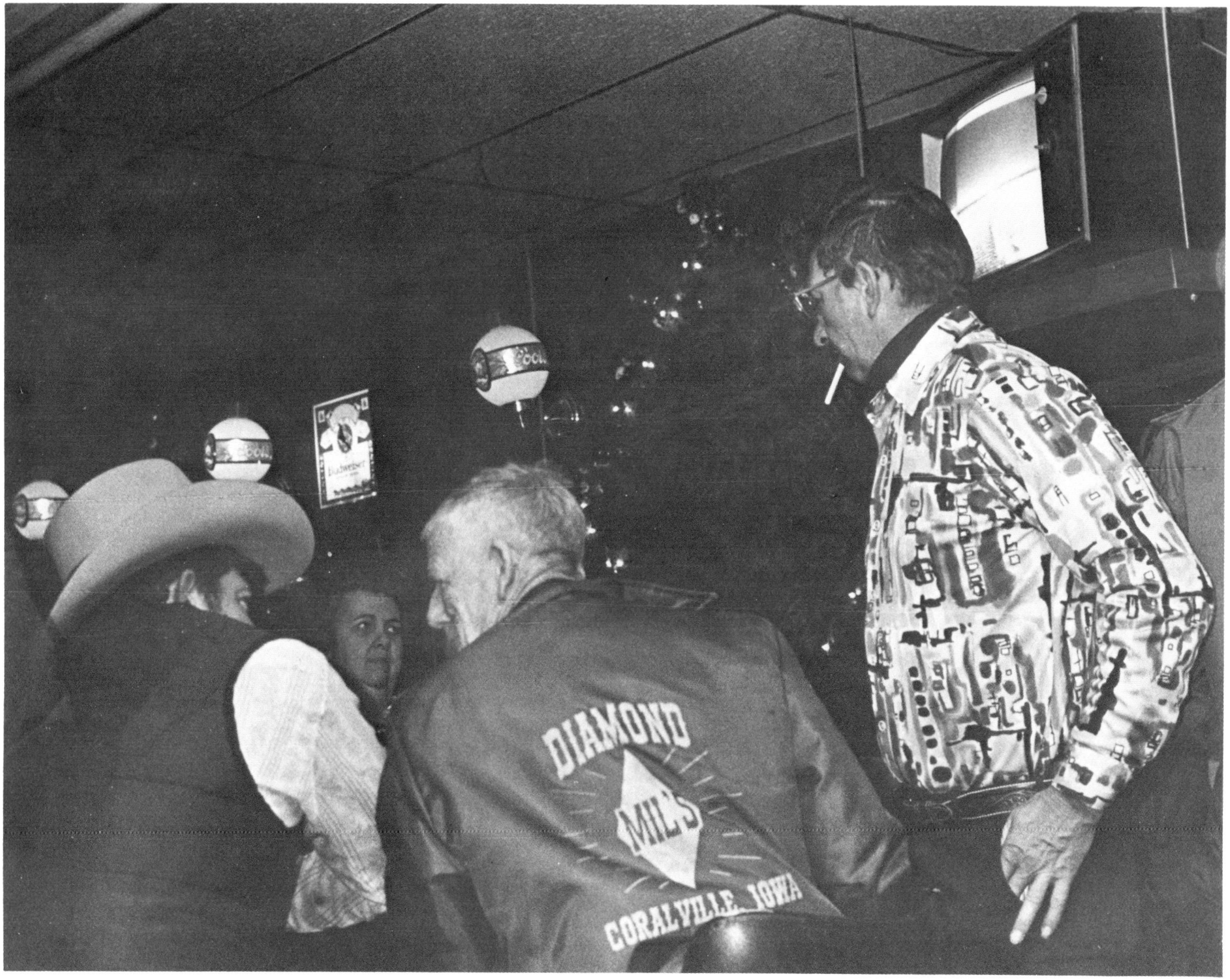
Budweiser
DIAMOND
CORALVILLE IOWA

get your clientele?" I said, "I don't know. But I have all kinds."

Well, just take a look now. That guy in the suit, he's talking to that guy in the coveralls. Look! They're talking about . . . who knows what they're talking about! He's a shoe salesman over at Wilbur's, lives in Cedar Rapids, and stops in every day. I bet he's never seen that guy before.

You know, you have young ones, you have older ones. To me, this is what's fascinating, to see people get along. This is what I really like. And I've always tried to maintain that this is what it's all about. So, I think it outweighs anything they do to you, as long as you have your thing you like and you enjoy it.

This is unmistakably *Millie's* establishment. She is there in the tap box, the piano and the juke, the decorations, the food, and the conversation. The strip outside may seem standardized and her tastes pure middle-American, but within these walls she has crafted a world distinctly her own.

Her success is making that world belong to her patrons and employees as well. They are a sort of family. There is no need for plastic grins or packaged greetings, no "have a nice day" or "have it your way." Instead, people cuss at the weather, the foreman, the Cubs, or each other, all the while expressing more genuine affection than industrial psychologists or Hallmark might imagine. Millie cannot explain how it happened nor can I. There are no operation manuals or schedules, at least none that are followed, just an alchemy of events and personalities.

In short, Diamond Mil's is a place with character, just the sort of place that strips are not supposed to house. It is, in fact, a kind of American ideal. Here are common men and women served good times by a woman whose gifts are luck and pluck. What could be more classically heroic? Here is democracy, success, and community under one roof. Its appeal in these respects is the same as that of cantinas, cafes, and general stores memorialized in lore. According to the same lore, nothing is quite so subversive of these traditions as a strip. But in Diamond Mil's and other mom-and-pop operations we can see that this need not be the truth. They suggest great continuities between small towns and business of the past and the modern strip. Character survives.

Yet, as Millie's story invites mythic interpretations, it diverts attention from the sheer labor involved. "Luck and pluck" on a daily basis look more like a bushel of potatoes being peeled, sliced, and country-fried before eleven in the morning and tables being wiped at two the next.

In addition to hours and exertion, there are more formidable obstacles. Every year along the Coralville Strip two or three independently owned businesses like Millie's fold. For example, after the oil embargo, a number of gas station owners were convinced to sell their properties to their suppliers, the majors. Instead of doing their own accounting and feeling driven to work long hours, they could just follow corporate instructions. Within five years, most of these owners-turned-managers were replaced or their stations simply closed, often with only a day's notice. Working-class bars and restaurants have been particularly hard hit since the early 1970s. There were about a half-dozen blue-collar bars to choose from a half-dozen years ago. Now there are two. Some of the regulars and owners of those defunct establishments are new regulars at Mil's.

Of course, small business has always been perilous. For decades almost as many of them have folded as have begun. Given the growth in the work force, this means a steady decline in the percentage of people working in mom-and-pop shops. The number of small businesses per capita has been falling for at least a century. Today a small number of corporations, fewer than 1 percent, control more than half the nation's corporate assets. Moreover, these large corporations, particularly

those with assets exceeding $100 million, annually enjoy both a greater rate of per capita growth and an increasing share of national sales. The losers in this story are smaller companies, and the smaller they are, the greater their collective loss. Even by conservative estimates, the average life expectancy of a small business is not long. Some say as short as a year, but nearly everyone agrees that most small businesses will not survive under the same management for more than three.[1]

This general trend toward big business should be news to no one. In fact, if you are a wage-earner, chances are better than even that you yourself work for one of the 750 largest corporations or for the government. Whatever the source of the threat to mom-and-pop operations, it is certainly older and more encompassing than the strip itself. Blaming the strip for the boom in franchises or the decline of neighborhood shops is a little like blaming your feet when your shoes pinch, the messenger for the message.

Millie Ollinger, like many small business persons, spends a good deal of time on the watch for such threats. It often sounds a bit paranoid (all this talk of "they" who are out to get you) but there certainly is real enough cause for worry. This is one of her strategies for survival. It may or may not figure in her success, but it is a regular part of life along the strip.

You'd be surprised what money can do. They can put you out of business. It's getting vicious in this particular locality, really vicious. I don't think people in this area realize half the stuff that's going on. They can get on you, pick and pick and pick. And it's mainly the little poor bars, the middle class, you know, like the Wagon Wheel, Mar-Kee, My Brother's Place, here, or Slim's over in Tiffin. They've got them almost beat up, beat out. They don't touch the big places, like the motels or the night clubs. That's where all the law officers have their big shindigs. You can't blame them for wanting to have a good time, protecting their own. They're human. But why pick on us little people?

And a lot of it is coming from out of state: Chicago. But you don't want to mess with it, and I don't want to mess with it. It's too big for you and I. There's nothing a little guy can do about it anyhow.

So I just do my job. I maintain that I got my hands full right here. What the next guy does I don't really care. You just keep your mouth shut, do your work from day to day, and take what comes along. Your best way is to smile, accept it, and do as they say.

But I'm a great person that I don't forget. I don't forget! A lot of them don't think I know what's going on, but I do. They even made a comment: "She wouldn't know the Mafia if it hit her in the ass." And this came from an "outstanding citizen" that's supposed to be protecting us. But I've got news for them! I know!

But it's getting bad. For example, I know the police used to watch this place. It was a well-known fact. They'd sit in the lot next door or across the street. If a car was here for a while they'd pull him over when he left and make him take a breath test. Think what that will do to your business!

Like last spring, almost a year ago now, Cecil was in here. He lives out at Western Hills. He went around back to get his car, but he came back and said, "They're at the Unibank. They're waiting for me!" So I said, "Fine. I'll drive you," and I told Patty to follow me in her car. Well, we got out, come around the Unibank, and, sure enough, they were back in there. Soon as we went by, they pulled out. When we got down by the Fruit Market, they gave me the red light and pulled me over. I wasn't driving erratical or anything, you know. So I rolled down the window, and he said, "Oh! . . . Millie! . . . Ah, would you get out?" He took me around the back and said, "When you get home, would you take his keys so he don't come back to town?" Now, what did he stop me for?! That's not entrapment?! I'm not going to take some-

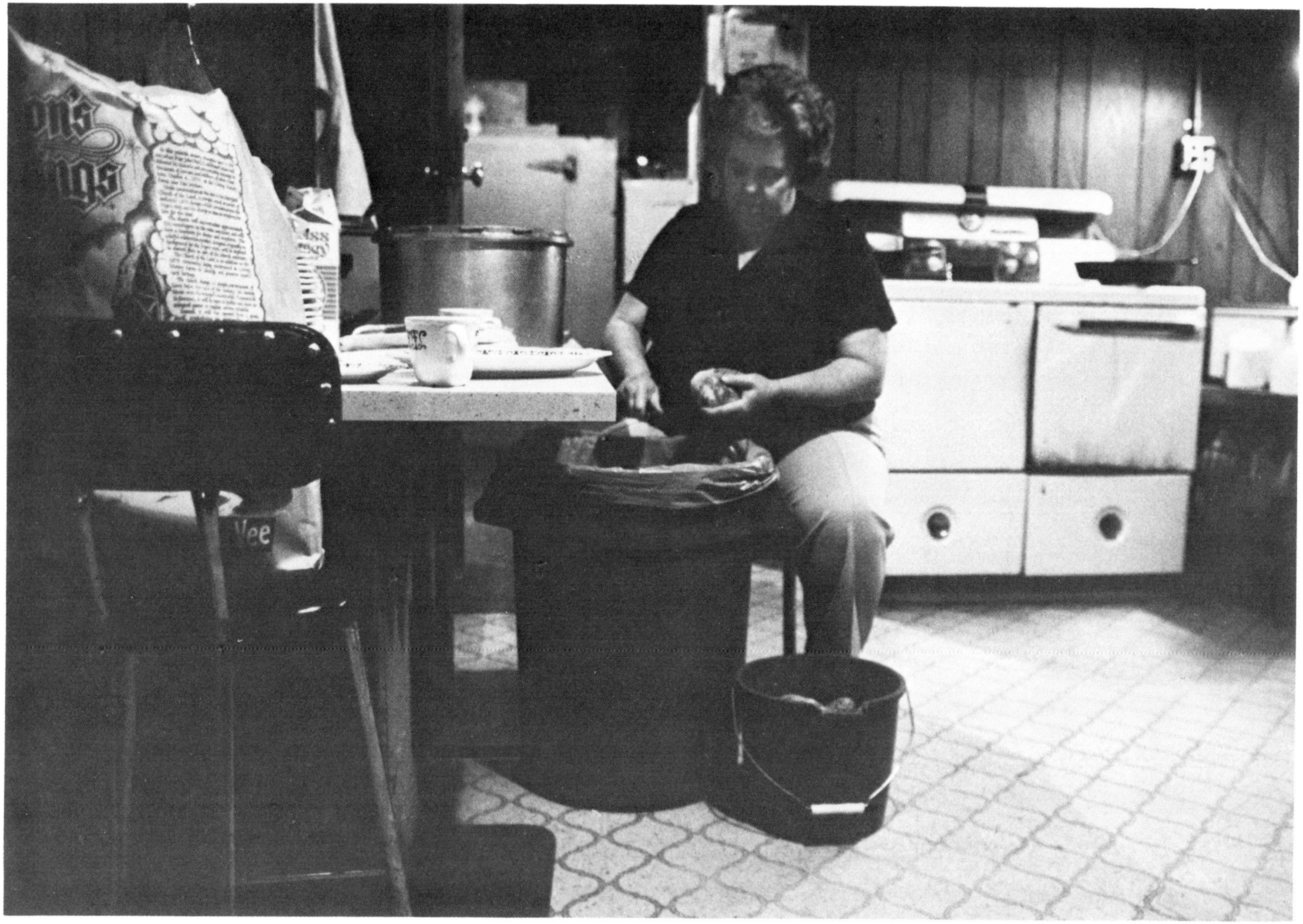

body's keys to their car. So I never said a word about it to Cecil. We just went, parked in the yard, and made sure he and his little boy (he had his boy with him) got in all right. We headed back in Patty's car. You know, when we come back to town, they were still sitting by the Fruit Market! You know? Now you figure it out.

They got some local people scared to come in. A lot of them have to go to little towns and drink. I just can't understand it. They're cutting off the hand that feeds them. You know, Coralville got like $31,000 in taxes last year just for liquor out of Coralville bars. And there's not that many bars here in town. That's quite a little tax money. Anyway, they can pick on me, but I'll always stand up for my customers.

It's funny. When people come in, they want to see me. And I have to be here in the daytime to cook and all night a lot. When I'm well, I'm here like eighteen hours a day. Sometimes I get so tired, I say, "Well, why do I have to be there in my business?" But people want to see me. Like, if I'm not here, people coming through leave notes. In fact, I got one today from somebody from Michigan: "You probably don't remember me, but we've still got your bucket." The first year I was here I gave little milk buckets away, buckets of beer with "Diamond Mil's" on them. This had to be more than six years ago that they was in here, and they stopped to see me!

But this means a lot, and it's worth it. It's worth all the friendship in the world. You know, these people stop by, or they've had somebody sick in the hospital. I've met so many nice families. There's one that lives in Colorado. I get Christmas cards from them. And there was a big family in Washington, Illinois. The brothers and sisters used to come out here at night when their dad was in the hospital. He was there for a long time. When he passed away, they sent me a card, and I sent flowers for his funeral. You just become so involved with people. I really enjoy people, and then, when somebody is trying to pick on you. . . . It's just too bad.

When I first opened the door here, my business took off right away. And some of them, town fathers and such, said, "She won't be there six weeks." "I give her six months." You know? Vern (he's a really nice guy; he used to run the Conoco Station by the Mar-Kee; now he's got a Dairy Queen), he said, "Millie, when you're successful you have to be ready for it, 'cause," he said, "success brings jealousy, and that's when you get the guff." And so I just made up my mind that you accept it, you try and smile.

Lots of times I get tired. I'm a little crabby. Maybe when I lose some weight I won't be so crabby. But, you know, I'm an Aries. An Aries is a go-getter. And I still would like to have my bar where I can have my Mickey Gilley, but I don't know. I don't know if it will be in this town, but it will be in this area. I'll have my bar and my Mickey.

True grit, Millie has her bar and her Mickey—the piano, the juke box, the softball team, friends and foes. She can be proud of her success though, I suspect, few others would call it more than "survival." Surely Mil's will never rival Gilley's Club. In fact, that may be part of its charm. If it were to look more successful, with brightly uniformed staff and furnishings, it would seem too "slick," too pretentious.

But why should a mom-and-pop operation like Mil's not make it by more conventional standards, become a "growth vehicle" to challenge the corporations that dominate the roadside and reactions to it? Business analysts would point out technical problems involved in bookkeeping, taxation, or cash flow. Macroeconomists would refer to larger "structures" or "factors" such as economies of scale that limit the potential of any small business in a competitive environment. The "big guys" may not be Chicago gangsters, but they are powerful.

Usually Millie and other small business owners tie their fortunes to more particular people and events. En-

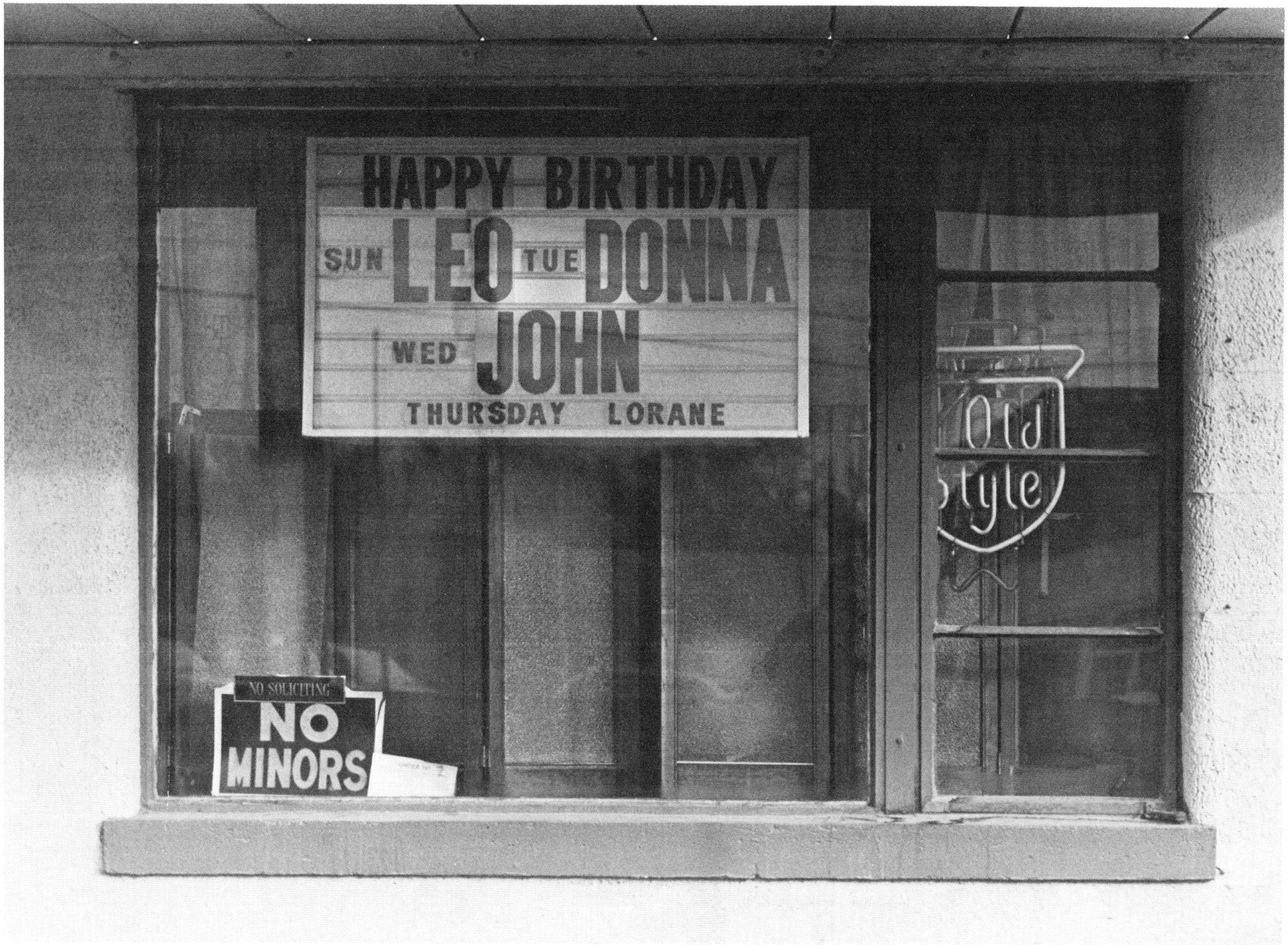
HAPPY BIRTHDAY
SUN LEO TUE DONNA
WED JOHN
THURSDAY LORANE
NO SOLICITING
NO MINORS
Old

couragement is a Christmas card or a full house on Saturday night, and danger, a cruiser at the Unibank. Some of these images are peculiar to an establishment of its kind. For instance, merchants in the liquor trade often complain of discrimination. State regulations put their product in a special category, "alcoholic beverage," requiring additional permits and taxes. To get a license to open on Sundays, a bar keeper must document that 51 percent of the gross receipts come from things other than alcohol, including beer. But when the Restaurant Association makes its assessment, again based on receipts, beer is considered a "food." There are also regular encounters with the law. The bar business is full of stories of conflict between owners, whose livelihood depends on attracting drinkers, and police officers, who must keep them off the road.

Other tales of misfortune, despite their particularity, have a familiar ring. Government regulations, for example, are a constant gripe. Large and small businesses may be equally required to keep extra records or install special fixtures, but the cost to small operators is proportionately higher. Such regulations represent a kind of regressive tax. In some cases they even more openly cater to big business. For instance, that 51 percent required for a Sunday license necessarily favors those who are less likely to need it, such as motel complexes or country clubs. Moreover, owners often complain of differential enforcement or outright harassment if they are not "in" with the local elite.

Anyone who has tried to borrow money will tell you that the more you need it, the harder it is to get. A bank loan to a big business is an "addition to the portfolio"; to a small one it is a "community service." Small business owners often speak of the world of capital as someone else's. Millie has even had trouble finding out who gets her rent check every month. Apparently local investors pass the property from one to the other as their tax situations change. You can imagine how much harder it is to find the owner when the building needs repair.

Running a small business means investing your own labor and risking your own cash. It means seeing an isolated case of vandalism or theft wipe out a month's profit. Or it means hearing your supplier demand cash while your well-heeled competitor gets credit and a discount.

Yes, Millie, they are out to get you, though I doubt it is anything personal.

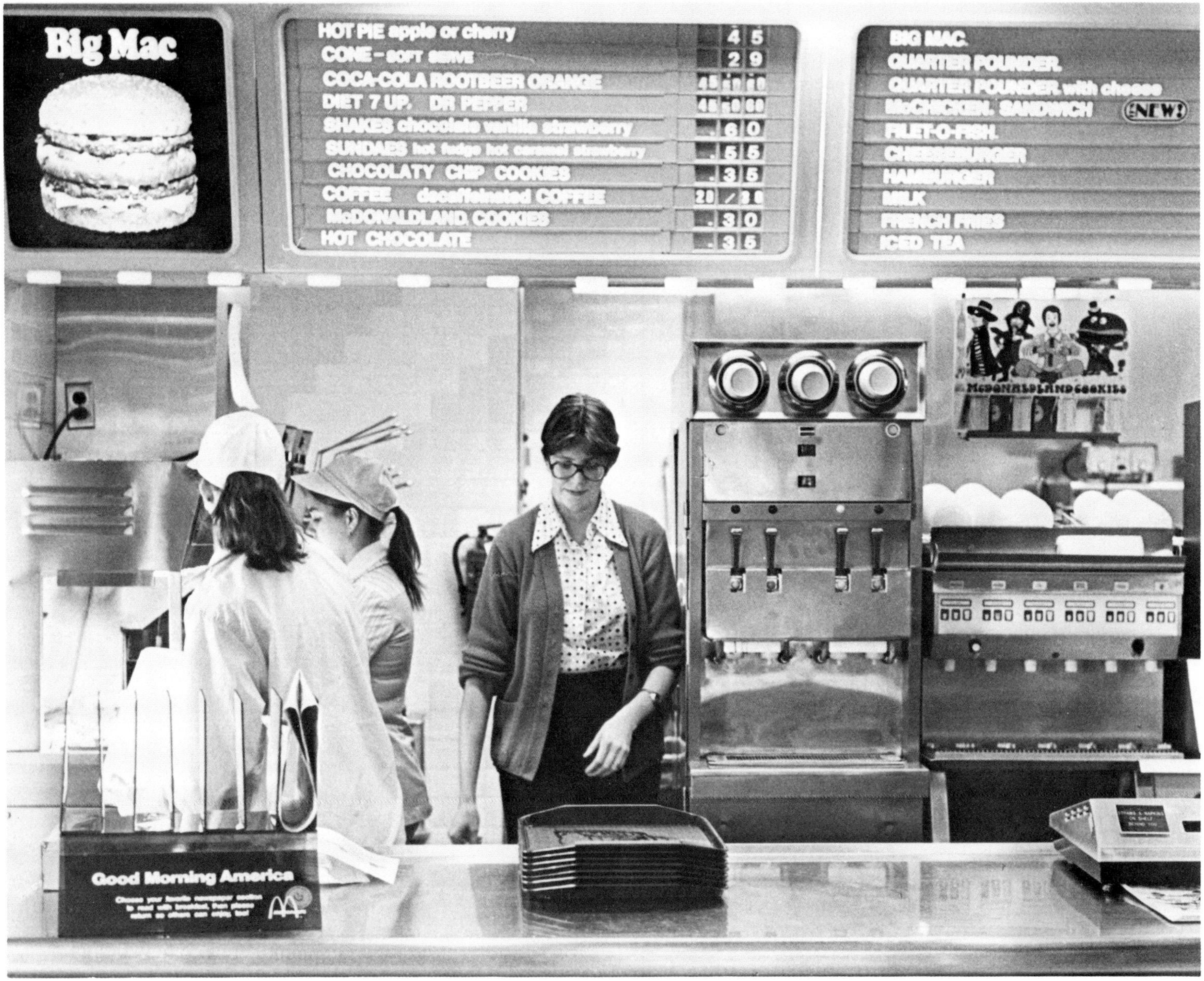

Big Mac
HOT PIE apple or cherry 45
CONE - SOFT SERVE 29
COCA-COLA ROOTBEER ORANGE
DIET 7 UP. DR PEPPER
SHAKES chocolate vanilla strawberry 60
SUNDAES hot fudge hot caramel strawberry 55
CHOCOLATY CHIP COOKIES 35
COFFEE decaffeinated COFFEE
McDONALDLAND COOKIES 30
HOT CHOCOLATE 35
BIG MAC
QUARTER POUNDER
QUARTER POUNDER with cheese
McCHICKEN SANDWICH
NEW!
FILET-O-FISH
CHEESEBURGER
HAMBURGER
MILK
FRENCH FRIES
ICED TEA
McDONALDLAND COOKIES
Good Morning America

Mac's and Mil's

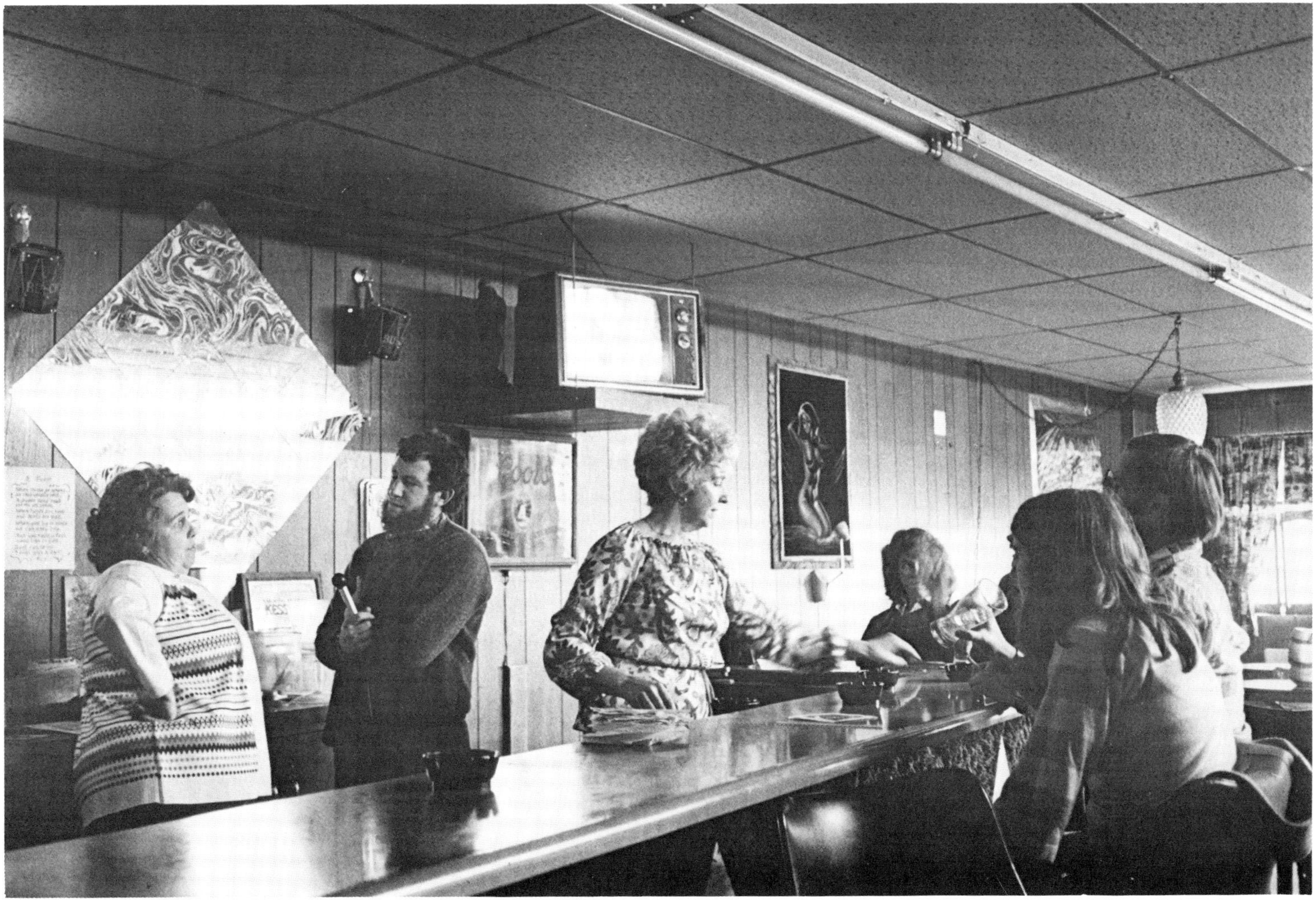

What lessons, then, can Mac's and Mil's provide?

Despite great differences in their trade and organization, they share success on the Strip. They contribute substantial services, wages, and taxes to a diverse citizenry. Their receipts turn directly over to neighboring suppliers, utility companies, and banks and indirectly to nearly every other sort of enterprise. Both provide a haven for motorists wearied by workaday life and highway travel.

But the differences are still substantial and well represent the direction of commercial development along the strip. McDonald's has rationalized every phase of service delivery. The decor, equipment, products, routines, appearance, and manner of employees have been engineered to their effective limits. In the store you, the customer, come first, no matter who you are. Diamond Mil's, on the other hand, shows more spontaneous compromise. With noticeably limited resources, the owner, employees, and patrons improvise on personal tastes.

These two businesses, then, suggest the larger motion of American culture from individual to corporate enterprise, from community to society. As the strip evolves from Mil's and Mac's (and thence to malls), it recapitulates the history of the industrial sector, from shop to factory, with attendant mixed rewards.

Such parallels are too grand to develop, much less prove, in only two sites. Moreover, the two are somewhat deceptive representatives. McDonald's is a well-recognized leader in its field. It is not so much typical of the modern strip as of the avant-garde. Nor is Diamond Mil's simply a relic, a survival of yore. The conditions surrounding its origin, particularly its competition, have changed substantially. More well-heeled establishments may, in fact, help secure a limited place for blue-collar bars. It is we, then, who *make* these places representative.

Even the photographs are made. Nothing wills itself onto film. With the permission of informants and their employers, Karin E. Becker and I composed, selected, and arranged photographs to portray the sites as accurately as possible but also to make a point. In some cases, particularly in the McDonald's sequence, we replaced our first choice to obtain subjects' consent. But in even more cases, we selected pictures that would advance our point, even where that meant some compromise in technical quality.

But technical considerations also affect the presentation. The use, insofar as possible, of a normal lens and available light reflects the canons of photographic realism as much as anything in the subjects themselves. McDonald's appears more angular, tidy, and metallic, in part because it is simply better lit. The bar is dark enough to require more grainy and hence softer images. Black-and-white film obscures some of the dreariness in Mil's decor and the gaiety in McDonald's.

But the most serious potential for bias lies in our approach to the two sites. We spent considerably more time in Diamond Mil's than in McDonald's. Our impression of Mil's evolved over more than a year of observations and interviews in the bar, where we enjoyed unlimited cooperation. The McDonald's pictures were based on an assignment: "Get shots that show regular tasks and contrast workers' and consumers' points of view." There were minimal background or follow-up interviews because of time constraints in our schedule, because of contextual constraints suggested by the management, and because the point seemed so thoroughly confirmed elsewhere.

It is possible that theoretical, technical, strategic, or unnamed factors significantly bias our impression, but I doubt it. The photographs still show much of the truth. The contrast between cast iron and stainless steel suggests simplicity turning high technology; between workers who touch their customers and those confined to stations and uniforms, advancing social stratification; between eclectic decor or celebration and omnipresent advertising, management replacing personal expression.

If together these suggest an alienating future foreshadowed in McDonald's, it is only right. This is not a bias but a judgment. Diamond Mil's has a warmth and spontaneity that no amount of engineering, smiles, themes, barnboard, or plants can recreate. The key ingredients are people who truly care about themselves and each other, who are able and willing to tolerate inconsistency and inconvenience to show they care.

This is not to counsel a halt to progress, much less a return to the past. Even if such a retreat were possible, there would be significant losses. Whatever their faults, giant corporations like McDonald's have helped raise the standards of quality, cleanliness, and fair play on the roadside. Look again at Mac's and Mil's, and ask yourself: Which is more likely to guarantee a dependable product? Which is less perilous for an investor or physically exhausting for a worker? As much as McDonald's portends spiritual impoverishment, it promises material rewards.

These sites, then, show a legacy of the strip remarkably like the legacy of American society as a whole. In the exchange of goods and services, truly human and material benefits are still to be found, but the balance between them seems in peril. Insofar as both sorts of rewards are to be prized in the future, we will have to look beyond the strip's stock critique and the purely cosmetic, consumer-oriented reform it implies. Waste and ugliness are surely worth combating, but before we turn our business districts into massive McDonald's, we have much to learn from both Mac's and Mil's.

Chapter 6. Learning from the Strip

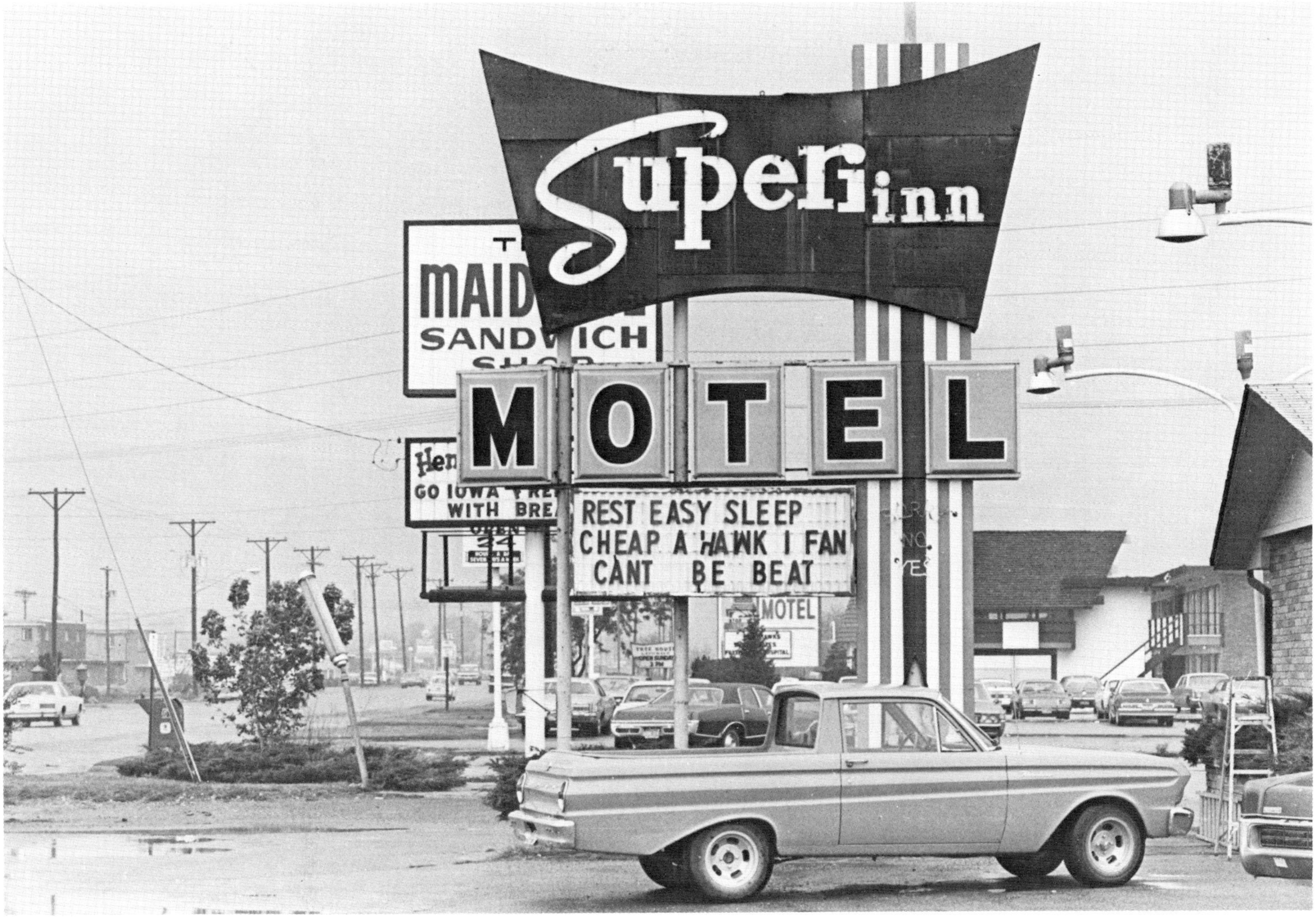
Super inn
SANDWICH
MOTEL
REST EASY SLEEP
CHEAP A HAWK I FAN
CANT BE BEAT
MOTEL

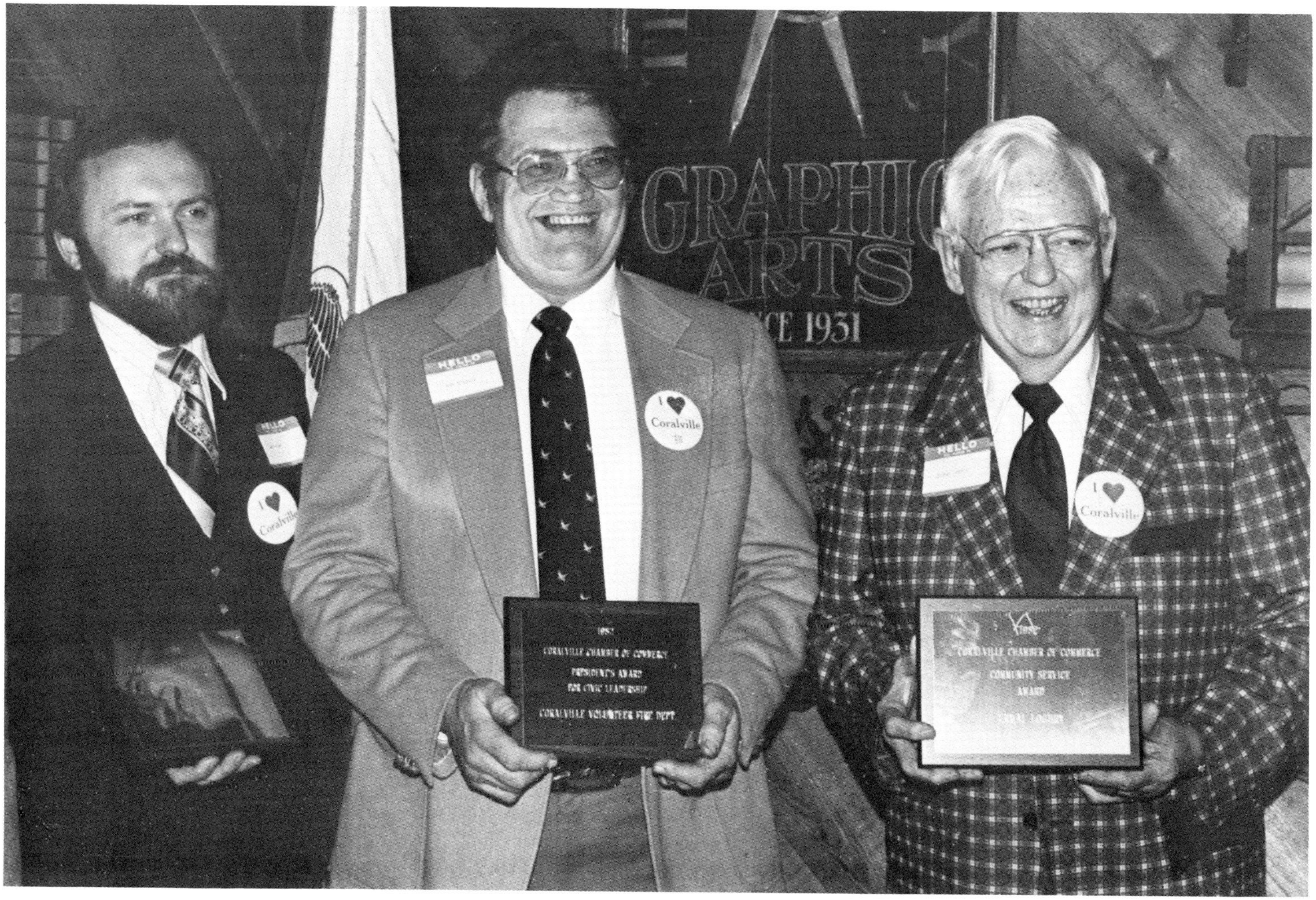
ARTS
CE 1931
HELLO
I Coralville
CORALVILLE CHAMBER OF COMMERCE
PRESIDENT'S AWARD
FOR CIVIC LEADERSHIP
CORALVILLE VOLUNTEER FIRE DEPT
CORALVILLE CHAMBER OF COMMERCE
COMMUNITY SERVICE
AWARD

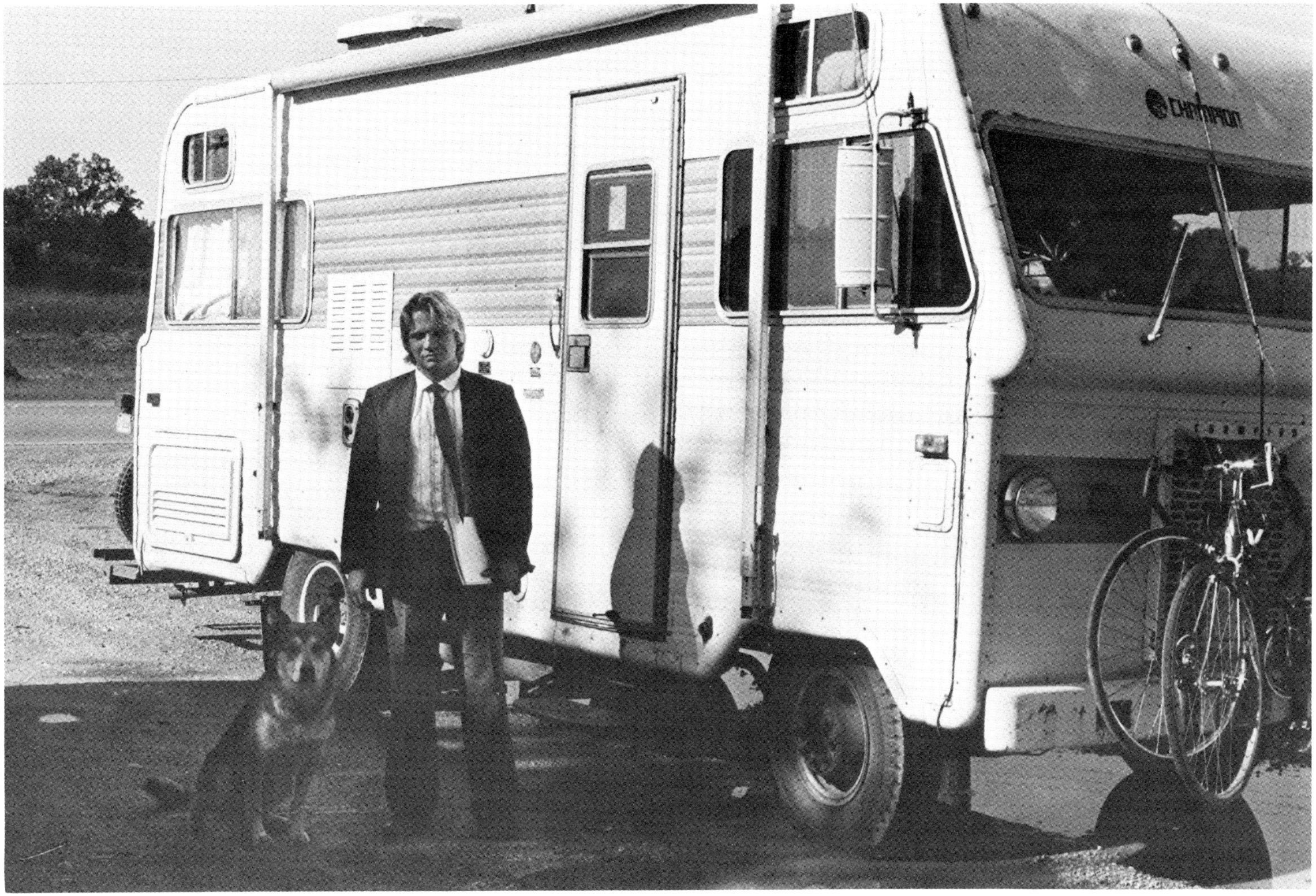

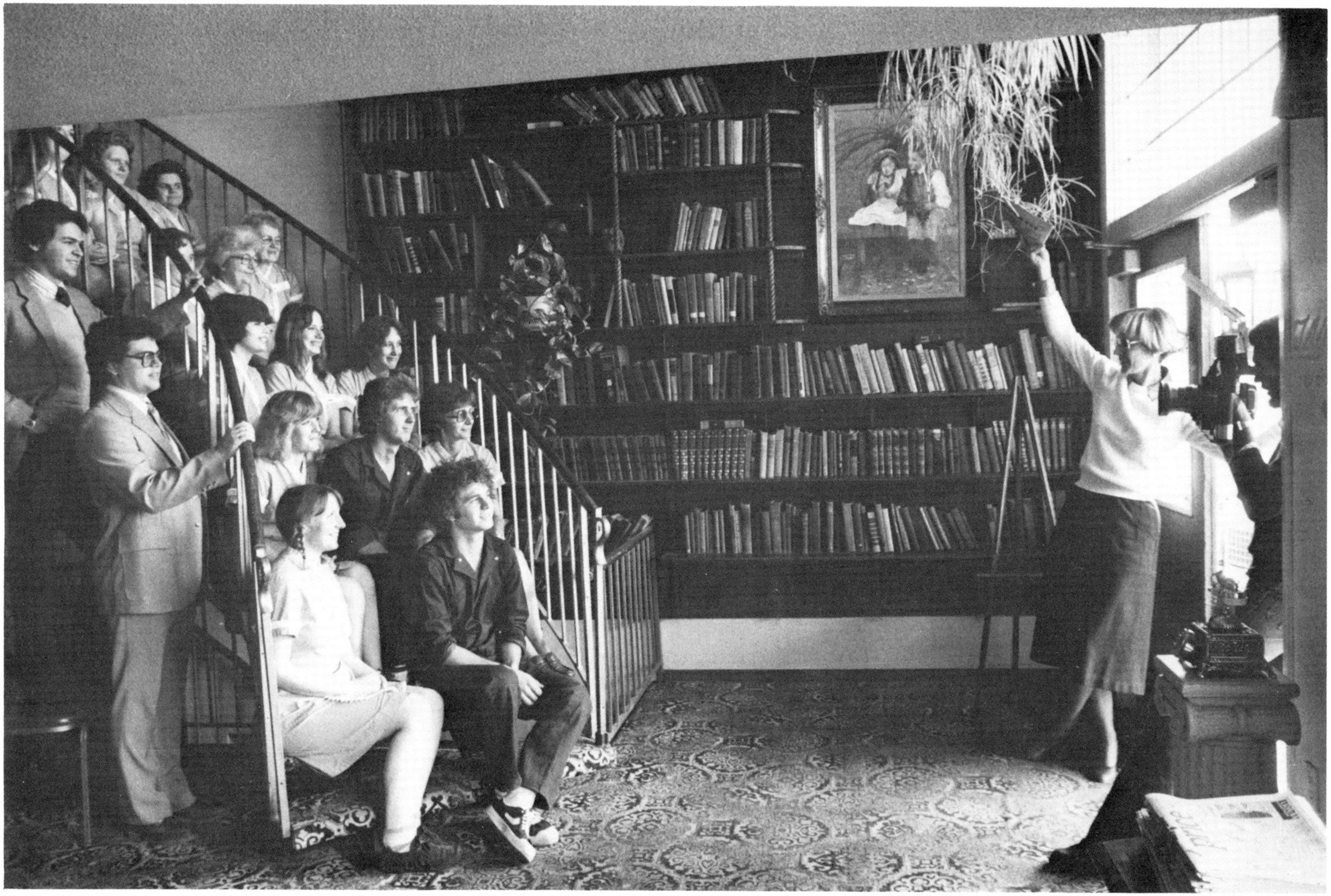

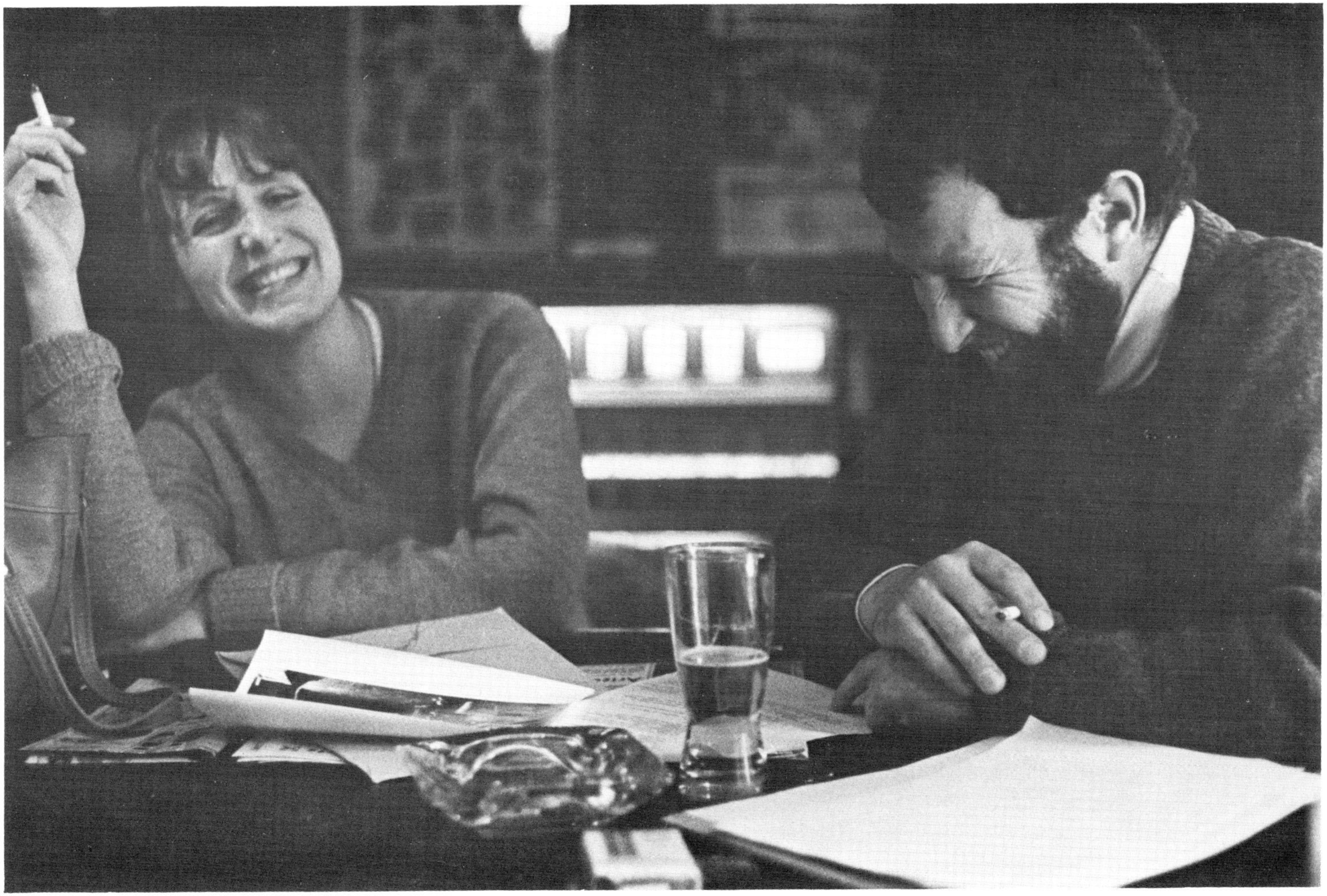

An American place is "around here" or "back home." It is the vista, the folks, and the climate we know best. "My place" could be as large and elusive as the South or as discrete as the county home. It is mountain, desert, tropic, and woodland, this side of the waterway, the beltway, or that side of the tracks. The land and its inhabitants show variety of which Americans can be proud. The sites that Americans have built show similar variety but less pride. Few evoke more outright disdain than urban slums and their roadside equivalent. Glaring lines of fast-food joints, motels, and gas stations are the ghettos of commerce.

But the strip is an ordinary place. Passing seasons and visitors leave their mark here as in the forest. Things rise and fall. They age and are renewed. Photographs seem instantly dated if only by fuel prices posted along the road. But even as it changes, the strip remains. For example, Coralville will probably have its "mistake" no matter how it is disguised or who makes the fries. It is more than a specific thing, some buildings, people, or socioeconomic arrangements. Nor is it simply symbolic, the embodiment of some purer idea. Particular human and economic events figure powerfully in its history. For example, the tackiness of old strips or recent gestures toward respectability are hardly aberrant. They are the work of individuals who constitute as well as respond to "larger forces." In this way, too, the strip touches main currents in American life ranging from wartime demographics to the popular arts. I have tried to highlight these connections as they appear in everyday life on a particular site.

Most of the facts, I suppose, are close to common knowledge, but I have presented them from an unusual perspective—unusual because it accents, not the consumers' experience, but the exchange between consumers and service providers. We see how the strip works, not for "The People," but for people, in particular, people on the job. The truth in their view comes from its concreteness and depth. People are more than carriers of variable "values," "opinions," or "behaviors." Supposedly "inarticulate" folk reveal a sense of place that does not leave biography behind. Their stories turn, not on some theory of the strip, but on a life and the minutiae it contains. I only regret that I could not recover more of the wisdom that surely lurked in their every gesture and quip.

I suppose this admission reveals as much about *my* perspective as anything else. It is hardly disinterested. As I learned about the Strip, I drew closer to Dean, Tammy, Millie, and the others who make it their place. "In the field," as elsewhere, it becomes hard to untangle your feelings from those around you. Even worse, it becomes hard to decide whose feelings are most justified, even when they conflict. Mike and Dean, Tammy and John, Dave and Millie—everyone seems to make sense in his or her way, largely because that is expected. In fact, I interviewed each person and edited my writing until sense had been made. I "got it right" when they and I agreed that our stories and workaday reality cohered.

My disposition, then turned method, amounts to a purposeful naivete. All people, I assume, make sense from some point of view, most likely their own. If they seem dishonest or dumb, I expect it is my failure more than theirs; I have not led us to a clearer, more honest and comprehensive truth. It may be happy or sad, perfectly simple or complex, but it must be there!

This is surely a bias but just as surely a necessary one. How can I probe the limits of my understanding unless I am willing to leave it behind? It requires a radical trust in my informants and distrust in myself. And I think it works. If nothing else, I hope to have shown that the customary views of outsiders are impoverished precisely because they are self-centered. With an empathic view the strip is more than its architecture or a reflection of American dreams. It is a place with people whose lives defy consumer reports, my own included. At stake are issues of freedom and dignity as well as material reward. If future developments in America's leisure industry are to avoid the mistakes of the past, more attention must be paid to its truly historical human lessons, alien or complex as they may seem.

But even this view cannot suffice. As we debate the meaning of the landscape, we cannot forget the land itself. For example, despite the recollections of Coralville pioneers, I cannot believe there was "really nothing out there" before Highway 6. It may have been nothing of direct human profit, but surely there was something. Under those decorated sheds, their foundations and surrounding pavement, beneath thousands of yards of fill, lie grounds that bore glaciers and rivers as well as untold cycles of birth and death. In an instant of its history the whole was buried. The water that graced the land and Virgil's corn is now annoying runoff. Whatever ecology remains has had to adapt to automobile fumes, noise, and litter. Fossil fuels are squandered on styrofoam, neon, and cruises down the strip. The land may be mute, but it cries for an end to commercial sprawl. From this

vantage, we can only applaud the efforts of engineers and planners to replace the strip with "nucleated" alternatives.

The strictly human side of the strip is more difficult to judge. All people may make sense in their own way, but some are more powerful than others. Judging from the roadside that developed through the 1960s, small-time entrepreneurs controlled the past. But the present belongs to an effective alliance of large corporations and consumer and environmental advocates. Restoration zones, mega-malls, and other alternatives to the strip promise more profit, rationality, and good taste. Even the oldest of strips show improvement. The signs and buildings are less garish. Services are more reliable. Wages and tax revenues have increased. It is still possible to ravage the land for profit but not without more consideration of the consequence.

By most accounts this represents a break with the past. But by others it is merely an extension of the industrial revolution. Mil's, the Carousel, Mac's, and malls are like archeological layers of human loss amidst material gain. While trade increases in scale and productivity, people are driven apart from each other and themselves. For managers and investors this is a necessary evil. For consumers it is a petty annoyance. But for workers it is a tragedy registered in small humiliations that mount week by week.

I emphasize this view because it is so often neglected and because I have come to know the victims so well. But this is not simply to advocate my friends, the underdogs. We are all producers as well as consumers and, through a dependence on "prosperity," share the interests of capital. The fact that some people are winners and others losers in the game is a result of rules that predate and extend far beyond the strip. And sensible justifications can be heard on all sides. In fact, one of the most touching overviews of the Strip I ever recorded came not from some weary employee but from Ermal Loghry, one of Coralville's most successful and distinguished pioneers.

I know there are a lot of people who think this is just an "asphalt jungle" or whatever they call it. They look at the Strip and think, "Boy, all they're interested in is making a buck." They don't see the other things we do or how hard it's been—part of an antibusiness attitude the past ten or twelve years. It probably started with the automobile makers and big corporations, but it has filtered down to the little guy, the businessman on the street. I'm sure my legislator in Des Moines thinks I'm just coining money in this place. They don't see how tough it is just to keep in the black. I'm not complaining, because I've been successful. I'm not extremely wealthy or anything like that, but I've built up a little to retire on. And it's not that business is completely innocent. A lot of things like the Strip happened because they were only interested in making a buck.

But people didn't come out here to create "the asphalt jungle." They came here because it was where they could do business. I see people's point in wanting things to look pretty. But I don't know if we can have everything, either. Who knows if downtown Iowa City will look any better when it is twenty or thirty years old? I'm not sure there is anything you can do to please some of them. Of course, my group of people over the years would say, "They're those eggheads who don't understand business. That's what makes money and pays for everything else."

At one time I would have said that, too. Maybe it's my age or living here, but I've become more moderate on

that. I realize that they've got some good points. There are some things I wish we had done differently. But it was a tough, tough thing just trying to survive and grow out here over the years. And it's going to get tough again.

Nobody could go in business now like I did in 1949, on a shoestring. It was different financial era. That's the basic reason growths like this happen. People come in to try to make a buck, and they don't worry about what it looks like. Now, all of a sudden, it does make a difference, and that takes money. They're looking for decorations, surroundings, what they call "atmosphere" as much as anything else. We've got the Power Company in Coralville, the Broom Factory in Waterloo, and in Des Moines the Court Street Station. In the East they've got a lot of them. It's just the in thing right now, even more than food and service, which at one time was all you needed.

Like, once I started a pizza house, Rodrigo's, with another guy. We didn't worry about the building and stuff like this. And it never worked. Pizza Hut came in and just killed us. Actually we put out better pizza than they did, but they had the whole package sold. And that's what's happened nowadays. You can't just pick up a building and start it out. You've got to make it look like something. And I'm sure that's good. Yet in some ways I feel badly about it.

These new types of businesses do serve a purpose, at least the good ones. I know myself, if I travel, I don't mind stopping in McDonald's for breakfast. It's quick, it's fast, it's informal, it's good, and the price per meal is cheaper. But they're serving you less food. They're running about thirty percent food cost, while I'm running about forty.

And a good franchise can teach you how to be a successful businessman. When you get into it as an independent, it's just hit and miss. You learn the hard way. Things might slow down a little now with the high interest rates, but I think the future belongs to these new types of businesses. As long as labor costs rise, you need them. The guy comes in with a package: "Serve these ten things; buy them in this way; lay them out like this. . . ." He teaches you how to do it and how to do it fast. Basically he's trying to cut labor because he can't control other things like food costs. But he can have control on labor.

Since 1969, my labor has risen seven percent on every dollar I take in, and I can't seem to find ways to lower it. We try to be more efficient, not to have anybody on a stand-around basis. I'm sure that some people think we're a Gestapo-type operation. Like, I saw a kid in the kitchen the other day breading shrimp. I said, "You know, if you bread shrimp that way, I can't afford to serve them." I don't think he understood what I was talking about, but this is what it gets down to. So, maybe I won't bread those shrimp anymore. I'm going to buy them all breaded and ready to drop in the fryer, because I can cut my labor costs. Somebody else can do it on a larger basis better than I can. And these are the things that the guy with the package does for you. He's researched products and done a lot of things that, as an independent, it's damned hard to do.

But a lot of these new places are owned by someone outside. I call them "parasites." A group in Minneapolis hires a manager to run the place here, and they aren't community-minded. They don't meet the people. They don't give anything; all they do is take. Like, if you have a ticket to sell for a good cause, you get nothing out of those people. You only get it out of independent people who live in the area. This is what I object to. They won't belong to your Chamber of Commerce. They won't belong to your Restaurant Association. You rarely see their managers in a service club.

To me, there is an importance to being in a community. I want to do something and be part of it, not just take money out of it. I still work on it, like with the Coralville Chamber of Commerce and the Iowa Licensed Bever-

age Association. In fact, I helped start them, so I've seen how it's changed. Of course, there are exceptions. Like, the O'Briens and McDonald's are real community-minded. But with most of them now, I just find it really irritating.

But you can see how it happened. Our business is rough. Over the years we didn't worry about volume that much. It was a family operation. We didn't really care if we made all the money in the world. We had the things I wanted for my family, to send my daughter to college and stuff. I wasn't really interested in much more. Now you can't hardly operate that way. You've got to have that volume.

I guess I'm kind of down on our service right now. I'm sixty-four years old and had some sickness the past couple of years. I had a small stroke and the medicine affects my blood pressure. So I'm trying to ease out. My son-in-law and daughter are taking over. I tell you frankly, he's a graduate of the university and a talented young man, but I told him I think he's nuts. There are other things he could do, maybe work for the other fellow. He's working awfully hard just to pay the bills. And I did that. But, you know, when you get to talking about your children, you kind of hate to see that happen to them. I mean, I never got to go home and eat dinner with my daughter. And I'm doing that now, and I can see how much enjoyment it is. I hate to see him keep at it like that.

And it's hard on the help, too. We're almost always short on help, especially when we have the business. The only time we can get enough help is when business isn't as good as it should be, like in the dead of winter. The rest of the time you don't have enough people to do the proper things, the things you want to do. So somebody has to work fourteen or even eighteen hours. And we've had some people who do this for us. God help us if we didn't have them.

Now I'm the first to say that they probably haven't been paid enough, but it's tough to make that dollar. We *just put in a new kitchen at $82,000, and we didn't have that money laying around. We borrowed it. It's tough to pay that off, and some of the new equipment doesn't last as long as the old stuff we replaced. Now, anytime we buy equipment, we try to cut our labor. It's the same throughout the service industry, the oil stations, the hotels and motels. You just can't pay people that much. It's too bad. But there are things that no one wants to do, no matter what you pay them. For instance, in our kitchen cleaning is the biggest job we have. We have to fight to get it done constantly. Nobody wants to hire out to do that. Well, some things have been improved, but nobody's yet figured out how you push a button and it cleans itself.*

But, as I say, it has changed a lot. In 1969, when we built the motel, I don't think I had more than a waitress or two who hadn't been with me at least two years, some of them for eight, ten, or twelve years. And the cooks had been with me for . . . just a long time. It was, to a certain extent, like a family. You looked at those people differently than I look at employees now, because I don't get acquainted with them that well. Maybe more pressure's on me due to volumes. I'm a different type of boss than I was then. Now I haven't changed much, but as I watch my son-in-law I see that he doesn't have the patience that I had. And I thought I was impatient, see? He doesn't understand their shortcomings like I used to. I used to tell my sister, "If they were as good as we were, they'd be running the business." You know? But you got so you liked those people. And, I think, basically they had respect for us. Now I don't think that's true at all, on both ends. The help are just there to get their dollar. And the boss doesn't care about them. He's only interested in making a profit, and that's all he can be interested in. And the customers don't care about either one of them. Hell, no. They don't care. "Look pleasant and give me my stuff." And I think that's real sad.

Our type of business is hard. It's a hard business for

people to run, make a profit, and be able to do what they want to do. And it's hard work for the help. I think service people, the whole service industry, has more problems right now than any other industry. I'm sure the automobile makers wouldn't say that, but that's how I see it. It's hard to say what we can do about it, but we need to do more. Maybe we just need to think about other people's problems a little more.

I cannot recommend a simple solution, either, but certainly Ermal is right. Compassion could help. It could help us see in the strip how much we all have lost in the race to modernity, how rapidly we have become alienated from ourselves and those around us.

It can also help us see the shallowness of modern reforms. More perfect dining or shopping experiences, more earth tones and sprouts, may bring greater beauty and responsibility to the land, but they also show the same slavery to the marketplace that has driven us apart. Unbridled consumerism is not only utopian but also spiritually suicidal. Instead of supporting "real life" in our work, our association with workmates, or exchanges across the counter, we scramble for "authentic experience" that is a decadent fantasy. In generous moments I believe the fantasy is a natural compensation for the emptiness of most workaday life: "My job is meaningless, but at least I can cash it in for other pleasures." In more paranoid moments I attribute it to the sinister designs of capitalists. What could be more convenient than a work force at once taught to surrender control of production for wages and to develop an insatiable demand for things only wages can buy? Yet, whatever their origin, more tasteful alternatives to the strip are hardly remedies. As we bypass the strip or beautify it, we engage in collective amnesia, blotting out the small freedoms and dignity it once housed.

But historic preservation does not seem to be an answer, either. Strips are dangerous for motorists, irrational, and, I must admit, ugly. They are interesting only in comparison to the oppressive unity of more respectable developments. I cannot see how any place that so depends on the automobile can be defended in the future, except as a reminder of the environmental arrogance and wastefulness it displays. Moreover, saving the strip, the thing itself, will hardly rescue its inhabitants. Classic cabin courts, diners, or filling stations are worth remembering less because of their design than because of the ways of life they accompanied. They were far from idyllic, but they did prove that powerlessness, alienation, and decadence are not, in fact, eternal necessities. Turning the strip into a nostalgic shrine would be just as truly a flight from the past as its obliteration.

To improve on the strip significantly, we will have to look beyond architecture or cuisine. Instruments of reform such as building and zoning codes, easements, or subsidies will help, if they are truly responsive to the land and all of its inhabitants. But to date they have done little to alter the social and economic processes that make "progress" a mixed blessing.

The problem, I believe, is that they have been product- rather than process-oriented. Reformers define ends for public policy without challenging the means by which the "public" is represented. Expert opinion tends to preserve the interests of capital and, to a lesser extent, consumers to the neglect of workers.[1] In effect, the ways we have conceived and enacted the lessons of the strip preserve the very inequities that fuel our disaffection.

Students of planning and business administration as well as labor leaders have recently called for more "participatory" decision making, as seems only proper.[2] What is wrong with the strip and even more with its remedies is the way they harness resources to benefit one group at another's expense. Economic democracy would surely help.[3] Its absence is visible on the strip, but it originates in the organization of our society, and that is where it demands redress. Power and wealth must be more equally distributed and decentralized so citizens can regain control of their lives. We must treat the disappointments of workaday life as realistically as its rewards. Even as we struggle for mutual understanding, we cannot and should not accept the "necessity" of compromise with ecological and spiritual destruction.

These, to me, are the main lessons of the strip. Yet, even if I could deduce from them some more concrete proposals, I am not so naive as to believe they would have much effect. Besides, what we need are not more utopian plans but action informed by the simple recognition that basic change is possible and desirable. That is the least I can ask as you choose where to shop or dine,, how to tip a waitress or treat a clerk, or as you make more patently political decisions. Remember Dean, Brad, Millie, Jan, Ermal, and all the others who share with us not only the strip but also humanity.

Notes

Preface

1. J. Hector St. John de Crèvecoeur, *Letters from an American Farmer and Sketches of Eighteenth-Century America* (1782 and 1925), ed. Albert E. Stone (New York: Viking, Penguin Books, 1981), p. 69.

2. Emile Durkheim, *The Rules of Sociological Method* (Chicago: University of Chicago Press, 1938). See also Anthony Giddens, *New Rules of Sociological Method: A Positive Critique of Interpretive Sociologies* (New York: Basic Books, 1976).

3. See James Clifford, "On Ethnographic Authority," *Representations* 1, no. 2 (Spring 1983): 118–46, and George E. Marcus and Dick Cushman, "Ethnographies as Texts," *Annual Review of Anthropology*, ed. Bernard J. Siegel, 11 (1982): 25–69. Models for this sort of ethnography include Jean-Paul Dumont, *The Headman and I: Ambiguity and Ambivalence in the Fieldworking Experience* (Austin: University of Texas Press, 1978); Paul Rabinow, *Reflections on Fieldwork in Morocco* (Berkeley and Los Angeles: University of California Press, 1977); Henry Glassie, *Passing the Time in Ballymenone: Culture and History of an Ulster Community* (Philadelphia: University of Pennsylvania Press, 1982); and Barbara Myerhoff, *Number Our Days* (New York: E. P. Dutton, 1979).

Chapter 1

1. John Fisher, general manager of Iowa River Power Company, quoted in Sal Lopez, "The Iowa River Power Company: An Unlikely Franchise" (seminar paper, University of Iowa, 1979).

2. Sandy Alexander, *Franchising and You: Unlimited Opportunities for Success* (Los Angeles: Lawrence Publishing Co., 1970), p. 189.

3. Wright Morris, *The Home Place* (Lincoln: University of Nebraska Press, 1968), p. 76.

4. Peter Blake, *God's Own Junkyard: The Planned Deterioration of America's Landscape*, new and updated ed. (New York: Holt, Rinehart and Winston, 1979), p. 14.

5. Alexander, *Franchising and You*, pp. 225–31.

6. Preliminary attempts to quantify strip development include the following: Brian J. L. Berry, "Ribbon Developments in the Urban Business Pattern," *Annals of the Association of American Geographers* 49, no. 2 (June 1959): 145–55; F. N. Boal and D. B. Johnson, "The Functions of Retail and Service Establishments on Commercial Ribbons," in *Internal Structure of the City*, ed. Larry J. Bourne (New York: Oxford University Press, 1971), pp. 368–79; John A. Jakle and Richard L. Mattson, "The Evolution of a Commercial Strip," *Journal of Cultural Geography* 1, no. 2 (Spring/Summer 1981): 12–25; and Paul R. Merry, "An Inquiry into the Nature and Function of a String Retail Development: A Case Study of East Colfax Avenue, Denver, Colorado" (Ph.D. diss., Northwestern University, 1955).

7. Tom Wolfe, *The Kandy-Kolored Tangerine-Flake Streamline Baby* (New York: Farrar, Strauss, and Giroux, 1965), p. 8.

8. Interview with representative of Nesper Sign Advertising, Inc., Cedar Rapids, Iowa, June 1980.

9. Quoted in D. Daryl Wyckoff and W. Earl Sasser, *The Chain-Restaurant Industry* (Lexington, Mass.: D. C. Heath and Co., 1978), p. 100.

10. Ray Kroc with Robert Anderson, *Grinding It Out: The Making of McDonald's* (Chicago: H. Regnery Co., 1977), p. 143.

11. Alan Gowans, *Images of American Living: Four Centuries of Architecture and Furniture as Cultural Expression* (Philadelphia and New York: J. B. Lippincott Co., 1964), p. 270; see also pp. 267–84.

12. Yi-fu Tuan, *Topophilia: A Study of Environmental Perception, Attitude, and Values* (Englewood Cliffs, N.J.: Prentice-Hall, 1974), passim; see esp. pp. 92–122. See also Leo Marx, *The Machine in the Garden: Technology and the Pastoral Ideal in America* (New York: Oxford University Press, 1964), and Barbara Rubin, "Aesthetic Ideology and Urban Design," *Annals of the Association of American Geographers* 69, no. 3 (September 1979): 339–61.

13. Christopher Tunnard, *Man-Made America: Chaos or Control? An Inquiry into Selected Problems of Design in the Urbanized Landscape* (New Haven: Yale University Press, 1963); Blake, *God's Own Junkyard*; and David Plowden, *The Hand of Man on America* (Washington, D.C.: Smithsonian Institution Press, 1971).

14. Blake, *God's Own Junkyard*, p. 24.

15. Pierce F. Lewis, David Lowenthal,

and Yi-fu Tuan, *Visual Blight in America* (Washington, D.C.: Association for American Geographers, Commission on College Geography, 1973), p. 4.

16. The role of government in affecting land use has a complex legal history. Even now, specific judgments are likely to depend both on the costs and benefits for the principals and the particular type of situation (e.g., planning vs. variance procedure, public vs. private property, residential vs. commercial zone, and so on). My summary of the law, then, is very general, but I believe it is well supported. For a thorough, annotated survey of relevant jurisprudence, see Robert M. Anderson, *American Law of Zoning*, 2nd ed. (New York: The Lawyers Cooperative Publishing Co., 1976), vols. 1–5, and his *Cumulative Supplement* (August 1983), vols. 1–5. I have heavily relied on vol. 1, pp. 556–96, updated in vol. 1 of the *Supplement*, pp. 263–68. See also vol. 1, pp. 78 and 552; vol. 2, pp. 74–75; and vol. 3, pp. 278–81, 318–22, 372–79, 403–9, and 591–92. Anderson concludes: "It is clear that the courts have become tolerant of land-use restrictions which to some extent are intended to conserve or improve community appearance. It is less clear that the courts, even in those jurisdictions where architectural controls have been upheld, will sustain a limitation on the use of private land where its sole relation to the police power is its tendency to enhance or protect community appearance" (1:578).

17. Blake, *God's Own Junkyard*, pp. 156, 27. Blake refers to an article in the *Wall Street Journal* of April 14, 1960.

18. Robert Venturi, Denise Scott Brown, and Steven Izenour, *Learning from Las Vegas: The Forgotten Symbolism of Architectural Form*, rev. ed. (Cambridge, Mass.: MIT Press, 1977), pp. 3, 18, 51.

19. Ibid., pp. 117, 107.

20. Ibid., pp. 146–47, 118.

21. Ibid., pp. 154–55, 162.

22. Ibid., p. 149.

23. Ibid., p. 150, 161.

24. Ibid., pp. 167–83.

25. Frank Rowsome, *The Verse by the Side of the Road: The Story of the Burma-Shave Signs and Jingles* (Brattleboro, Vt.: S. Greene Press, 1965); John Baeder, *Diners* (New York: Harry N. Abrams, 1978). See also Warren H. Anderson, *Vanishing Roadside America* (Tucson: University of Arizona Press, 1981); Richard J. S. Gutman and Elliot Kaufman in collaboration with David Slovic, *American Diner* (New York: Harper & Row, 1979); Paul Hirshorn and Steven Izenour, *White Towers* (Cambridge, Mass.: MIT Press, 1979); John Margolies, *The End of the Road: Vanishing Highway Architecture in America* (New York: Viking, 1981); Martin Pawley, *Garbage Housing* (London: Architectural Press; New York: Wiley, 1975); Rudi Stern, *Let There Be Neon* (New York: Harry N. Abrams, 1979); Daniel I. Vieyra, *"Fill 'er Up": An Architectural History of America's Gas Stations* (New York: Macmillan Publishing Co., 1979); Jan Wampler, *All Their Own: People and the Places They Build* (New York: Schenkman Publishing Co., 1977).

26. Robert Venturi, *Complexity and Contradiction in Architecture*, with an Introduction by Vincent Scully (New York: Museum of Modern Art, 1966). It was translated into Japanese in 1969, French in 1971, and Spanish in 1972.

27. Venturi, Scott Brown, and Izenour, *Learning from Las Vegas*, p. xii.

28. Ibid., plates 73 and 74, pp. 88–89, and Blake, *God's Own Junkyard*, plates 101 and 109, pp. 120 and 124. Blake gives credit for use of the photographs to Standard Oil Company of New Jersey.

29. Blake, *God's Own Junkyard*, pp. 157–58.

30. Peter Blake, *Form Follows Fiasco: Why Modern Architecture Hasn't Worked* (Boston: Little, Brown and Co., 1977).

31. Blake, *God's Own Junkyard*, pp. 9, 14, 19.

32. Ibid., pp. 14, 20, 21.

33. Ibid., pp. 20, 19, 22.

Chapter 2

1. Barry Gordon, "The Commercial Strip as an Indicator of American Cultural Themes" (M.A. thesis, George Washington University, 1969). For a critical survey of the literature on streets and their significance from nearly every imaginable perspective, see Stanford Anderson, ed., *On Streets* (Cambridge: MIT Press, 1978).

2. Constance Perin, "The Symbolic Landscape: Authority and the American Way," in *The Arts in a Democratic Society*, ed. Dennis Alan Mann (Bowling Green: Popular Press, 1977), p. 51.

Chapter 3

1. See Michael Agar, *The Professional Stranger: An Informal Introduction to Ethnography* (New York: Academic Press, 1980), pp. 119–36.

Chapter 4

1. The social history of the industrial revolution and its current repercussions is, of course, a massive subject. For a critical starting point, I would recommend Alan Dawley, *Class and Community: The Industrial Revolution in Lynn* (Cambridge: Harvard University Press, 1976); Alan Trachtenberg, *The Incorporation of America: Culture and Society in the Guilded Age* (New York: Hill and Wang, 1982); Harry Braverman, *Labor and Monopoly Capital: The Degradation of Work in the Twentieth Century* (New York: Monthly Review Press, 1974); and Richard Edwards,

Contested Terrain: The Transformation of the Workplace in the Twentieth Century (New York: Basic Books, 1979).

2. The history of Best Western International, Inc., is drawn from business periodicals. In particular: Robert Ashton, "Best Western Booms as Independent Alternative," *Institutions*, March 1, 1979, pp. 33–36, 40; "Best Western Is Thinking Big," *Hotel and Motel Management*, December 1979, p. 17; "Best Western Markets Its New Image," *Hotel and Motel Management*, September 1976, pp. 25–27; "B-W Financial Services Is Off and Running," *Hotel and Motel Management*, October 1979, pp. 58–59; C. E. Curtis, "Somebody Must Be Wrong," *Forbes*, April 14, 1980, pp. 86–87; H. D. Menzies, "What Willy B. Prosperous Likes about Best Western," *Fortune*, December 31, 1978, pp. 66–68; and "Why Big Hotels Are Joining Up," *Hotel and Motel Management*, January 1977, pp. 20–21. Additional data on the lodging and service industry in general came from the U.S. Department of Commerce, Bureau of the Census, *Statistical Abstract of the United States*, 1979, pp. 437, 439, 841, and 843. For more historical background, see Warren James Belasco, *Americans on the Road: From Autocamp to Motel, 1910–1945* (Cambridge: MIT Press, 1979).

3. For a similar analysis of retailing, see Barry Bluestone, Patricia Hanna, Sarah Kuhn, and Laura Moore, *The Retail Revolution: Market Transformation, Investment, and Labor in the Modern Department Store* (Boston: Auburn House, 1981). On page vi they note, "Surprisingly, the transformation of department stores from locally owned and operated 'petite bourgeoisie' enterprises to billion-dollar international conglomerates [including those specialty shops in the mall] is chock-full of the same kind of intrigue that characterized the development of small 19th-century manufac-

tories into the mammoth multinational industrial conglomerates that dominate today's economic landscape." Of course, the service economy is responding to both human and institutional imperatives. For a compelling synthesis, see Arlie Russell Hochschild, *The Managed Heart: Commercialization of Human Feeling* (Berkeley and Los Angeles: University of California Press, 1983).

4. Most of my discussion of chains and food service is drawn from D. Daryl Wyckoff and W. Earl Sasser, *The Chain-Restaurant Industry* (Lexington, Mass.: D. C. Heath and Co., 1978), esp. pp. xxiii–lxix. See also Robert V. Emerson, *Fast Food: The Endless Shakeout* (New York: Lebhar-Friedman, 1979). With these authors, I depend heavily on statistics collected by the U.S. Department of Commerce, the Bureau of Labor Statistics, and the National Restaurant Association. Among the most useful sources they cite are Bureau of Labor Statistics, *N.R.A. Washington Report*, October 10, 1977, pp. 1–3; W. Earl Sasser and Ivor P. Morgan, "The Bermuda Triangle of Food Service Chains," *The Cornell H.R.A. Quarterly*, February 1977; U.S. Department of Commerce, *Franchising in the Economy*; and J. Whitmarsh, "Chains within Chains: Foodservice's Unseen Power," *Institutions/Volume Feeding*, September 1, 1975, pp. 60–64.

There are a wide variety of published perspectives on chains and fast-food franchises in particular. A sample might include the following: Boosterism—Sandy Alexander, *Franchising and You: Unlimited Opportunities for Success* (Los Angeles: Lawrence Publishing Co., 1970); and Ray Kroc with Robert Anderson, *Grinding It Out: The Making of McDonald's* (Chicago: Henry Regnery Co., 1977). Feature journalism—Ada Louise Huxtable, "Architecture for a Fast-Food Culture," *New York*

Times Magazine, February 12, 1978, pp. 23–25, 30, 32, 36; and Lynn Langway et al., "America: Out to Eat," *Newsweek*, October 3, 1977, pp. 86–90. Fiction—Stanley Elkin, *The Franchiser* (New York: Farrar Straus Giroux, 1976). Home economics—"Fast-food Chains," *Consumer Reports* 44, no. 9 (September 1979): 508–13; and Coleen P. Greecher and Barbara Shannon, "Impact of Fast Food Meals on Nutrient Intake of Two Groups," *Journal of the American Dietetic Association* 70, no. 4 (April 1977): 368–72. Humanist scholastics—Marshall Fishwick, ed., "Focus on the World of Ronald McDonald," *Journal of American Culture* 2 (Summer 1978): 334–471; and Kay Mussell and Linda Keller Brown, eds., "Focus on American Food and Foodways," *Journal of American Culture* 3 (Fall 1979): 392–570. Muckraking—Max Boas and Steve Chain, *Big Mac: The Unauthorized Story of McDonald's* (New York: E. P. Dutton, 1976); and John L. Hess and Karen Hess, *The Taste of America* (New York: Penguin Books, 1977).

5. Wyckoff and Sasser, *The Chain-Restaurant Industry*, p. lxvi.

Chapter 5

1. Ted S. Frost, *Where Have All the Woolly Mammoths Gone? A Small Business Survival Manual* (West Nyack, N.Y.: Parker Publishing Co., 1976), pp. 9–18. See also Richard Edwards, *Contested Terrain: The Transformation of the Workplace in the Twentieth Century* (New York: Basic Books, 1979).

Chapter 6

1. See, for example, Marshall Kaplan, *Urban Planning in the 1960s: A Design for Irrelevancy* (Cambridge: MIT Press, 1973); Jane Jacobs, *The Death and Life of Great*

American Cities (New York: Random House, 1961); Constance Perin, *Everything in Its Place: Social Order and Land Use in America* (Princeton: Princeton University Press, 1977); and especially Robert B. Riley, "Speculations on the New American Landscapes," *Landscape* 24, no. 3 (1980): 1–9. For a similar analysis with a different moral, see Dean MacCannell, *The Tourist: A New Theory of the Leisure Class* (New York: Schocken Books, 1976).

2. See, for example, Robert B. Reich, *The Next American Frontier* (New York: Times Books, 1983); Michael J. Dear and Allen J. Scott, eds., *Urbanization and Urban Planning in Capitalist Society* (London: Methuen, 1981); Pierre Clavel, John Forester, and William W. Goldsmith, eds., *Urban and Regional Planning in an Age of Austerity* (New York: Pergamon, 1980); and Robert W. Burchell and George Sternlieb, eds., *Planning Theory in the 1980s: A Search for Future Directions* (New Brunswick: Rutgers University Press, 1978).

3. For an accessible survey of the relationship between land use and economy, see Brian J. L. Berry, *The Human Consequences of Urbanisation: Divergent Paths in the Urban Experience of the Twentieth Century* (New York: St. Martin's Press, 1973). For an introduction to the massive and growing literature on economic democracy, see Frank Lindenfeld and Joyce Rothschild-Whitt, eds., *Workplace Democracy and Social Change* (Boston: Porter Sargent Publishers, 1982).